DURBAR

DURBAR

Tavleen Singh

with best wishes,

hachette
INDIA

First published in 2012 by Hachette India
(Registered name: Hachette Book Publishing India Pvt. Ltd)
An Hachette UK company
www.hachetteindia.com

1

ISBN 978-93-5009-444-0

Hachette Book Publishing India Pvt. Ltd,
4th & 5th Floors, Corporate Centre,
Plot No. 94, Sector 44, Gurgaon 122003, India

Typeset in Sabon 10/13.6
by Eleven Arts, New Delhi

Printed and bound in India by
Gopsons Papers Ltd., Noida

durbar /ˈdəːbɑː/ ▸ **noun historical** the court of an Indian ruler.

■ a public reception held by an Indian prince or a British governor or viceroy in India.

– ORIGIN Urdu, from Persian *darbār* 'court'.

CONTENTS

AUTHOR'S NOTE

When I was sixteen years old I first became aware of being a foreigner in my own country. It happened on a train. The incident remains so fresh in my mind that I can almost smell the pine-scented air that came through the open windows of the second-class compartment with its frayed green Rexine seats. I was coming down from Simla at the end of the summer term in St Bede's College and with me were other girls from my college. We were on our way home to Delhi for the holidays. At a station on the way to Kalka a group of boys entered our compartment. They were what we called 'Hindi-speaking types' and they tried to attract our attention by making cheeky remarks and singing romantic songs from Hindi movies.

We ignored them at first but when their efforts to draw our attention became a nuisance someone in our group stood up and reprimanded them in English. She told them they had no manners and that they had been so badly brought up that there was no point in trying to teach them any. They clearly did not understand a word of what she said but when she finished her lecture on etiquette one of them said with a sneer on his face, in refined Hindustani, '*Angrez chale gaye, apni aulaad chhod gaye.*' (The English have gone but they left their progeny behind.)

The other girls were not bothered by this remark but it troubled me enough to remember it more than forty years later. At the time I looked around at the girls I was travelling with and became aware of how very 'foreign' we were. We wore Western clothes and talked of Western things in English. In the train compartment that day we had been discussing a new record by Elvis Presley and a new Hollywood film. Those who brought books to read on the long train journey were reading Georgette Heyer and Agatha Christie. I liked to think of myself as a more serious reader and had brought with me a beautifully bound copy of the first Russian novel I ever read. It was *And Quiet Flows the Don* by Mikhail Sholokhov that my roommate, a woman of high literary tastes, had gifted me for my birthday that year. I read it zealously without understanding the story or its context, and without finding it strange that I should be reading a Russian novel without ever having read an Indian one even in translation. If I had been asked to name a single book in Hindi, Urdu or Punjabi that I had read I would have had to admit that I could not read in any of these languages and that the only Indian author I had heard of was Munshi Premchand. It was the way it was in those first decades after the British Raj ended.

The best schools were those that taught Indian children to be British and they did a good job. I left Welham Girls' High School speaking fluent English, and with a head filled with English literature and poetry, but without being able to speak more than basic Hindi. I relearned Hindi, Urdu and Punjabi only after becoming a journalist and now write Hindi well enough to write two columns a week. But it saddens me that I never learned Sanskrit. This language that is the key to India's civilization and her ancient texts was mocked in the little English world in which I grew up.

If my foreignness had been an individual flaw it would not have been worth mentioning at the beginning of this book. It becomes important because people brought up just like me have ruled India since 1947, perpetuating a twisted continuance of colonial rule. I would go so far as to say that my generation of Indians was possibly more colonized than those who lived in colonial times and our tragedy was that most of us lived out our lives without ever finding out.

This memoir begins in the summer of 1975 when Indira Gandhi used the Emergency to declare her younger son, Sanjay, as her political heir. That summer I first met Rajiv Gandhi and his wife. He was a pilot in Indian Airlines and a devoted family man with a small circle of friends. In this circle were the privileged scions of businessmen and former ruling princes. And, there were those of slightly humbler origin whose parents had been in government service and the army. What bound them together was often that they had been to the same schools, spent summer holidays in the same hill stations and shared the same cocoon of privilege that kept out India's realities. They belonged to a tiny class of Indians who, like me, had grown up without any awareness of the country in which they lived.

If someone had said, when I first met them, that Rajiv would one day become prime minister and that his close friends would become the most powerful men in India I would have laughed at the improbability of people so removed from Indian political and cultural realities ever being in such a position. Yet, this is what happened. Rajiv was given a unique opportunity to make the sort of changes that could have made India a very different, more confident, country. But because he was only an elected prince surrounded by people who could not have been more distant from India's complexities he ended up leaving as his political legacy only his Italian wife and their children.

India's oldest political party did not hesitate before accepting this legacy gratefully and since the Nehru–Gandhi dynasty is revered as India's royal family its example was emulated. Today there is almost not a single political party in India that does not practise hereditary democracy of a peculiarly Indian kind. Legislative assemblies have turned into private clubs with limited access except for those who consider themselves entitled by birth. There are political families in other democracies but outside the Indian subcontinent the widow or the children of a political leader do not automatically claim the dead man's legacy as if it were their birthright. This distortion of democracy may not have happened if Mrs Gandhi had not introduced it in that long hot summer of the Emergency.

Durbar has been difficult to write. I started to write it soon after Rajiv Gandhi died. I knew him well from the days when he was not a politician and found myself in a unique position to tell the story of how a prime minister with the largest mandate in Indian history ended up as such a disappointment. Not just because I happened to be a part of the same tiny social set in which he moved, but because my career as a journalist, that so changed the way I saw India, ran almost parallel with Rajiv's career as a politician. I believed then that he had failed India but when I started to write the book I realized that he was not the only one who had let India down. An entire ruling class had. A ruling class to which I belonged.

As the story unfolded it became as if a mirror of my own life, a memoir not just of the short life of Rajiv as a politician and how the seeds of dynastic democracy were sown, but of my own as a journalist. I discovered how much the clear lens of journalism had changed my understanding of the country in which I had lived all my life. And this fundamentally changed the way in which I saw the people I had grown up with. I saw how aloof they were from India, how foreign her culture and history were to them, and how, because of this, they had failed to bring about renewal and change. I saw how my life as a journalist opened up doors that made me constantly ashamed of how India has been betrayed by people like me. I believe that it is because India was let down by her ruling class that she failed to become the country she could have been. If we had been less foreign and more aware of India's great wealth of languages and literature, of her ancient texts on politics and governance and her scriptures, we would have wanted to change many things. But we failed and instead brought up our children, as we had been, as foreigners in their own country. Fascinated by all things foreign and disdainful of all things Indian.

A new ruling class is slowly replacing the old one. A newer, rougher breed of politician has come to control the levers of power. The sons of peasants and peons and the children of castes that were once considered untouchable have ruled some of India's biggest states. But in emulation of the old ruling class they teach their children English and send them to Western universities. There would be no harm in this if they did not also bring them up removed from their own languages and culture.

The possibility of an Indian renaissance, that as the first generation of Indians to grow up in post-colonial India should have been ours to ensure, recedes further and further away. Dynasty, a political tool in the hands of the ruling class, has become the catalyst for a new colonization of a country whose soul has already been deeply scarred by centuries of it. This is the main reason why an expanding and increasingly educated middle class is becoming disenchanted with democracy and democratic institutions.

New Delhi
2 October 2012

PART 1

1 AN UNTIMELY DEATH

On the night of his funeral there was a storm. It began quietly, a gentle swirl of a dust storm and then with great rumbles of thunder and flashes of lightning came the rain. Hard, heavy, angry rain. It does not rain in Delhi in May and as I sat on my terrace watching the violent unseasonal storm I thought of it, despite my better judgement, as some kind of omen. An unseasonal storm for an untimely death – a death so terrible that not the worst person in the world should die that way.

The fact had not fully registered in my mind even though I had spent the day at Rajiv Gandhi's funeral. It seemed hardly possible that he was dead – and yet he was. Killed by an assassin who killed herself just seconds after murdering him.

The night Rajiv was killed I talked to Jayanthi Natarajan, a Congress Party member of the Rajya Sabha who was with him in Sriperumbudur, to find out what had happened. She had just come back to Madras (not Chennai then) from Sriperumbudur and she was in shock.

'I noticed her standing there,' she said, 'she looked like such an ordinary sort of girl. Dark, stout and with those big glasses. She had a garland in her hands. I remember seeing her clearly, then Rajiv told me to go back to the car and fetch something, and I had barely walked ten steps when there was this terrible explosion. When I turned around, he had disappeared and there was a big hole in the ground.

'He saved my life,' Jayanthi kept repeating, 'he saved my life by sending me back to the car or I would have died too. I was walking alongside him. I would have been dead. I would have died with him because I was right there by his side.'

Jayanthi was a lawyer from Tamil Nadu who had joined politics at Rajiv's behest and worshipped the ground on which he walked. Between tears and hysteria she told me how the policemen had run away and how she had been the only one to go back and look for him. Pictures of her in a red sari, with her hands cupped over her mouth, standing at the edge of the black pit, the crater made by the bomb, appeared in newspapers across the world.

'It took me a few minutes because there were so many bodies – bits of bodies – scattered around. There was no sign of him and then I noticed his shoes – I recognized them, and there was the back of his head… But when I tried to turn him over I realized there was nothing to hold. His body no longer existed. Some party workers helped me gather the remains and wrap them in some cloth we found. We called Delhi when we got to the hospital.' The other person with Jayanthi was Suman Dubey, a journalist who had been editor of *India Today* and was one of Rajiv's closest friends. He had recently taken over as Rajiv's media advisor.

It must have been minutes after Rajiv was killed that someone called me from the *India Today* office and gave me the news. The next person to call me was Nina Singh, an old friend of Sonia Gandhi, though now estranged. Nina's husband, Arun Singh, was Rajiv's oldest and closest friend. They had known each other as young boys in the Doon School and then been at Cambridge University together. They remained friends after their marriages and the friendship had deepened when their wives became close friends. They grew apart soon after Rajiv became prime minister and the reason why Sonia dropped her was never clear to Nina or anyone else.

'I can't believe this has happened. I just can't believe it,' Nina said on the phone that day. 'If you're going to the house I'd like to come along. I feel I ought to be there for Sonia.'

By the time we got to 10 Janpath there were many people there. Party workers in white standing sullenly in small groups, socialites in carefully coordinated mourning colours, sundry fixers and shady businessmen. They stood together in the cul-de-sac outside the house with confused expressions on their faces, not quite sure what they should do next.

Then H.K.L. Bhagat, a Congress MP with a reputation for being a thug, arrived with a group of political workers, shouting, '*Khoon ka badla khoon se lenge.*' Blood will be avenged with blood. Their shouting converted the sadness that had hung over the cul-de-sac into something ugly and violent. Some of the more hot-headed in the group said there would not be a Sikh left alive in India this time, while Bhagat, small, dark and beetle-like behind his ever-present dark glasses, watched with a half smile on his thin lips. I knew him well, from before he became notorious for being involved in the 1984 massacres in Delhi in which more than 3000 Sikhs had been killed to avenge the assassination of Indira Gandhi. So I went up to him and asked if he was preparing his supporters to participate in another massacre.

'No, no,' he said, looking a little embarrassed, 'they are just venting their anger, you know, just letting go of their emotions.'

'Well, tell them to stop,' I said. 'There is no evidence that Sikhs were involved in killing Rajiv.'

He made a small gesture with his right hand and the young men stopped their 'venting' and stood silently behind him, alert and ready to spring back into action.

The narrow cul-de-sac that separates 10 Janpath from the Congress Party's old headquarters at 24 Akbar Road quickly filled up. I was there as a reporter, but Nina was there as a friend and wanted to find someone who could help her go into the house to see Sonia. When she saw Satish Sharma, Rajiv's friend from his days as a pilot who became a politician when Rajiv did, taking some people into the house, she got into the white Ambassador that he was driving.

Within minutes she was out again. 'He told me to get out of the car,' she said, looking puzzled and hurt. I led her away.

Nina was silent and sad on the drive to her house, and I found myself unable to stop memories of Rajiv from filling my head. Memories of long ago. Of Rajiv as he had been before he became a politician, before he started to make the compromises that politicians make. I remembered how unassuming, open and honest he had been, so totally unaffected by being the son of the prime minister and the grandson of one of India's most revered political leaders. I felt happy that in his last days we had met and talked about the barriers that had come up between us in the years he was prime minister. In 1987 I had started writing a political column in the *Indian Express* and often criticized his policies and this led to relations between us becoming frosty. I told him at that meeting that when I criticized him in my column it was in his role as prime minister. As a political journalist that was my job and I could not understand why he had taken it personally. He smiled and said that he had never held anything I had written against me, and agreed to give me an interview in Amethi, his constituency, where he was going soon. It was there that I met him for the last time.

After dropping Nina home I drove back to 10 Janpath. There were hundreds of people there by then and the cul-de-sac had been closed off. Party workers, reporters, TV crews and ordinary people had gathered in large numbers, and the atmosphere was tense because of Bhagat and his men. They were no longer shouting their slogans but whispering among themselves about how it had to be the Sikhs who had done it. We did not know then who had killed Rajiv but the crowds outside his house assumed that it was Sikhs. Rajiv had made no known enemies in the nearly two years that he had been leader of the opposition and in his time as prime minister the only people who had hated him were the Sikhs because they blamed him for allowing the 1984 massacres and justifying them afterwards. I remember thinking that if the Sikhs were responsible for his assassination, there really would not be a Sikh left alive in Delhi this time. I thought it might be best for me to go home before the mourners turned violent, but as I was about to leave a colleague told me that the Congress Party's working committee had met and a decision had been taken to make Sonia party president.

'But she is a foreigner,' I gasped, 'she doesn't even speak Hindi. She never reads the newspapers. It's a crazy idea.'

The colleague who gave me the news of Sonia's new political role said he was going next door to the Congress Party's office to get more details of the working committee's decision. I went with him. It was close to midnight but the lights were on in all the rooms of the squat, yellow-washed bungalow and the grounds were filled with party workers. They were mostly villagers and had probably been camping in the party office because the election campaign was not yet over. Somehow we found our way through the crush of workers and in the hectic corridors of the party office located a general secretary who told us that Arjun Singh, former chief minister of Madhya Pradesh, had proposed Sonia's name for party president and the working committee had unanimously decided that she would be the best choice. He gave us a copy of the working committee's resolution.

The next day Rajiv Gandhi's remains arrived in Delhi in a big wooden coffin, which was placed in Teen Murti House, where his grandfather had lived as India's first prime minister and where Rajiv and his brother Sanjay had spent their childhood years. It was one of those Delhi summer days when the heat is so intense it becomes incandescent. Outside Teen Murti House the queues were long and the mourners angry. Plump, middle-aged women and grey-haired government servants talked of the need for revenge. It was not clear yet who was behind Rajiv's assassination and the general assumption remained that it must have been Sikhs.

The queue I stood in moved slowly. It took me an hour to get into the high-ceilinged hall where the closed coffin lay, a large portrait of Rajiv at its head. Hindu, Muslim, Buddhist and Sikh priests sat beside it murmuring a babel of prayers and the scent of burning sandalwood filled the room. Sonia, her daughter and other ladies of the family sat in white saris on the floor. Sonia's dark brown hair was tied back and covered with her cotton sari and her face was carefully made up. Even the lower eyelashes she painted on to make her eyes look bigger were in place. I reached out and held her hand, but she pretended to greet someone else. When our eyes met, she looked at me as if I were a total stranger.

How much had changed. What a long way we had come from those days of long lunches in my little flat in Golf Links when she would laugh and gossip and urge me to tell her what was going on in the city. There were so few people, she used to say, who dared speak freely to her and she had got tired of listening to sycophants. Did they think she was so stupid that she could not see through their lies?

After Rajiv became prime minister, our friendship lasted for the first two years and then deteriorated for reasons that to me remained obscure. Except that perhaps Sonia, as the prime minister's wife, probably wanted around her only people who totally supported her husband. My support for him had waned after the Bofors scandal. When fingers started being pointed at him for corruption in the Bofors arms deal Rajiv seemed to lose confidence. Much was lost because of his inability to do anything to rectify the damage done to Indian democracy and to the fabric of Indian politics during the two decades that his mother ruled India with the populism of a demagogue.

By the time Mrs Gandhi was killed, a deep cynicism had infected not just Indian politics but the soul of India. People had lost faith that things would ever change for the better. One of the reasons why Rajiv won his first election with the largest majority in Indian parliamentary history was because he had become for one brief, shining moment the embodiment of hope.

What had gone wrong?

2 BEGINNINGS

I was born almost exactly three years after India became an independent country. My father's family was landed aristocracy from that part of Punjab which is now Pakistan. They lost their estates and everything else in 1947 when India was divided. Believing that they would be able to continue living in Pakistan, they made no preparation to leave until they were forced to by the violence. My grandmother, a young widow at the time, explained that they had 'opted' for Pakistan because their home and their lands, in a village called Rajkot, near Gujranwala, went to Pakistan. She had never been to Delhi, she said, or worn a sari or spoken any language other than Punjabi. My uncle, only seventeen but already a cynic, said, 'We thought that in Pakistan there would be Muslims ruling us but that was all right because before the British ruled us we were ruled by Muslims – so what difference would it make to us if they became rulers again?' My father, two years older than his brother and a young army officer, said one of his considerations for wanting to stay in Pakistan was that his regiment, Probyn's Horse, had been given to Pakistan when the Indian Army was divided.

My mother's family is from Delhi. Her father was one of the five Sikh contractors who helped Edwin Lutyens build the city of New Delhi. Among the buildings he built was South Block, which houses the Indian prime minister's offices as well as the offices of the ministers of defence and foreign affairs. As children we used to be taken for walks from Jantar Mantar Road to South Block where our ayahs would read out our grandfather's name imprinted in a sandstone wall of South Block.

The Sikh contractors who worked with Lutyens stayed on in the new city. They built big houses for their families along the wide, tree-lined avenues, contributed to the building of Sikh temples and owned most of

Connaught Place. These contractors became rich enough to graduate from being nouveau riche to becoming part of the aristocracy of Delhi, replacing the prominent Muslim families that left for Pakistan. When millions of Punjabi refugees came to Delhi from Lahore and Rawalpindi, rich Sikhs like my grandfather helped many resurrect their destroyed businesses and broken lives.

Among the lives my maternal grandfather helped revive was that of his future son-in-law, my father. My father had got engaged to my mother before Partition and the date for their wedding was set for 15 December 1947. After his family was driven out of Pakistan he became both penniless and homeless and it was in a house in Dehra Dun that belonged to my maternal grandfather that he married my mother.

It is my maternal grandfather's house, 5 Jantar Mantar Road in Delhi, that I remember as being the only permanent home in my childhood. That is where we came from boarding school every summer holiday. My father's entire extended family were refugees from Pakistan who seemed always in the process of building their new homes. In Karnal, itself a broken down sort of half town, they lived in half-built houses on plots that had been marked out in the fields. My parents moved constantly from one army cantonment to another and I never got to thinking of the houses in those army bases as home. They always had about them the atmosphere of a transit camp. So 5 Jantar Mantar Road with its Persian carpets and hunting trophies on the walls, its carefully decorated bedrooms and its manicured gardens seemed to my childhood mind like a sanctuary. I remember the house on Jantar Mantar Road as vast, filled with more rooms than we could count and bursting with cousins and aunts and uncles. My mother used to be allotted the rooms she had lived in before she was married. They opened on to a red sandstone courtyard on one side and a garden with colourful swings on the other. Sadly, we never stayed there for long and seemed always to be on the verge of leaving for yet another army cantonment to move into yet another empty, charmless house.

The India of my childhood seemed full of people rebuilding disrupted lives in a country where every commodity seemed always to be in short supply. I can remember grown-ups complaining constantly about shortages. Even such ordinary things as sugar, milk and bread seemed every other day to become unavailable. Sometimes it would be kerosene and petrol that would be rationed. Everything about life in India had a rundown, makeshift quality about it as if life itself had seen better days, but we saw this as an acceptable price to pay for Independence. If we blamed anyone for India being such a shabby sort of place in which even rich people lived in genteel poverty, we blamed it on 'colonization'. We were building a new India, after all, and when new things are built there is about them an unfinished quality. In the army messes and the musty old British clubs conversations were often about 'falling standards of cleanliness and discipline'. Men in immaculately pressed evening clothes lamented, in clipped British accents, about how things had declined after the British left. The circles in which my parents moved blamed this on our new socialist rulers, though nobody blamed the prime minister.

When I was eight I was sent off with my sister to a boarding school that had about it that same new and unfinished feel.

Welham Girls' High School was six months old when my sister and I became its ninety-ninth and hundredth students. It did not have proper classrooms or dormitories but functioned languidly out of two old-fashioned houses with tin roofs and long verandas. The houses, we heard, had once belonged to a nawab. When I finished school two years too early at the age of fourteen (because they put me by mistake in the wrong class), India was still a dilapidated, unsure sort of place but it had about it the innocence of a country that believed in its dream of democracy and freedom.

As an army child it was the war with China in 1962 that I remember as the moment when things began to change. I turned twelve that year and was not capable of fully understanding how the Chinese had defeated us, but I remember Krishna Menon, the defence minister, and General Kaul, the Army Chief, being talked of as the villains of the war. Nobody blamed Prime Minister Jawaharlal Nehru but what I remember repeated in conversations about the war was 'that scoundrel Menon was making coffee percolators in defence factories'. It made a deep impression on my twelve-year-old mind because it seemed so extraordinary that a factory meant to make guns should be making coffee percolators instead.

By the time of the next war, with Pakistan in 1965, I was in St Bede's College in Simla which was so removed from politics and current events that even when the sirens went off signalling an air raid we were never sure what was happening. We knew that we were at war with Pakistan and that Simla, as the headquarters of the Western Command, could be a target but we never really understood what the war was about. A Kashmiri friend called Poornima Dhar would tell us, as we ran excitedly down to the basement when the sirens went off, that it was about Kashmir and we believed her. We had no interest in why the Pakistanis wanted Kashmir. We just knew that they must be wrong and that they were the enemy. I confess that I grew up with such a limited understanding of the world that when I, aged twenty-one, first met a Pakistani in London it surprised me that he spoke Punjabi (not Urdu) and that his Punjabi accent was just like my grandmother's Lahori accent.

After completing an education that left many, many gaps I ended up doing a course in journalism at the New Delhi Polytechnic only because it was the shortest course on offer. Textile designing was a three-year course and interior design took two years, but journalism you could supposedly master in a year. At some point during that year I realized that I really wanted to be a journalist. So, once I got my diploma from the Polytechnic I started wandering about the offices of the four main English newspapers in Delhi – the *Times of India*, the *Hindustan Times*, the *Indian Express* and the *Statesman* – to offer my services as a reporter.

It did not take me long to discover that women were not popular in the reporting business. There were, I was told, only five women reporters in Delhi at the time and only one of them, television journalist Barkha Dutt's mother, Prabha, had the temerity to try and do the hard reporting that men did. Defeated and despondent, and only nineteen, I gave up on journalism and took a job as a secretary in a travel agency that had its offices in the newly opened Oberoi Hotel. This was not a good choice. The Oberoi Hotel with its glistening new coffee shop was the favourite watering hole of my mostly idle friends. So many friends came by to ask my grouchy boss if they could take me out to coffee that I got sacked in less than six months. At this point, a kindly, older secretary at the travel agency felt sorry for me and suggested I apply to the Ford Foundation for a job. She knew someone there and could put in a good word for me. I was exceptionally good at shorthand and the fastest typist she knew, she said. For this I must acknowledge the mysterious option we had in Welham to drop geography for shorthand typing. As a result, I did not discover that the earth moved around the sun until I became a journalist but I learned how to type.

The job at the Ford Foundation came through, and I found myself working for a nice Englishman called Kevin Mansell. After several months of watching me hiding one book or the other under my desk when he walked in, he told me that I was truly the worst secretary he had ever had. Was there not something else I would rather do? When I told him about wanting to become a journalist, he said he had a friend who might be able to help me get on to a training programme run by the Thompson Group in England. A few days later he said I should send an application letter to his friend who worked for the *Evening Mail* in Slough, a town I had never heard of until then. He asked me to mention that as an Indian I would be able to understand the language and the problems of the Indian and Pakistani immigrants flooding into Slough. I followed his advice and, to my amazement, got accepted to work as a trainee reporter for the *Evening Mail*.

Slough was a dismal, ugly town but close enough to London for me to be able to live in the big city and commute to work. In the two and a half years I spent at the *Evening Mail*, I learned to speak English in a Slough accent because I had to phone copy over to copy-takers who found my Indian accent incomprehensible. I learned accuracy from covering magistrates' courts, speed from covering police and fire stories, and I learned to understand the dreary concerns of local government from reporting on the proceedings of local councils. I could have continued to work in British journalism if I had wanted, but in a short time I got bored with my job and homesick for India. In early 1974 I came home only to find that it was still very hard for women to get jobs in journalism. I had returned confident that since I was a foreign-trained journalist in a country that revered all things foreign it would be quite easy for me to get a job. I was wrong.

As I did not write in Hindi at that time my choices were limited, as before, to the four English-language newspapers that were published in Delhi. I discovered quickly the reasons why there existed an open prejudice against women. The women who joined journalism took a man's job without doing it in full measure, and usually left once their priorities shifted to marriage and babies. I tried freelancing, and sent off a few long and passionate articles to the *Illustrated Weekly*, the famous Indian magazine, and received brutal rejections from Khushwant Singh who was its editor.

After many months of rejection I succeeded in getting an article published in a youth magazine that the *Times of India* used to bring out. But when I asked its editor, Anees Jung, for payment she laughed in my face and said that I should be grateful that she had been good enough to publish the article. I could hardly believe my luck when I got my first job with the *Statesman,* a small but influential English newspaper, and when I finally set foot in the red brick offices of the newspaper on a hot day in the first week of May 1975 it was with gratitude and great excitement.

It was a month before Mrs Gandhi declared the Emergency. I had been in England for nearly three years and it was only after joining the *Statesman* that I became aware of the political turmoil caused by a general unhappiness with Mrs Gandhi's rule. There had been student riots in Gujarat the year before that sparked off a larger movement called Nav Nirman, protesting against rising living costs and corruption, that forced Mrs Gandhi to get rid of the state's chief minister Chimanbhai Patel. The movement found its echo in Bihar where Jayaprakash Narayan, a veteran Gandhian, led a movement that he called Total Revolution or Sampurna Kranti against corruption in public life. His movement was supported by most opposition parties. By May 1975 the opposition leaders had begun to hold angry rallies in Delhi, which made Mrs Gandhi very nervous. Then came the judgement of the Allahabad High Court on 12 June 1975 anulling Mrs Gandhi's win in the Lok Sabha elections of 1971 and disallowing her from holding elected office for six years. The complaint against her had come from a man called Raj Narain, who had contested against Mrs Gandhi in Rae Bareli and after his defeat had gone to court, charging her with electoral malpractice.

It was on the day that this judgement came that I met Sanjay Gandhi for the first time in his political avatar. I had seen him two or three times at parties in the days when he was more interested in making an Indian car for the masses than being in politics. Charges of nepotism were made by opposition leaders and the press when the Congress government in Haryana donated many acres of land for Sanjay Gandhi's car factory. But for all the bad publicity Sanjay Gandhi seemed only to become a more glamorous figure. In Delhi's social circles he was the more popular of Mrs Gandhi's sons because of his reputation for liking fast cars and fast women. He was small, slightly pasty-looking and had a feminine quality about his features, but there was a peculiar magnetism about him. It may have been just because he was the prime minister's son but where women were concerned he seemed to possess a special allure.

Sanjay was more sociable than Rajiv, and could be seen often at parties and in restaurants. In the late sixties, Delhi's first discotheque, The Cellar, opened in a basement in Regal Building and instantly became the city's most fashionable rendezvous. Most of the other restaurants in Connaught Place had fallen into a state of decay when prohibition laws took away their licences and The Cellar became a beacon for Delhi's small circle of rich and idle youth. It did not have a liquor licence but the food was good and it enhanced its appeal by organizing poetry readings and plays. It was at one such event that I once saw Sanjay Gandhi standing near the entrance, in a white kurta–pyjama, looking sulky and bored. I cannot remember who he was with but the girls who were with me were mesmerized and kept trying to sidle up to him to somehow attract his attention.

When he chose Maneka as his wife, the salons of Delhi were littered with broken hearts and bile. Disappointed aspirants said cruel things about Maneka's claim to fame being limited to having modelled in a towel. When I asked my mother about her supposedly 'low background' she was outraged and told me that Maneka came from a perfectly respectable Punjabi family. It was the aura of aristocracy that enveloped the Nehru–Gandhi family that made people believe that Sanjay should have married someone higher born. When Rajiv had married a few years earlier nobody noticed that Sonia Maino came from a very ordinary Italian family because she was a foreigner.

On the afternoon of 12 June 1975 what took me to Mrs Gandhi's house at 1 Safdarjang Road was a rally that was being organized by her to protest against the judgement of the Allahabad High Court. People had gathered at a roundabout at the end of Safdarjang Road, which was lined with neem and gulmohar trees. The orange of the gulmohar flowers took on a blinding lustre in the white, white heat. On the roundabout was a thin covering of scorched, yellow grass outlined by beds of dying flowers. I stood with my face covered with a wet dupatta and even then it was so hot that I eventually took shelter under the neem trees outside the Gymkhana Club.

From there I watched the rally that was being organized. Buses were parked, discreetly and out of sight, in another street. Out of them poured sweating, barefoot men and women who looked exhausted. When they got to the roundabout, they were made to sit in rows on the brown grass. They sheltered their faces from the burning sunlight with frayed saris and turbans, and waited patiently.

Every few minutes someone would emerge from Mrs Gandhi's house and tell them that she would be coming out any time now. I waited, feeling increasingly sorry for the people on the roundabout (and myself) as the day got hotter and hotter. I thought a few times of going back to the office and returning later but nobody knew exactly when Mrs Gandhi would emerge and as I had been a reporter with the *Statesman* for less than five weeks I was eager to prove my worth. By late afternoon more busloads of people arrived.

It was early evening, and I was nearly at the end of my tether, when men in khaki uniforms emerged from the prime minister's house, carrying white plastic chairs that they placed in front of the people who had by then waited all day. Behind them came a short, balding young man with very white skin and very pink lips. Big, horn-rimmed glasses covered half his face and his kurta–pyjama was so white and starched the people on the roundabout gaped in wonder. I almost did not recognize him as the man I had last seen in The Cellar.

I rushed up eagerly, notebook at the ready, and introduced myself to Sanjay Gandhi. I asked if he would give me an interview, and to my surprise he agreed. I wanted him to comment on the Allahabad High Court judgement and he said he thought it was a 'stupid' judgement. I asked him what the prime minister planned to do next, to which he responded with some comment like 'we shall see', and then he was gone. It was not much of an interview but I thought it was important. He seemed so obviously to be playing a political role. Everyone was taking orders from him, including Mrs Gandhi's secretary, R.K. Dhawan, at the time one of the most powerful men in India.

At around 6 p.m. Mrs Gandhi emerged in a cotton sari, a worried frown on her face. Her skin, normally shiny and glowing, looked sallow and grey and the lines on the sides of her mouth looked deeper. But as she approached the people on the roundabout, a smile spread across her face and instead of going to the podium she went to the people and greeted them. Old ladies jumped up and embraced her with their dark, wrinkled arms. They smiled toothlessly when she apologized for keeping them waiting. Old men in grimy turbans fell at her feet. She looked like a higher being compared to 'the people' with their withered skin, their bare feet and their dirty clothes. After greeting them and graciously accepting their adulation she went up to the rickety wooden podium. Shading her eyes with one perfectly manicured white hand she made a short, uninspiring speech but seemed to understand that it made little difference what she said. Her listeners were bewitched by her because of who she was and not because of anything she had to say. It was the first time I had seen her at a public rally and the effect she had on these people fascinated me. They were nearly all illiterate and had probably been paid a small sum to attend the rally but their reverence for the tiny woman in her plain cotton sari was real. Dark, sweaty faces, mouths hanging open to reveal paan-stained, blackened teeth, they stared up in wonder as if in the presence of a goddess.

As I was the only reporter present, I should have had the only account of the speech she made that afternoon. But I was new to the job and the notebook in which I recorded what she said is long lost. I remember she said she came from a family of freedom fighters and could never betray the interests of the people. She spoke of the attacks on her by the opposition parties and accused them of attacking her because they knew she would fight to the end for the poor. As far as I remember she did not mention the judgement of the Allahabad High Court, except obliquely. When I got back to the office I told the chief reporter, Mr Raju, that I had an exclusive interview with Sanjay Gandhi and that he had criticized the judgement. He was unimpressed and continued typing with two fingers on his battered typewriter.

'Write it up and send it to the news editor,' he said, without looking up. 'They'll decide what to do with it.' It appeared as a few paragraphs on page three the next day.

Two weeks later, on the morning of 26 June 1975, my mother came into my bedroom early in the morning with a transistor in her hand. I heard Mrs Gandhi's thin, quivery voice saying, 'The actions of a few are endangering the rights of the vast majority… The forces of disintegration are in full play and communal passions are being aroused, threatening our unity.'

'She has declared a state of internal Emergency,' my mother said, looking shocked and puzzled. 'Fundamental rights have been suspended and the press has been censored.'

3 THE EMERGENCY

It was a hot evening in June, a few days after the Emergency was declared, when I first met Rajiv and Sonia Gandhi at a dinner party given by my friend Mapu, or Martand Singh to give him his full name. He used this name so rarely that I knew nobody who called him anything but Mapu. I had known Mapu since I was sixteen and studying journalism at the New Delhi Polytechnic. We met through a friend called Bapa whose father, the Maharaja of Dhrangadhra, was at the time a member of Parliament and lived in a house on Thyagaraja Marg. HHD, as we referred to Bapa's father, was away a lot either in his constituency in Gujarat or attending a Parliament session, so his house became a place where we congregated often. It was a large bungalow with verandas on all sides that led to a garden full of leafy trees. Mapu, a prince from the state of Kapurthala, was a friend of Bapa's brother, Jai, from the Doon School and seemed to be a permanent fixture in Thyagaraja Marg. I knew he had an older brother called Arun Singh who was married to someone called Nina from a prominent Delhi family, but I had never met them.

That evening, I went to Mapu's with Naveen Patnaik, a glamorous socialite who went on to become the chief minister of Orissa. Naveen and I had met recently through Mapu in Thyagaraja Marg and had taken to going out together in the evenings after we discovered that we were neighbours. Naveen lived on Prithviraj Road at the end of the vast garden of his father's house on Aurangzeb Road, which stretched between these two arteries of Lutyens's Delhi. Biju Patnaik, his father, bought the house from the Maharaja of Jubbal many years before I knew Naveen. It was one of a handful of private houses left in this area. By the seventies almost all the colonial bungalows in the tree-lined avenues of this most exclusive part of Delhi were occupied by senior government officials, ministers and political leaders. The most 'socialist' of our political leaders had acquired a taste for living like the white sahibs of yore and once they got a 'government bungalow' were loath to leave it even after they lost elections. Naveen's house was set in its own small garden whose most beautiful feature was an old Mughal pavilion. Later, when a rich businessman bought the house from Naveen's father, who sold it to finance an election, he tore the pavilion down. Even today when I drive past Naveen's former house in Prithviraj Road, I silently curse the vandal.

My parents lived in what used to be called Southend Lane, a narrow lane between Aurangzeb Road and Prithviraj Road, in a house my mother inherited from her father. The Indian contractors who worked with Edwin Lutyens to build New Delhi were given different sections of the new city to develop and my grandfather ended up owning several houses on Aurangzeb Road, including number 10, which he sold to Mohammed Ali Jinnah when my grandmother threatened to move into it after he secretly married again. My grandmother had been unable to give him a son and heir.

Delhi's social life in the seventies revolved around its drawing rooms. There were very few restaurants and these were expensive. The only affordable entertainment was to watch the latest English film playing in the Odeon or Plaza Cinema in Connaught Place, but once the Emergency was declared there were so many policemen on the streets of the city that we hesitated to go to public places after dark. Instead, we met regularly in someone or the other's house to drink Indian whisky and rum, and gossip into the early hours of the morning. We did not fully understand why Mrs Gandhi had needed to declare an Emergency but secretly found it interesting how Delhi had suddenly changed to become a city of policemen and fear. In the drawing rooms of Delhi there began to appear with alarming frequency a new breed of self-effacing but surprisingly inquisitive officials, who we concluded were Mrs Gandhi's spies.

Delhi's drawing rooms in those socialist times had about them a shabby sameness. Terrazzo floors that had seen better days were usually covered with Persian carpets now a little worn at the edges, the sofas looked as if they had been made by a carpenter working in the garden and the upholstery and curtains were perpetually dusty and frayed. The people who gathered in these drawing rooms were a motley lot. Princes, recently de-recognized by Indira Gandhi, scions of high officials, the occasional business tycoon from Bombay (not Mumbai then), young married couples of little distinction and single young women looking to get married. Almost nobody in these drawing rooms had a serious job or a serious interest in getting one. All they had in common was that nearly all the men had been to the Doon School and all the women to Welham Girls' High School or some convent in Simla or Mussoorie. We who had been to Welham viewed girls who had studied in convent schools like Tara Hall and Waverly with disdain for reasons that had to do with us considering ourselves more Indian than them. I remember going to Tara Hall in Simla for a sporting event with other Welham girls and laughing openly at the way the girls sang the national anthem with a British accent.

On the way to Mapu's house that evening, Naveen told me that Arun and Nina were Rajiv and Sonia Gandhi's best friends and that it might be embarrassing for him to run into them since Rajiv's mother had just put his father in jail. I think I said something to the effect that it might add some excitement to what could otherwise be a dull evening. I remember that on the short drive from Prithviraj Road to Sundar Nagar both of us noticed that there were more policemen on the streets than we had ever seen before. This was Delhi before it had witnessed terrorism and political violence of any kind, so policemen were a rare sight. To see them standing in the shadows of nearly every gulmohar tree we drove past was both exciting and a little scary.

Mapu lived in an old-fashioned, stolid, double-storeyed house that looked on to the high walls of the zoo. All you could see from his tiny front garden was the wall and the tops of the tall trees on the other side of it, and sometimes distant sounds of animals roaring or cackling could be heard. The drawing room windows had been left open and a hot, dusty wind blew in, tossing the white muslin curtains about and drawing them on to the veranda. At that time only rich businessmen could afford more than one air-conditioner and this was most often reserved for the bedroom. Mapu's drawing room was not air-conditioned so most of his guests had settled down in an alcove close to the windows where there was a hint of a breeze that brought in the summer scents of jasmine and raat-ki-rani.

While Naveen got himself and me a drink I spent a few moments looking around Mapu's large, high-ceilinged drawing room and noticed that the only people I knew there were Romi Chopra, whom I met at parties and who I knew was a friend of Rajiv Gandhi from Cambridge, and Vicky Bharat Ram, who belonged to a famous Delhi business family. Mapu introduced me to his brother, Arun Singh, and Arun's wife, Nina, while Naveen was still getting our drinks. My first impression of Arun was that he had a dour, intimidating reserve about him and Nina I noticed was elegant, friendly and full of laughter. She wore a brightly coloured chiffon sari, expensive French perfume and magnificent Cartier rings on her fingers.

Mapu was passionately interested at the time in reviving Indian textiles and in pursuit of this passion had made a whole new group of friends. Most of the other people in the room were from this group. They were a distinct type. The women all wore handwoven cotton saris and cheap Kolhapuri slippers on feet that looked like they were in need of a pedicure. Their hair was uniformly left long and loose and their only concession to make-up was a large bindi. The men wore kurta–pyjamas and had an unwashed quality about them. The feature they had in common with the women was their ridiculous effort at being 'Indian'. They were so affected in their ethnicity that their conversation was pointless and dull. They talked about Indian culture and music with fake intimacy. Conversations were usually about the latest Ravi Shankar concert or the latest performance by Yamini Krishnamurthy or Sonal Mansingh that, of course, they had attended, all of this discussed in English heavily interspersed with the Sanskrit names of ragas and dance forms. Most of them had studied in the best private schools in India and many had gone on to Oxford or Cambridge, but somehow this turned them into 'professional Indians', as a British friend once described them. That evening Naveen made his disdain for 'the ethnarks' more than apparent, so after we had said hello to Arun and Nina we wandered off to a quiet corner of the drawing room with our drinks.

It must have been a few minutes after Naveen and I had repaired anti-socially to our distant corner that I saw Rajiv and Sonia walk in through the open French windows. Rajiv wore a white kurta–pyjama and Sonia a lacy white dress that just reached her ankles. The first thing I noticed about Rajiv was his skin. It was pink and shiny, as if he had been in a sauna. He was not very tall but was slim and, despite his thinning hair, very good-looking. She was small and slim, with a prominent, sulky mouth and thick brown hair that hung loose down to her waist.

Had they been royalty they could not have got a more reverent reception that evening. Romi and Vicky rushed forward, abandoning whoever they were talking to and everyone else in the room slowly followed. Rajiv and Sonia sat down, holding hands, in the alcove near the open windows and a circle formed around them. Naveen made a joke about us having been left out of the 'magic circle' but reiterated that it would be embarrassing for him to go up and talk to Rajiv. We were still dithering over what to do next, when Mapu's sister-in-law, Nina, came sailing up to us and said with a gay laugh that Sonia had asked 'if that wasn't Naveen Patnaik standing in the corner'. After saying this, she sailed gaily back to the circle around Rajiv and Sonia without noticing the effect her words had had on Naveen.

'My drink has turned to ash in my mouth,' he said melodramatically. 'What should we do now? They might think we are very rude not to join the magic circle.'

'Yes. Maybe we should,' I agreed.

When we got close enough for Sonia to say hello to Naveen and for me to be introduced to her, Naveen, in a feeble attempt at polite conversation, decided to compliment her on her white frock. 'Is it a Valentino?' he asked with a friendly smile, to which she said unsmilingly, 'I had it made in Khan Market by my *darzi*.' There was something in the way she said this that prevented further conversation.

Despite the Emergency having just been declared and the city seething with political tension, nobody talked about politics that evening. There was talk of Corbett Park and children's schools and holidays abroad, and about handloom cloth and handicrafts, but nobody brought up even once the political situation in the country. I sensed that this unstated conspiracy of silence had to do with nobody wanting to embarrass Rajiv and did not bring up the subject either. Mapu told me later that his brother disapproved of the Emergency and was close enough to Rajiv to have been able to write Mrs Gandhi a letter giving her his views. Later, at another dinner party when I asked one of the people regularly invited to dinner parties for Rajiv and Sonia why nobody mentioned politics in front of them, he said it was because Rajiv was not at all interested in politics. He was very happy being an Indian Airlines pilot and a family man even if he was Jawaharlal Nehru's grandson and Indira Gandhi's son.

That first evening, though, I found it extraordinary that nobody mentioned the Emergency even after Rajiv and Sonia left. In the nearly thirty years that India had been an independent country we had failed to deal with most of our problems but the one thing that we were rightly proud of was that we were a democracy. The average Indian may have remained poor, illiterate and living in the most primitive conditions but he had the right to vote and this we considered a huge achievement when we compared ourselves to the military dictatorships in most other developing countries. So, you would think that as educated, privileged Indians at least the suspension of fundamental rights and the imposition of press censorship would have come up in conversations that evening. They did not. I realized later that the political changes in the country were never mentioned only in the set in which Rajiv and Sonia Gandhi moved.

During the Emergency, my social life seemed to become an endless series of dinner parties. The city had not extended as much as it has today. If we travelled to the still unfinished colonies of Shanti Niketan and Vasant Vihar it was considered a long way. Vicky Bharat Ram lived in Shanti Niketan and I found myself invited to his house quite a lot. At his dinner parties there were nearly always the same people. One of them was Romi Chopra, who remains a devotee of the Gandhi family to this day. I remember him from those evenings as a shy, effeminate man. Someone who knew him from his Cambridge days once told me that he had wanted to become a ballet dancer but had ended up working for an advertising company in Delhi. When Rajiv and Sonia were not present he would talk to me about politics, but his political views were limited to the unashamed, unstinting, unquestioning worship of Mrs Gandhi. In his eyes she could do no wrong and the Nehru–Gandhi family had a divine right to rule India forever and ever.

Vicky I remember as being full of bluster and social conversation. He was a lot richer than the rest of us so at his dinner parties he would serve French wine and fine Scotch whisky at a time when Mrs Gandhi's socialist economic policies made these things almost impossible to acquire. He was married at the time to a beautiful Mexican woman who hardly ever came to Delhi. This did not deter Vicky from giving wonderful dinner parties in his house filled with antique Indian sculpture and exquisite paintings. His family was famous for their contribution to Delhi's culture and some of the finest private concerts I have attended were in Vicky's father's house.

Another couple who were regular guests at these dinner parties were Satish Sharma and his foreigner wife, Sterre. She was blonde and spent most of the evenings chatting to Sonia. Satish Sharma was a surly, silent man who did not seem to have much to say. He came from a middle-class background and had not been at either school or university with Rajiv and his other friends. Satish worked for Indian Airlines and it was through flying together that Rajiv and he had become friends. He gave no indication that he was even slightly interested in politics or current affairs. If someone had predicted that he would one day become an MP from Indira Gandhi's constituency, Rae Bareli, and a cabinet minister it would have been taken as a joke.

The other close friends who were present at these gatherings when they were in town were Nina and Arun Singh, and Suman and Manju Dubey. Of them Nina was the most likeable because of her friendly, open nature. Arun, or Roon, as everyone called him, was impossible to talk to because of his forbidding reserve. I knew of Suman from journalistic circles, in which he was respected for having got himself a very well-paid job with a newspaper in Singapore or Hong Kong. Indian journalism in those days consisted of a handful of English newspapers, with a small circulation and big influence, and a handful of Hindi newspapers that had a larger circulation but little influence, and any journalist who could get a job in a foreign newspaper was hugely admired. Suman was fidgety and nervous and seemed permanently distracted, while his wife, Manju, was a legendary beauty but had about her a cold, supercilious air. Another couple I remember as being part of Rajiv and Sonia's inner circle were Nimal and Thud. I never found out his real name because everyone called him Thud, short for his surname, Thadani. It was only after Rajiv became prime minister and Thud became well known as one of his close friends that I discovered that his first name was Mohan. His wife was a plump, blowsy former airline stewardess who looked as if she may once have been pretty.

Then there were the foreign friends with whom Sonia seemed most comfortable and relaxed. Ottavio and Maria Quattrocchi were the ones who were nearly always invited where Rajiv and Sonia went. Not much was known about them, except that Ottavio worked for an Italian company and lived in Friends Colony. Sonia's parents stayed with them when they came to Delhi. The other foreign friends came and went. There were Teresa and Brewster, whose surname I no longer remember, who lived in Marbella and had been introduced to Rajiv and Sonia by Mohammed Yunus, one of the Gandhi family's closest friends. Yunus was a tall, talkative Pathan who, during the Emergency, became one of Mrs Gandhi's most vociferous spokesmen. Teresa was very glamorous and always dressed in the latest clothes by Yves Saint Laurent or whoever was the designer of the season, and Brewster was a tall, bald ex-model. They disappeared soon after the Emergency ended, when it was discovered that they were involved in smuggling antiques out of India. There were other foreigners who came and went but were too itinerant to be important.

Drifting in and out of this inner circle of friends would be the occasional prince from Rajasthan or Punjab, a business tycoon or two from Bombay and other friends of Rajiv from the Doon School. It was a closed circle of people who lived an upper middle class Indian existence. Nobody spoke Hindi well but that did not matter. What mattered was if you spoke the sort of English you may have learned in a public school in Dehra Dun. If some newly rich businessman drifted by speaking English with difficulty, he was instantly treated as an object of fun.

Sonia did not speak English well but because she was a foreigner it did not matter. We were deeply impressed by all things foreign not just because we had been ruled by white men for so long but because secretly we believed that Western culture and civilization was superior to ours. It may sound like a funny thing to say, but Sonia's foreignness made it easier for her to be accepted in Rajiv's circle of friends. Had he married an Indian woman of her background, she would have been permanently held in contempt by the broken-down aristocrats and aspiring grandees who were Rajiv's closest friends.

It is an indication of how deracinated our little set was, how removed from even popular Indian culture, that we did not notice that a few weeks after the Emergency was declared, a film called *Sholay* was released and made history as the biggest hit ever from the Bombay film industry. Rajiv's childhood friend Amitabh Bachchan was one of the stars of the film and would go on to play a political role when Rajiv became prime minister.

While people in Delhi's drawing rooms, including Rajiv and Sonia and their friends, lived through the Emergency years blissfully oblivious to the new political realities that the suspension of democracy created, most Indians were learning in different ways to understand the meaning of repression.

On the morning my mother woke me up to tell me that a state of Emergency had been declared in the country all I could think about was getting to the office as soon as possible to see if the consequences of censorship meant that I would no longer have a job. Press censorship brought with it the possibility of retrenchment in newspapers and the thought of becoming unemployed again and so soon terrified me.

When I got to the reporters' room I found it packed with senior journalists who had descended from their fine offices at the other end of the corridor to explain the meaning of the Emergency to us humble reporters. A Bengali editor, who shall remain nameless, was in full dissertation mode and in lengthy sentences filled with big words was explaining why Mrs Gandhi had to do what she did. He supported the Emergency, he said, because no country could tolerate opposition leaders who openly incited the police and military to disobey the prime minister. His reference was to a rally in Delhi's Ram Lila Maidan that the opposition leaders had held a few days earlier, at which Jayaprakash Narayan urged soldiers and policemen to disobey government orders. I had not been at the rally but heard from colleagues who had that it was the biggest political rally ever held in Delhi. This rally alone would have frightened Mrs Gandhi enough to declare an Emergency, nervous as she already was about the political movements against her government that seemed to be spreading across the country.

The Emergency came into effect at midnight on 25 June 1975 when the President was 'persuaded' to sign the declaration without asking questions. Mrs Gandhi's cabinet ministers were forced to go along with her plan. That night every major opposition leader in Delhi was arrested. This did not seem to bother the Bengali editor.

When someone asked about press censorship, he said it was a temporary measure and then, with a wave of his hand, vanished back up the corridor where senior journalists had offices much grander than our crowded, hot and stuffy reporters' room. It had a glass wall through which we could see the grubby balcony on which the peons sat all day, breathing fumes from the relentless traffic in the outer circle of Connaught Place. The reporters' room seemed to have been designed with the specific purpose of making reporters feel the worst of the heat during summer and the iciest cold in winter. Our desks were crammed together, making life even more uncomfortable, and the room always smelled of newsprint and south Indian spices.

That hot June morning there was too much excitement in the air even for someone as finicky as me to notice the smells and the heat. Journalists, especially junior reporters, love big political stories, and this was as huge a story as anyone had ever covered. What made the day even more exciting was the news that our paper had decided to defy censorship. Surinder Nihal Singh was the editor-in-chief of the paper at the time and made it clear to the senior staff at that morning's news conference that we would carry on the front page details of the arrest of opposition leaders. When this was conveyed to us, I have to say that I was thrilled. I saw our battle against press censorship as a small but vital part of the struggle for democracy that the Emergency had provoked.

That morning most of the city's newspapers had failed to come out because Mrs Gandhi ordered the power supply to be cut in Bahadur Shah Zafar Marg where they had their offices. But, with typical Indian ineptitude, the officials had forgotten that the *Statesman* and the *Hindustan Times* had their offices in Connaught Place, so we began our defiance of censorship by bravely bringing out a special edition that had blank spaces on its front page where the story about the opposition leaders being arrested would have been. This got us into trouble with the censors but we continued bringing out the paper with blank spaces until the censors, sitting in the Press Information Bureau, ordered the newspaper to be submitted to them every night for what they called 'pre-censorship'. On some days it would be returned so late at night that it could not be sold the next day until after 8 a.m.

It did not take long for the *Times of India* and the *Hindustan Times* to start obeying government orders. But, the *Statesman* and the *Indian Express* fought valiantly on until the minister of information and broadcasting was changed at Sanjay Gandhi's behest. Sweet, mild Inder Gujral was replaced by Vidya Charan Shukla. The story of the minister's sacking that drifted around newspaper offices was that Mr Gujral, an old friend of Mrs Gandhi, had objected to Sanjay ordering him around and Sanjay had responded by ordering his immediate dismissal. The unsmiling, brutish Shukla warned us at the first press conference he held that any defiance of press censorship would be dealt with harshly. He was soon dictating which stories we should give 'prominence' to and these were usually related to an event attended by Sanjay Gandhi or an idea that had come from him.

Every day in that first month of the Emergency political rallies were organized in Delhi in support of Mrs Gandhi. At these rallies, her close aides made long, sneering speeches about the opposition leaders. They were reviled as the villains of the Emergency for supposedly inciting anarchy and violence while Mrs Gandhi was praised as India's only hope, the saviour of India. I remember one of these rallies in particular because the star speaker was Mrs Gandhi's former stenographer, Yashpal Kapoor, the man chiefly responsible for the Allahabad High Court's judgement against Mrs Gandhi as the official indicted for managing her election campaign without resigning from his government job. His presence at a political rally so soon after the Emergency was a sign that Mrs Gandhi had decided to be brazen. My most vivid memory of this rally is of Yashpal Kapoor's wife, who was also present on the stage, and the large, dangling diamond earrings that she was wearing. This was unusual in those socialist times when the richest of our political leaders pretended to be poor, but as we were soon to discover the Emergency was a most unusual time.

Another rally I remember from those first days of the Emergency was one that was meant to be addressed by the Rajmata of Gwalior, Vijaya Raje Scindia, an opposition leader who had managed to give Mrs Gandhi's policemen the slip. One day the reporters' room buzzed with the rumour that the Rajmata was going to emerge in old Delhi that afternoon and after making a speech would allow herself to be arrested. I spent a burning hot day waiting in Chandni Chowk for her to arrive. Mark Tully, already the most famous foreign correspondent in India and the voice of the BBC in South Asia, was there along with reporters from Delhi's newspapers.

We waited in an old Mughal square at the end of a cluttered, ugly street in front of an old mosque. Political workers from the Jana Sangh, the party the Rajmata represented, tried to rally people by shouting slogans and 'courting arrest'. After waiting all day we were told that the Rajmata would not be coming after all and that she had probably been arrested. I remember going home and telling my mother that I had spent a whole day waiting for the Rajmata of Gwalior and she had not shown up. My mother listened politely but seemed less interested in what I was saying than in the trays of food that were being carried to a guest room by maids I had never seen before.

'We have guests?'

'Yes.'

'Who?'

'You don't know them.'

'Oh.' The house was often filled with relations from Punjab whom I spent a lot of my time trying to avoid so I asked no more questions.

It was only when the Rajmata of Gwalior was arrested some weeks later that my mother told me that on the day I had waited for her in old Delhi, she had been the mystery guest in our home. In the days that she remained 'underground' the Rajmata was on the move constantly and stayed a few days with my parents because of their friendship with Jaswant Singh who was then one of her political aides. He was in the same regiment as my father but left the army to enter politics and went on to become India's foreign minister when Atal Behari Vajpayee became prime minister in 1998.

Mrs Gandhi used the Emergency to teach the nation, in instalments, the lesson that not even the smallest act of defiance would be tolerated. First it was politicians and journalists who were taught what the Emergency meant. Then came the turn of judges to be taught that they would owe allegiance to the government or find themselves in trouble. So when the Supreme Court was asked to rule on whether the suspension of fundamental rights was valid, they quietly submitted that it was. Only one judge dissented and paid for his defiance by remaining out of favour as long as Mrs Gandhi ruled. India's political culture changed forever during the Emergency. It was on account of the absolute power that the prime minister was seen to wield that an atmosphere of servility and sycophancy came to surround her and her family. Dissenting voices were no longer heard in government, in Parliament or in the judiciary.

After this came the turn of rich Indians to learn what the Indian government could do to them. Their ranks had already been decimated by high taxes and a virtual economic dictatorship but now they were forced to realize how dangerous it could be for them to oppose the government in any way. In Delhi it was the sudden intrusion of unknown but important officials into people's homes that first made people wonder what was happening. The officials were polite but asked a lot of questions and had no hesitation in admitting that they represented various branches of the Indian government's intelligence agencies. Then came the tax raids.

Mrs Gandhi had long used the income tax raid as a weapon against her political opponents but now raids were carried out randomly against almost anyone. Tax inspectors appeared one morning in Mapu's house in Sundar Nagar and started questioning him about the silver chairs in his drawing room that belonged to a Gujarati prince. He tried to explain that the chairs did not belong to him and had been brought to Delhi for repairs but Mrs Gandhi's tax inspectors had little time for explanations. After this they wandered down the road to the house of a rich businessman and questioned him about how he could afford to own and run seven air-conditioners. Stories of these raids were deliberately leaked by officials to the offices of censored newspapers and Mapu's silver chairs got bigger headlines than the businessman's seven air-conditioners. Journalists covering the story were somehow bedazzled by the idea of silver furniture.

The most famous of these tax raids took place in the palaces of the Maharaja of Jaipur. The Nehru–Gandhi family, who had pretensions to aristocracy, were famous for their antipathy to the Indian princes. In Mrs Gandhi's case this antipathy was believed to be intense on account of her personal dislike of the Rajmata of Jaipur, Maharani Gayatri Devi. Those of us who knew the Rajmata also knew that though she had contested a Lok Sabha election in the early sixties and won with such an astonishing margin that she found herself in the *Guinness Book of Records*, her political aspirations were less than serious. We often wondered why Mrs Gandhi disliked someone who was no political threat to her and concluded that it could be because she was the only Indian woman, other than Mrs Gandhi herself, who was well known outside India in the seventies.

The reasons for the raid on the Jaipur royal family were not obviously political unless Mrs Gandhi was playing a card she had played with great success before. Three years before she declared the Emergency, she abolished the titles, privileges and privy purses of the Indian princes. The Government of India had signed a treaty with the princes guaranteeing them their personal privileges and a privy purse when they merged their kingdoms with the Union of India in 1947. The size of the privy purses varied according to the size of the state and diminished with every generation but Mrs Gandhi decided to put an end to the princes' privileges altogether. This was the first instance of the Government of India breaking a sovereign treaty.

Once India's fabled maharajas were no longer ruling princes they lost touch with the people and when Mrs Gandhi abolished them, they went mostly unmourned. The urban middle classes saw them as feudal anachronisms and their poorer subjects no longer respected them as givers of jobs and deliverers of justice. By the seventies, the princes hardly mattered to anyone and Mrs Gandhi was seen as the great socialist heroine by the people who lived in desperate rural poverty. The princes ruled 40 per cent of India in the days of the British Raj and it was in this 40 per cent that Indian culture was kept alive. The maharajas created schools of music and painting, built museums and kept Indian languages alive through their promotion of Indian literature and poetry. But there were also stories of debauchery, decadence and indolence, of toadying to the British and betrayals of India that they became more known for.

Mrs Gandhi liked to depict herself as a person of simple living and socialist beliefs. State-controlled television channels, the only kind that existed until the nineties, portrayed her as a sort of people's maharani whose family had donated their 'palatial' family home in Allahabad, Anand Bhawan, to the nation. When I finally saw Anand Bhawan during an election in Allahabad, it surprised me to find it was not a magnificent palace but an ordinary house of little charm. It was a museum by then and to perpetrate the myth of Nehruvian aristocracy, Pandit Nehru's laundry bills from some European laundry were on display in glass cases along with other artefacts from the days when Anand Bhawan was one of the centres of the freedom movement.

Mrs Gandhi's socialist officials went out of their way to humiliate the real maharajas after they were 'derecognized' in 1971. Senior bureaucrats and petty officials took to marching into palaces in Rajasthan on 'inspections' and if some objet d'art or piece of furniture caught their eye, they would order it to be sent to their own homes. With their privy purses taken away, most maharajas were unable to maintain their palaces. At the time they could not even turn the palaces into the hotels they were to eventually become since there were few foreign visitors to India in the seventies. Princely India fell into genteel decay. This did not stop Doordarshan programmes and Bollywood films from routinely depicting maharajas as venal and duplicitous and our new socialist rulers as paragons of virtue.

Doordarshan programming was entirely controlled by the government and Bollywood was controlled by writers of leftist persuasion who liked to depict princes and rich businessmen as enemies of the people.

The raid on the Jaipur royal family confirmed all the myths and created many more because of the 800 kilograms of gold found in a hidden cellar in the Moti Doongri fort. The discovery validated Mrs Gandhi's tax raids. The funny thing is that the gold was found by accident and it seems more than possible that even the Jaipur royal family did not know of its existence. A friend who was close enough to the royal family to have been present through the raid told me afterwards that the tax raiders 'just got lucky'.

'They went through all the big palaces and forts with a fine-toothed comb,' she said, 'and they found nothing at all. I think all they found was $70 in one of Rajmata Sahib's handbags and it was because of this that she was arrested under COFEPOSA under which they arrest smugglers and those who deal in foreign exchange. Then, on the last day they went up to Moti Doongri and again found nothing that was illegal. The man who was leading the raid was quite frustrated at finding nothing so he stamped his feet and the paving stone made a hollow sound. That's how they found it. I tell you nobody knew it was there or when it was hidden there. If they had, do you think it would have still been there?' What the 'lucky', foot-stamping tax inspector stumbled upon was a wall of gold bricks. Nothing like this hidden treasure has ever been found either before or since, and the excitement it caused during the Emergency is almost indescribable.

Delhi's reporters finally had a really good story they could actually report on. The Jaipur gold sent such a tremor through dreary, censored newspaper offices that usually stingy editors opened their purse strings to pay for reporters to go to Jaipur and do some 'investigative' journalism. I was not lucky enough to be assigned this story but I happened to be in Jaipur for other reasons shortly afterwards and found the city full of new myths. In the bazaars they talked of how this was 'Mughal gold'. The maharaja who built the fort was commander-in-chief of the armies of the Emperor Akbar, they said, and it was at that time that the gold was brought here and buried. Suddenly, everyone had an ancestor who had personally seen 'long lines of mules laden with gold going up the hill to Moti Doongri'.

Mrs Gandhi's tax inspectors were so encouraged by the success of the Jaipur treasure hunt that they started looking for hidden treasure in other palaces and forts. Almost next on the list was Gwalior. Vasundhara Raje Scindia and her sister Yashodhara were the only two members of the Gwalior royal family who were around when the raid happened. Their brother, Madhav Rao Scindia, escaped to Nepal when the Emergency was declared because, as a prominent member of Parliament of the Jana Sangh at the time, he was an obvious candidate for Mrs Gandhi's jail cells. Vasundhara Raje's mother, Rajmata Vijaya Raje Scindia, was in jail by the time of the raid. Vasundhara was in the family home in Delhi when the raiders came. They threw all the furniture out of the house, she told me later, and said that she could take what she wanted from it but could no longer have the house. It was taken over by Navin Chawla, who soon became known as one of Sanjay Gandhi's hatchet men and, much later, when a government came to power under the dispensation of Sonia Gandhi, was appointed the chief election commissioner of India. At the time of the raid on the Gwalior family he was an unknown municipal official. Vasundhara became homeless overnight and had to move into a manager's cottage on the premises of an abandoned ceramics factory her family owned. Yashodhara told me afterwards that the taxmen seemed more interested in going into the cellars under the Gwalior palace than in anything else. It was hidden treasure they were looking for and after the Moti Doongri discovery they had good reason to hope that they would find something. They found nothing, but the raids on businessmen and opposition leaders continued.

The Emergency shattered the safe little world in which I had grown up and threw me into another world altogether. In my secure, privileged India of boarding schools, Gymkhana Clubs, summer holidays in the hills and Enid Blyton books, I had been taught to respect our political leaders and never question the authority of the government. In that first month of the Emergency I learned to understand brute political power and the terror that the Indian state could instil in those who chose to defy its will.

4 TURKMAN GATE

As the months went by it became clear that beneath the talk of discipline and development the main reason for the Emergency was to ensure that no questions were asked about Sanjay Gandhi's new political role. Until that summer of 1975, Sanjay Gandhi was known only for being the prime minister's more controversial son. He had shown little ability to succeed at anything. His academic record was unremarkable and instead of going to university, as his older brother had done, he chose to do an apprenticeship at the Rolls Royce factory in England. I knew from friends, who were with him when he was briefly at the Doon School (he left for unknown reasons), that he had a mechanical bent of mind and that his taste in reading was limited to magazines for amateur mechanics.

After he left for England not much was heard of him except for the occasional bit of gossip about reckless behaviour and a taste for fast cars. Sanjay's activities only caught the public eye after it became known that the prime minister had granted her younger son a licence to build a 'people's car' for India to be called Maruti, after the Hindu god of the wind. This was the height of the licence raj when not only were licences and quotas hard to come by but industrialists could face criminal charges for producing manufactured goods beyond their quotas. Only two or three Indian companies were licensed to make cars so for Sanjay, with no experience of automobile manufacturing, to be given a licence was so irregular that Maruti became a big issue in Parliament and in the media. What added fuel to the furore was the Congress chief minister of Haryana's gift to Sanjay of hundreds of acres of public land on the outskirts of Delhi to set up his car factory. Sanjay supposedly got to work but never succeeded in making a single car.

Until the Emergency Sanjay showed not the tiniest interest in politics. When the first stories about his interference in matters of government and his influence over his mother began to filter into newspaper offices many people dismissed them. If I took them more seriously it was only because of my acquaintance with Rukhsana Sultana, a celebrated socialite, whose access to the rich and powerful was legendary. Rukhsana had once been married to the brother of a school friend of mine but the marriage had not lasted. I did not see her for many years after this but heard of her often in Delhi's social circles and always because of her connections with powerful politicians and rich businessmen. She was much older than me and we moved in different circles, so I may not have met her at all had I not gone with Naveen Patnaik to dinner at Biki and Goodie Oberoi's farmhouse.

The Oberoi Hotel was by the mid-seventies not just the most glamorous hotel in Delhi but had enhanced its allure by giving Delhi its first nightclub. It was called Tabela and, because the word means 'stable' in Urdu, its interior was designed by a singularly unimaginative designer to resemble a stable. Every table had its own stall and there was real straw and paintings of horses on the walls. It was outside Tabela one evening that Naveen introduced me to Biki and Goodie Oberoi as they wafted into the nightclub in a cloud of expensive perfume and cigar smoke. They were with a baron from Germany whose private plane had been seized by Indian customs. Rich foreigners rarely came to India in the seventies and the customs officials had never seen a private plane so they confiscated it. It was as simple as that. They then spent many days examining it closely for reasons that remain unexplained. The baron was on his way to a more enticing eastern destination like Bali and was annoyed to be stuck in Delhi instead, worried that Indian customs may have plans to sell his plane in bits and pieces to smugglers. I remember him being very puzzled about why it should take so long for customs officials to release it. In a misguided attempt to defend India and blame it all on the new rules of dictatorship, I tried hopelessly to explain the Emergency to him in a few short sentences. In the course of this conversation I found myself invited to dinner at the Oberois's farmhouse the next day, when Goodie leaned across me to order Naveen, 'Bring her with you.'

Rural land on the edge of Delhi was cheap and Rai Bahadur Oberoi had bought more than a hundred acres of farmland in Bijwasan village near the airport to grow food and dairy products for the Oberoi Hotel. In one corner of this farm, Biki and Goodie had built themselves a modernistic glass palace and filled it with beautiful things. There were Persian carpets on floors of Italian marble, elegant European furniture, paintings by famous Indian artists and a luminous view of lit-up gardens and a swimming pool through walls of glass. Not many people lived like this in socialist Delhi and I admit to gaping like a villager as I picked up a glass of champagne from the uniformed waiter at the entrance.

No sooner did Naveen and I enter the drawing room than I noticed Rukhsana Sultana resplendent in a dark chiffon sari and very much the belle of the ball, possibly because it was by now well known that she was a close aide of Sanjay Gandhi. She wore sunglasses that were tinted blue and I remembered that my school friend had told me she wore them all the time because she was short-sighted. I had not seen her for more than ten years and was struck by how good she still looked. She was in her late thirties and had gained a few pounds so there was a soft dumpiness about her body, but her skin was as clear as that of a young girl and she had a femininity about her that was, according to men of reliable expertise, her real allure. 'Look at the way she always smells of wonderful perfume,' one of them said to me that evening. 'Look at how her hands are always perfectly manicured, look at how beautifully she is dressed... You women should learn from her.'

That evening she sat surrounded by an audience of businessmen and socialites whom she was regaling with stories of the 'social work' she was doing 'for Sanjay' in the old city. He wanted her, she said with a sweet smile, to introduce Muslim women to modern ideas like family planning. The fragment of this conversation that remains etched vividly in my mind is her saying, 'You know, these women are ready for change, darling, but they do not know how to defy their men. So when they see me, a Muslim woman, wearing chiffon saris and pearls and French perfume they like it... They see me as someone they would like to be.' They were words I was to remember well, some weeks later, when Rukhsana's efforts at coaxing Muslim women to plan their families caused riots in the old city and I was nearly attacked by a mob because my sunglasses caused some people to mistake me for Rukhsana.

Why Sanjay Gandhi chose an apolitical socialite to influence conservative Muslim women to stop having babies remains a mystery but what soon became evident was his personal touch when it came to running the government. In the very first weeks of the Emergency, after he appointed a tough information minister of his choice, a concerted effort began to introduce Sanjay to India as her future leader. Photographs of his thin-lipped, bespectacled face started appearing nearly every day on the front pages of newspapers. Doordarshan, state-controlled and obedient, followed him on his travels around the country with the prime minister. He suddenly seemed to be accompanying his mother everywhere she went.

He started his own political activities as well with the creation of a new youth wing of the Congress Party. It soon became hard to ignore in Delhi. Thuggish young men in white became a worrying feature of life in the city. They moved in large, noisy groups and terrorized restaurants and shops in Connaught Place and Janpath. If they chose not to pay their bills or create a disturbance nobody objected, because everyone knew that these were Sanjay Gandhi's men. Sanjay made no effort to hide his growing political power or his influence on government policies. He announced a 5-Point Programme that was given more publicity than Mrs Gandhi's own 20-Point Programme. The 5-Point Programme turned big policies into short sentences.

Plan your family.
Plant a tree.
Clean your street.
Remove poverty.
Remove slums.

Delhi's walls were soon covered in posters advertising the political thoughts of the new leader in snappy, one-line slogans.

Each one, teach one.
We two, our two.
Clean India, dream India.

The one that urged Indians to stop having more than two children. '*Hum do, hamare do*', which literally translated is 'We two, our two', survived beyond the Emergency as a family planning message.

Along with Rukhsana's efforts to teach Muslim women the joys of having fewer babies, another point in Sanjay Gandhi's programme that began to manifest itself in Delhi soon was the injunction to remove slums. If Rukhsana Sultana was an odd choice as his family planning envoy, the person he picked to be his slum clearance envoy was odder still. He chose Jagmohan, a municipal official, whose family had come to Delhi as refugees in 1947 and who had a reputation for being bitter about the division of India in the name of Islam. Years later when he started writing regularly in newspapers, the thoughts he expressed had a distinct tinge of Hindu nationalism.

Jagmohan was a small, charmless man with a long nose and hair that he brushed upwards to cover his bald pate. He was head of the Delhi Development Authority (DDA) when the Emergency began and vain about his administrative abilities, perhaps because he had developed some parks in Delhi and had made efforts to 'beautify' the city. When Sanjay announced his slum removal plans, Jagmohan took up the task with unconcealed zest. Sadly, one of the first things he demolished in the old city was a lovely little air-conditioned restaurant called Flora, which was so close to the steps of the Jama Masjid that you could see the mosque through its big glass windows as you feasted on kebabs so delicate they melted in your mouth. When I made some inquiries about the disappearance of my favourite restaurant, I learned that it had been demolished on Jagmohan's orders because it was 'illegally constructed'.

It was around then that rumours started to spread in the old city about Jagmohan being a man who 'hated' Muslims. Bazaar gossip had it that a meeting of officials had taken place in Ranjit Hotel, a new hotel nearby whose higher floors offered a clear view of the old city. According to hearsay, it was at this meeting that Jagmohan said, 'I want everything cleared from here to the Jama Masjid because I will not allow another Pakistan to come up.' Jagmohan has since denied that there was ever such a meeting but because newspapers were censored at the time rumours were easily believed. This was especially true of the bazaars of the old city. Karim's restaurant put up a sign in Urdu that said: 'Political conversations are banned in this restaurant until further notice.' But rumours of Jagmohan's alleged plans to demolish huge sections of old Delhi continued to spread and somehow got mixed up with Rukhsana Sultana's exercises in family planning.

Rukhsana may have convinced herself that she was doing social work in old Delhi, but the residents of this conservative Muslim quarter of the city saw her as someone who had been sent to corrupt God-fearing Muslim girls. I heard this not from women in the old city but from Muslim men, particularly the older, bearded ones, who saw themselves as sentinels of Islam and its traditions. It was always easy in this part of Delhi to raise the cry of Islam being in danger and between Jagmohan's demolitions and Rukhsana's family planning forays it became easy for Muslims to believe that the Emergency was being used to target them as a community. Days before violence broke out at Turkman Gate, I remember wandering about the streets around the Jama Masjid and being conscious of a simmering rage.

Shahjahanabad, the old Mughal city, once existed where the Jama Masjid and the Red Fort now stand. At one time its population had been mostly Muslim. After Partition this changed because thousands of Punjabi refugees were settled in the homes vacated by the Muslims who left for Pakistan. But because of old tensions and differences in dietary habits the Hindus formed their ghetto on one side of the mosque and the Muslims lived on the other side, as they do today.

These are factors that Sanjay Gandhi seems not to have considered or cared much about. If the prime minister was trying to give him wiser counsel it did not prevent him from sending his envoys to this politically sensitive place to implement the two most contentious points of his 5-Point Programme. Rukhsana Sultana and Jagmohan went about their missions with zeal and insensitivity. And what happened at Turkman Gate on 18 April 1976 was an eruption of public anger that had been building slowly for months.

Turkman Gate is an old Mughal gate that was one of the entrances to the walled city, built by Emperor Shah Jahan when he moved his capital here from Agra. It is made of stone, more arch than gate, and would have been just another one of Delhi's forgotten monuments if it had not lent its name to the area in which it stands. Leading off from the gate is a maze of narrow lanes that twist and wind their way to the Jama Masjid. Until Jagmohan's demolition crews arrived, these narrow lanes were lined with old-fashioned havelis typical of this part of the city. Their architecture is distinct; they are usually tall, narrow structures built around a central courtyard. These grand, old buildings have now mostly disappeared but in the seventies there were many fine havelis hidden in old Delhi's squalid, cluttered alleys. Their narrow doorways opened to courtyards and walled gardens and into high-ceilinged rooms beautifully furnished with antique Persian carpets and dusty chandeliers. By the seventies, municipal neglect had turned old Delhi into so unsanitary a place that those who owned the grander havelis had moved to newer and cleaner parts of the city, but this did not mean that old Delhi could be described as a slum. It was, and still is, the most picturesque and romantic part of the city despite decades of neglect and civic decay. There were slums and shanties in newer parts of the city but, for reasons that remain mysterious, it was old Delhi that was targeted for 'slum removal'.

On 18 April 1976, it was one of those lazy afternoons in the reporters' room when news came of riots in the old city. Whoever brought the news said people had been killed in police firing. I assumed that it was a clash between Hindus and Muslims because this, sadly, is what the old city had become notorious for after 1947. There was some debate in the reporters' room whether it was even worth covering a riot since the story would be almost certainly censored but I decided to go anyway. After a series I had written on Delhi's hospitals was censored, I was given the task of writing an anodyne column called 'Passing By'. I had to find three people who were passing through Delhi every week and interview them. It was as tedious a task as I have ever had in my career. So I jumped at the idea of having a real story to cover, even if just for my own satisfaction.

The bulldozers had arrived before I got to Turkman Gate and were doing their work with remarkable speed. Clouds of dust and debris obscured the houses that were being demolished, so it took me a few moments to realize that the bulldozers were battering down old Mughal havelis, which may have looked rundown and shabby from the outside but were proper, furnished homes beyond the façade. The officials with the bulldozers did not care. They were interested only in carrying out their orders. Through the dust and debris I saw people standing amid their salvaged possessions, looking dazed and helpless. Women wailed and children wept as they stood among pots and pans tied up with string, clothes gathered in bundles made of old sheets, rolled up mattresses and small pieces of furniture that they had managed to save. They stared mesmerized at the bulldozers as they smashed down the walls of their homes. When the walls came down, there would be glimpses of beds and cupboards and carpets before the bulldozers smashed them to dust. At one moment it looked as if some men were on the verge of stopping the demolition by lying down in front of the bulldozers, but before this could happen a convoy of trucks arrived, into which they were herded.

While the officials supervising the demolitions were busy I managed to talk to some of the people whose homes were being demolished. They said they had been given no more than an hour's notice to move out of their homes. There had been rumours of possible demolitions for about a week but nobody had paid much attention to them because they did not think it was possible that the government would destroy their homes. It was only that morning, before the bulldozers arrived, that people realized they were about to lose their homes. They tried resisting but their protests had ended quickly when the police escorting the demolition squad fired into the crowd. Nobody knows how many people died in police firing that day. Figures range from twelve to 1200.

The people who were forced to move from Turkman Gate were taken to one of Sanjay Gandhi's 'resettlement colonies' on a wasteland beyond the Yamuna river where they were given small plots on which they were ordered to build their homes. Given the space provided, they could afford to build no more than one-room tenements, and since there were no provisions for drainage, electricity or water, what emerged from Sanjay Gandhi's 'slum clearance drive' were real slums that even today are places of open drains, flies, disease and degradation.

These shanties stretch from the banks of the Yamuna to the borders of Uttar Pradesh. If Jagmohan had been a real city planner he would have realized that by creating a wasteland of slums on the other side of the Yamuna he was throwing away forever the chance to use the river as part of Delhi's urban design. It could have been what the Thames is to London, the Seine to Paris and the Hudson to New York instead of turning into the poisonous sewer it is today.

Bizarrely, the place where I was to hear about the Turkman Gate incident next was, of all places, the unlikely surroundings of another Oberoi dinner party. Naveen called one morning to say that Sheikh Abdullah's son, Farooq, had returned to India after many years abroad and Goodie and Biki Oberoi were having a dinner party in his honour.

'We should go,' he said, 'it could be fun.'

One achievement Indira Gandhi can be given full marks for was the 'Indira–Sheikh accord' that she signed with Sheikh Mohammed Abdullah in 1974. As a result of this accord he gave up the demand for a plebiscite in Kashmir and agreed to elections within the democratic framework of India.

Sheikh Abdullah was Kashmir's most important political leader and the history of the subcontinent may have been different if the Government of India had not made its first big mistake in Kashmir by jailing him for nearly two decades. In 1953 Indians were still on an extended honeymoon with their political leaders so nobody seems to have asked too many questions about Jawaharlal Nehru's decision to imprison Sheikh Abdullah, who was not just Nehru's personal friend but the man directly responsible for Kashmir not opting to be in Pakistan.

Thirty years later, while I was doing research for a book on the Kashmir problem, I examined the reasons why Sheikh Abdullah had been jailed and found them hard to understand. The charges against him seemed flimsy. He had played golf with the American ambassador to India, met American officials in Saudi Arabia and visited Pakistan, and it was on the basis of these activities that he was charged with trying to bring about the secession of Kashmir from India with American help. All he appears to have wanted was Kashmir's right to retain the special status it was given when it chose to remain in India. Under the terms of its accession it was allowed to have its own prime minister, its own constitution and greater autonomy than other Indian states. These terms could have been conceded without any damage to the fabric of India.

Farooq Abdullah, Sheikh Abdullah's eldest son, left Kashmir after his father was jailed to go to a medical school in Jaipur. After becoming a doctor, he made a life for himself in England and returned only in 1975 after his father was released and allowed to return to Kashmir as chief minister. I remember this particular evening as being even more enjoyable than usual, possibly because Farooq was an old friend of the Oberois, returning after a long absence. It could as well have been because Sheikh Abdullah was now chief minister in Kashmir and the Oberois owned

Srinagar's grandest hotel. Farooq Abdullah, a very tall man, was a better-looking, lighter-skinned version of Sheikh Abdullah.

After drinks in the drawing room we went downstairs to the dining room. It had glass windows that opened on to the same landscaped gardens and a swimming pool that could be seen from the floor above but more intimately. The food, as usual, was excellent, starting with European hors d'oeuvres, a European main course that I think was capons from the Oberoi farm and then, to satisfy the Indian palate, there was spicy Goan prawn curry. Farooq and I were seated at the same table that evening and the conversation turned to politics, as it frequently did during the Emergency in drawing rooms that did not have government officials or members of the Gandhi family present. Most people at my table were supporters of the Emergency and made this clear. There was a retired military man who said that he liked the Emergency because he found it easier to park his car in Connaught Place and 'because the trains were now running on time'. This provoked me to say, with a sweet smile, that the trains had run on time in Hitler's Germany as well. There were protests from the military man and his wife about this 'odious' comparison. It must have been to deflect attention that I asked Farooq if it was true that his father had recently made a speech in Delhi criticizing the Emergency.

Farooq, who had listened quietly to the military man, looked straight at him and said that his father had indeed made such a speech after visiting the area where people moved from Turkman Gate were 'resettled'. It had made him very angry. It had shocked him, Farooq said, that they were living in the open in the rainy season. They had been dumped without shelter and without help, his father had said in his speech, adding that he could not believe that human beings could be treated this way. I cannot remember what the military man said in response but I do remember that we stopped talking about politics and went back to the sort of inanities usually discussed at dinner parties.

When I look back on Sanjay Gandhi's early exercises in governance I realize that it was the policy that interested him and not the people it would affect. Since he was a political novice and apparently uninterested in history, he never examined the reasons why the poorest, most illiterate Indians had the most children or why slums had come up in our cities.

He was interested only in ensuring that these things were stopped. The Emergency's suspension of fundamental rights suited his idea of governance perfectly.

On the need for 'slum clearance' Sanjay was correct in observing that cities that had once been charming and well-planned now looked like slums, but he never stopped to examine why this had happened. Had he done so he would have noticed that the blame for it lay in his grandfather's belief that central planning was the only way to urbanize India. Sanjay's solutions to the problem of slums may have worked better had he tried to understand what caused them.

It was not poverty that made migrants from rural India choose to live in flimsy dwellings in the midst of filthy, festering shanties it was the unavailability of affordable housing. The problem has reached crisis proportions today in cities like Mumbai and at its root is the Nehruvian idea of centrally controlling economic activity. Indian metropolises continue to be controlled by state governments instead of elected city governments and this is hard to change because of the mindset that Nehruvian socialism created. A mindset based on the fundamental belief that officials are benign, competent and beyond reproach.

Jawaharlal Nehru was a passionate democrat in political matters. Thanks to him, India's political institutions grew strong when dictatorships bloomed in every one of India's neighbouring countries. But when it came to the economy and building economic assets, he was a benevolent dictator. He believed that it was necessary for the state to control economic activity to prevent private entrepreneurs from profiteering, so one of the actions he took in the early sixties was to ban private real-estate developers in Indian cities. He set up the DDA to build affordable housing for the poor but since this was an impossible task for a single organization to undertake, slums developed when the number of migrants exceeded the supply of adequate housing. The DDA idea was copied in other Indian cities so that across the country slums came up in cities and towns. Then, when politicians realized that it was easy to find voters in the slums, they did nothing to stop them from growing. None of these things concerned Sanjay Gandhi. He wanted slums to be cleared and that was that.

Sanjay began his slum clearance exercises in Delhi because it was the capital and then made similar efforts in Agra. India had very few foreign visitors in the seventies but those who did come almost always went to see the Taj Mahal and while the Taj remained indescribably beautiful the bazaars around it had become indescribably squalid. In Delhi, why did he begin the demolitions in the old Mughal quarter between the Jama Masjid and Turkman Gate? I have asked myself this question many times and not found an answer. And I have no idea why it was in this part of the city that he sent his family planning envoy, Rukhsana Sultana. What is a matter of historical record is that his mother's health minister, the former maharaja of Jammu and Kashmir, Dr Karan Singh, had evolved a population policy, just before the Emergency, that was based on the premise that development was the best contraceptive. But development takes time and Sanjay Gandhi wanted instant results. The prime minister must have shared his impatience because she did nothing to prevent him from making a radical change in her health minister's family planning policy. Sanjay altered it to base it on targets that officials were ordered to meet. Everyone from teachers in villages to clerks in the government were enlisted and given sterilization targets. When the targets were found to be unrealistic, officials used the Emergency's suspension of fundamental rights, and the blanket of silence imposed by a censored press, to institute an undeclared programme of compulsory sterilization. This started to happen not just in Delhi but in villages across northern India. The peons in the *Statesman* office, our most reliable source of information from the rural areas, brought back to the reporters' room stories of relatives in villages in Uttar Pradesh who had been forcibly sterilized.

Newspaper editors in those times did not allow reporters to travel out of Delhi except in rare instances, so it was hard to know whether the stories the peons brought from their villages were true. What I did know was what was happening in old Delhi. Derelicts, rickshaw-wallas and others who slept on pavements at night were being picked up by mysterious officials who appeared in vans. They were taken to clinics where they were sterilized against their will. The very poor were easy 'targets', but despite their destitution they had tongues and they talked freely about being picked up in white vans with tinted glass windows and then waking up in hospital beds. It was only a matter of time before this 'point' in Sanjay Gandhi's 5-Point Programme became as notorious as slum clearance.

Sanjay Gandhi was so obviously the most important person in Mrs Gandhi's Emergency government that we in the media, who sat idling the hours away in reporters' rooms in Delhi, became obsessed with finding out what we could about him. We heard from 'reliable sources' that he had no time to read books but liked comics and technical magazines. We heard that he had a bad temper and got very angry if his orders were disobeyed. The sacking of his mother's information minister, Inder Gujral, was an example often mentioned. We heard that Sanjay was completely in charge of running the government and that the prime minister listened only to him. We had no way of verifying any of this information because he gave no interviews and our only contact with him was at public events like rallies where he said very little. He spoke in uncertain Hindi and in staccato sentences in a thin voice that was not made for public speaking.

Mrs Gandhi was not a popular prime minister by the summer of 1975. The high moment of her career had been the Bangladesh war in the winter of 1971 that ended with the division of Pakistan. India had not won a war in more than a thousand years, Mrs Gandhi's admirers like to say, and so if she achieved nothing else in her life she had done more than enough by winning the Bangladesh war. More than two decades after that war ended, I interviewed one of Mrs Gandhi's most ardent supporters, the industrialist Rama Prasad Goenka, for a television programme. When I asked him why he admired Mrs Gandhi so much he said without a moment's hesitation that it was because she had won India her first war in more than a millennium. In the immediate aftermath of the war even her opponents, like Atal Behari Vajpayee, exalted her publicly as Durga, the goddess of war. India's most famous artist, M.F. Hussain, painted her riding on the back of a tiger as the goddess Durga. But by 1975 Mrs Gandhi's lack of administrative skills and her misguided economic policies led to general unrest. The slogan of '*Garibi hatao*' (Remove poverty) that won her a spectacular victory in the 1971 general election had begun to ring hollow because her economic policies had failed to make the smallest dent in India's poverty.

By the summer of 1975 the mood in India was defeated, bleak and desperate. Every economic indicator told a bad story. Literacy was less than 50 per cent, infant mortality higher than in almost any other country, GDP growth so slow that it was mocked as the Hindu rate of growth. The richest Indians did without clean water and regular electricity. In Mrs Gandhi's own neighbourhood, long power cuts became the bane of burning hot summer nights. The water that came out of taps was undrinkable unless boiled. India seemed incapable of dealing with the most fundamental human needs like clean water to drink and enough food to eat.

Meanwhile, in the drawing rooms of Delhi, life went on as it had always done.

Without exchanging more than a few words with Sonia during the Emergency I noticed that none of the Indian women in what was considered her inner circle of friends were ever informal with her, except Nina, Arun Singh's wife, and she was not in Delhi much. The other ladies seemed to be in awe of Sonia and their simpering attempts to make conversation always seemed, at least to me, to be stilted and false. Sonia guarded her privacy fiercely and this gave her a reserve that was forbidding. I remember just one instance of trying to engage her in conversation at this time at one of Vicky's dinner parties. I asked her if she had ever missed Italy after coming to live in India and her answer was, 'No. Not at all. Sometimes maybe some food...some kinds of bread.' She made it so clear that she was not interested in the conversation going any further that I scuttled off and found someone easier to talk to. I personally found Sonia as foreign as any foreigner I had ever met. In those days she never wore Indian clothes, and was always in skirts or frocks, which added to the impression that she was different from the rest of us.

One thing I gathered from overhearing a conversation she had with the ladies who surrounded her was that she seemed terrified of India in a deep, deep way. It was summer and there must have been a new outbreak of malaria that the ladies were talking about. I heard Sonia say that when her children were babies she was so worried about them being bitten by mosquitoes that she would put anti-mosquito coils under their cradles. She only stopped when the family doctor told her that they were more in danger from the smoke of the repellent than from mosquitoes. None of the ladies found the story funny. None of them had the courage to tell her that when you grow up in India, you learn to live with mosquitoes just as you learn to live with undrinkable water in your taps, filthy streets, flies and an unreliable supply of electricity.

Another memory I have of Rajiv and Sonia in the Emergency days was when a group of us went to Tabela after a dinner party. Romi Chopra was in the group and Sonia's brother-in-law Waltair Vinci, who worked for Fiat in Italy. We were too early for Tabela to be open so as we sat on loungers by the Oberoi pool and I heard Sonia's brother-in-law chatting to her in Italian with an informality that was refreshing. I think he asked her to come and dance with him and she said, '*Doppo*' which someone translated for me as 'later'. There was no dancing, though, and neither Rajiv nor Sonia ever drank anything stronger than juice while the rest of us drank what we could get from the bootlegger.

It was from the group of friends that surrounded them that I got to know more about Rajiv and Sonia. These friends loved talking about their friendship with Rajiv and Sonia and competed with each other to show how close they were. I learned from them that Sonia hated politics and politicians and was very loyal to her friends, and that Rajiv was a 'very good person'. When I asked for an example of his goodness I was told, more than once, that Rajiv saw a beggar in rags on a cold night and immediately stopped his car and gave him his own coat.

Delhi in the seventies was a city in which everything was changing. All kinds of social and political barriers were breaking down. In the most conservative drawing rooms young people I had grown up with were smoking hashish and talking of revolution. This was partly because the winds of change that began to blow across the West in the sixties were bringing new music, new ideas and hippies to Delhi. Suddenly, girls from 'good families' were running off to Kathmandu and Goa in pursuit of free love and freedom.

There were indigenous influences as well that were beginning to change the way we thought. Political influences that came from the Naxalite movement that had spread across West Bengal and Bihar had many sympathizers in Delhi University. When seen from the safety of smoke-filled student canteens, the Naxalite revolution seemed most romantic. The allure of revolution was heightened by the repression the Emergency brought to Delhi and because Mao and Marx had not been discredited yet. The brutal, mindless violence that the Naxalite movement would later spawn had not yet begun to happen.

The students I knew who joined this Maoist armed struggle were well born, well educated and full of revolutionary zeal until they actually went to join the 'people's struggle' in the jungles of eastern India and had their first brush with the law. No sooner did they get arrested for taking up arms against the Indian state than they came home chastened and shaken up by the torture and brutality they faced in police stations. I remember meeting girls who showed me scars on their bodies that they said had been made by policemen putting their cigarettes out on them during torture sessions. I was not a political reporter yet nor did I fully understand such things as revolutions, but it was hard not to notice that outside the drawing rooms in which I spent most of my evenings, India was changing and that the people I met in those drawing rooms were oblivious to these changes. As a reporter I met different kinds of people and got a sense of what was happening. Revolution was so much in the air that for a moment I was personally seduced. I remember going off to a little shop in Connaught Place that was owned by the Embassy of the Soviet Union and sold Marxist literature of all kinds. I think it may have been my failed attempts to plough through *Das Kapital* that prevented me from joining my more revolutionary friends. But I continued to meet them for long, political discussions made languid with hashish or volatile with Old Monk rum in small, one-room barsatis in Nizamuddin and Golf Links.

There were other changes happening. There was a new kind of cinema coming from Bollywood, new young artists who tried to depict changing realities in their paintings and writers who were beginning to question what was going wrong in India. Everyone loved gossiping about Sanjay Gandhi and speculating about why the prime minister was letting her son rule India in her place. So when I met the friends of Rajiv and Sonia Gandhi I found it most curious that they seemed completely unaffected by India's social and political changes.

Perhaps it was because these changes had no impact at all on their mundane lives. They had nearly all married young, nearly all produced a child or two by their early thirties and their conversations were not very different to the conversations that my parents' generation would have had. When the occasional foreign visitors turned up in Vicky Bharat Ram's drawing room, there would be talk of the latest fashions in Europe or a new film from Hollywood and this would hugely elevate the level of discourse. Then the foreigners would disappear and it would be back to talk of holidays and children and occasionally spicy gossip about someone's private life and even that was not really spicy.

Nobody talked about books. These were people who had been to the best schools in India and gone on to the best universities abroad and it was as if they had remained impervious to the fine institutions of learning they had passed through. It was as if they had never even tried to look beyond the banality of their own lives to discover the larger canvas of existence with its drama, newness and constantly changing realities.

By the second year of the Emergency, Delhi's newsrooms had become accustomed to the rules of censorship. We devised ways to pass our censored time. One of these was to do 'human interest' stories.

Raghu Rai, who worked for the *Statesman,* and was already India's most famous photographer, became for me a handy accomplice in these exercises. In the summer of 1976 we went off on an excursion with some Americans who wanted to go white-water rafting on the Ganga. It was easy to forget the Emergency once we got to Devprayag, where the dark and treacherous Alaknanda meets the bubbly, dancing Bhagirathi to become the Ganga. Having gone to school in Dehra Dun, I felt a little as if I were on a mid-term trip. We followed the river up beyond Tehri, where its colour became that of the clearest emerald, and we camped at night on the cold white banks of the Bhagirathi.

In September that year we drove from Srinagar to Leh where the Dalai Lama was going to deliver his sixth Kalachakra sermon. This is a Tantric rite of initiation into Buddhist practice that is so special that most Dalai Lamas only give one in a lifetime. The strange circumstances of the fourteenth Dalai Lama's exile from Tibet altered this tradition. This sermon was all the more special because Ladakh had once been a part of Tibet.

A glass temple was built in Leh on the banks of the rust-coloured waters of the Indus for the Dalai Lama to preach from and thousands of devotees gathered from all over Ladakh. The riverbank teemed with monks in maroon and saffron robes and ordinary Ladakhis in their traditional clothes. Raghu took wonderful pictures and I would have stuck to writing a human interest story full of descriptions of moonlight and monasteries if Mao Tse Tung had not died on the day the sermon ended. My interview with the Dalai Lama happened to be on the day that news of Mao's death reached Leh. We met in the sunny garden of the local army commander's residence. Throughout the interview, the General stood behind me to make sure I did not disobey his injunction to not ask political questions. Mrs Gandhi was celebrating a moment of friendship with China and the General appeared to believe that it would embarrass the Government of India if the Dalai Lama made a political remark at this time.

As the interview began I said, 'Your Holiness, the General who is standing behind me has warned me not to ask you any political questions so we will have to talk about religion despite the news ...'

The Dalai Lama spoke almost no English then but when his interpreter told him what I had said he laughed and replied, 'Mao Tse Tung's death has just been announced, but if you want to talk about religion then that's all right.'

By early 1977 Delhi was beginning to boil over with anger and rebellion. After the violence in Turkman Gate the old city became a place where small explosions of rage occurred at regular intervals mostly due to the compulsory sterilization programme which continued although Rukhsana Sultana became less visible. Every time I went to Karim's for lunch I would hear more stories, from ordinary residents of the old city, of people being compulsorily sterilized. It was clear to most people I spoke to that tensions were building towards a violent explosion and the night it finally came happened to be a night on which I was on late duty in the *Statesman*'s reporters' room.

As a woman reporter I was assiduous about fulfilling my late-duty obligations. It was a new practice in Delhi's newspaper offices for women to be allowed to stay late at work. Because of the general hostility and disdain from our male colleagues, we made it a point to prove that we could do everything that they did, and late duty was one of these things because refusing to do it meant that some male reporter had to do double his share.

It was a particularly hot and sticky night and I had spent most of the evening fanning myself with a magazine. I was about to go home at around 10 p.m. when one of my contacts in the old city called to say that there had been police firing near the Jama Masjid and that he had seen some bodies lying near the steps of the mosque. It took me no more than ten minutes to drive through Daryaganj and get to the road that led to the main entrance of the mosque. A worrying silence hung over what was usually a noisy, bustling place and I noticed that the rickshaw-wallas who slept on the pavement opposite the Zenana Women's Hospital were missing. They could usually be found chatting and smoking late into the night. There were lights on in the hospital, but nobody was around. I left my car on the main road and walked to the Urdu Bazaar, stumbling over broken bricks. The street was covered with them. When I got close enough to be able to see the sandstone steps that led up to the mosque, I noticed a group of policemen standing beside two dark patches. One of them was outlining the patches with chalk in the dusty, yellow light of a street lamp.

When I met my contact, who had been waiting in one of the dark bylanes near the mosque, he said the riot started because of the sterilization drive. A young rickshaw-walla had been taken away by men in a white van and sterilized although he was unmarried and only twenty years old. When he was dropped back to the rickshaw stand he told everyone what had happened to him and said he had seen other victims in the clinic. It did not take long for an angry crowd to gather and turn violent. The next morning I returned to the old city and met victims of the sterilization drive. They were mostly very poor rickshaw-wallas from distant villages in Bihar and Uttar Pradesh and so frightened of what could happen to them that they were planning to go back to their villages. Their stories could not be told during the Emergency because of censorship.

This is one reason why later, when there were commissions of inquiry into the Emergency, it became almost impossible to establish that there had been a compulsory sterilization drive under Sanjay Gandhi's direction. The victims were not the sort of people who could come forward at an inquiry commission and give evidence. They were too poor and too powerless to dare to take on officials of any kind.

In politics, perception matters more than reality and the perception of the Emergency towards its last months was one of repression and brutality. Matters got so serious that a vaccination programme in Delhi's schools could not go ahead because parents were convinced that it was a secret programme to sterilize their children. No amount of official reassurance dispelled this idea. When school principals insisted that the vaccinations had to go ahead, terrified parents started withdrawing their children from municipal schools.

5 ELECTIONS, 1977

In the second week of January 1977, underworked and bored, like every other Indian journalist during the Emergency, I went to the Kumbh Mela in Allahabad for want of anything better to do. Little did I know on that bitterly cold night, as I took the Prayag Express from the old Delhi railway station, that what I thought was going to be yet another human interest story would turn out to be the biggest political story I had covered in my short career as a journalist. I was lucky to have a cold but cosy coupé to myself. I wiped the grit and dust off the green Rexine bunk, looked underneath for hidden cockroaches and ordered tea for 5 a.m. Then I laid out my sleeping bag and fell instantly asleep.

It was still dark when a sleepy attendant brought me tea in a plastic thermos the next morning. I noticed that we were on a bridge over a wide river and took this to mean we were approaching Allahabad. The tea was too sweet and too milky and had a thermosy taste, nowhere near as delicious as the railway tea I remembered from my childhood which tasted of spices and the terracotta cup in which it was served. As the first light of dawn broke, I saw wretchedly poor villages built along the edge of pools of stagnant water. As we got closer to Allahabad, shanties appeared where the fields had been. At least the hovels were 'pukka', I thought. In Indian government language this meant that they were made of brick and cement, which made the residents of these shanties count as relatively prosperous compared to villagers who lived in mud huts.

Allahabad railway station was crowded with sadhus of all manner and description. Ash-covered sadhus, saffron-robed sadhus, sadhus with strange objects twisted into their filthy dreadlocks and naked sadhus impressively unaffected by the freezing weather. They were unwashed and unattractive but old ladies collapsed before them in obeisance and young brides bowed their veiled heads and stretched their bangle-covered arms to touch their feet. The real India, I thought, getting into the first autorickshaw I could find, the real India of superstition, blind faith, wretchedness and misery.

We rattled off at an alarming pace through grubby bazaars and a city that seemed to have grown organically without any thought to aesthetics or town planning, no different from other cities of socialist India. Mrs Gandhi's fundamental economic principle was that the 'poorest of the poor' must be helped before money could be spent on luxuries. Town planning was considered a luxury, as were properly constructed roads and modern airports. Consequently, beautiful towns and cities from India's colonial and princely times crumbled into ruin.

The autorickshaw driver seemed to have guessed that I was a reporter because without any instructions from me he dropped me at the entrance of the press enclave. It was a cordoned-off area just below the ramparts of the old Mughal fort that towers over the confluence of the Ganga, Yamuna and the mythical Saraswati, which Hindus revere as the *sangam*. Every foreign correspondent in India, as well as an unusually large number of Indian journalists, seemed to be eating breakfast in the press enclave's tented dining room. I spotted Raghu Rai, Mark Tully from the BBC and American journalists from *Time* and *Newsweek* whom I vaguely knew. As I helped myself to hot tea, toast and a spicy omelette, I asked a colleague from one of the other Indian newspapers why every journalist in Delhi seemed to have made the effort to come to the Kumbh Mela and he said, with a furtive look around, that there were rumours that Mrs Gandhi was going to come to the mela and make an important announcement. 'Elections,' he whispered, 'they say that elections are about to be announced and she will make the announcement here.'

After breakfast I wandered down to the river. The press enclosure was at the top of a slope at some distance from the pilgrims and to get to the river I had to walk down a dirt path that had become squelchy and embedded with rose petals, marigold flowers and other offerings that pilgrims had dropped on their way to the river. On both sides of the path stretched the tents of the pilgrims. The sound of prayers rose above the din of voices and the smell of dirty toilets overpowered the aroma of incense.

Accommodation at the mela was arranged in accordance with the rigid hierarchy of the Hindu caste system. Rich pilgrims and wealthy gurus were given luxury tents at the top of the slope where the press enclosure was, while the poor were left to fend for themselves in clusters of dormitory tents lower down and closer to the river. Cheap rugs were laid out on dirt floors and whole families huddled together to keep warm. The tents smelled of unwashed clothes and kerosene oil.

Over the sound of prayers, on a crackly public address system, came the announcements for lost children. They were all for lost girls. 'Meena, aged five, wearing red frock is in tent number two. Parents are requested to please come forward. Sonia, aged three, wearing white frock. Divya, aged six …' It was always little girls that got lost at the Kumbh, often because their parents wanted to get rid of them. I found myself outside the tent for lost children and went in to see if there was a single boy among them. There were none. A row of little girls with tear-stained cheeks and frightened eyes sat on a wooden bench. They were barefoot and none of them wore warm clothes. Their hair was tangled and unwashed and they had the confused look children get when they sense something bad is about to happen. They looked sad and frightened.

I approached the officials in monkey caps and woolly sweaters who sat sipping tea and warming their hands in front of an electric heater. They had not bothered to feed the girls or helped them keep warm, and I asked if it would be all right for me to give the girls some biscuits.

The two men in monkey caps stared at me for a minute as if they thought I was mad, then one of them said, 'Suit yourself. It's not our job to feed them. But if you want to…go ahead.'

I had a packet of biscuits in my bag which I distributed among the little girls. They ate them hungrily and I think it shamed the officials into paying more attention to the lost children because one of them sent for some tea and breakfast. 'We were going to give them breakfast a little later,' he said with a surly look in my direction 'but they may as well get it now.'

When I asked him what would happen to the girls if their parents did not come looking for them he said with a sneer, 'They will not come for them. They never do. We will have to send them to a children's home. It is their kismet…' I thought of the children's homes in Delhi with their squalid dormitories that smelled of urine and were filled constantly with the sound of crying. A children's home in Allahabad would be much worse.

If the girls were lucky they would find someone to adopt them, if not they could end up in brothels.

India's children are the worst victims of bad governance. Those who grow up in poverty are lucky if they get one meal a day. Most grow up without ever eating vegetables or drinking milk. According to statistics collected in 2011 by the United Nations 45 per cent of India's children are malnourished. The government schools that they are sent to provide education of such abysmal standards that most children leave school without being able to read a story or count to a hundred. If girls get sick they are often left to die because their parents consider it a waste of money to pay medical bills for girls. The situation was a hundred times worse in the seventies but nobody talked about it. In the reporters' rooms of Delhi's big newspapers subjects like this never came up because we did not think people wanted to read about these things. As I walked on to the river I found myself wondering how much the media was to blame for what had gone wrong in India. Had we given more coverage to India's real problems, would our political leaders have paid more attention?

On that first day of the mela I got as much material as I needed for the 'colour' story I planned to write and would have returned to Delhi earlier than I had intended if the rumour of Mrs Gandhi's possible arrival had not acquired a new seriousness. The rumour, now half confirmed by mela officials, was that Mrs Gandhi planned to arrive on the most auspicious bathing day, which was on the *amavasya* or moonless final night of the Kumbh Mela on 19 January. It seemed stupid to leave, especially since there was so little happening in Delhi. Besides, there were many of my friends at the mela and in the evenings much fun to be had drinking and merrymaking in our cold and damp tents. Drinking alcohol was strictly prohibited, but if the officials knew what was going on they pretended not to.

The last day of the mela was rainy and cold. I would have happily skipped the morning worship and stayed in bed but my tent was leaking so it seemed like a better idea to have a quick breakfast and get on with the day. As I headed towards the river under a cloud of black umbrellas I was surprised to find that a new road, wide enough for a car to drive along, had come up overnight connecting the fort to the river. Soldiers from the regiment garrisoned in the fort had been deployed to put up barricades that sealed the road from intrusions by ordinary pilgrims and everyone else.

'Is this a private road?' I asked one of the officials who ordered us to take an alternative route. 'If it isn't, why can't we walk on it? Why are we being pushed off it and made to walk in the mud?'

'It's for the prime minister,' he said simply, 'she is coming here tonight.'

'What is she coming for? To take a holy dip?' My attempt at irony was wasted.

'Yes.'

'Great. So what time will she be taking her dip? We are reporters from Delhi.' I pointed to the small crowd of journalists standing under black umbrellas around me.

'We are not to speak of such details,' he said with a suspicious scowl.

'But we are reporters. We have a right to know.'

'Then find out from the press information desk.'

We went back to the press enclosure for more information, and got none. The rain became heavier. We decided that our best bet was to cancel the daily trip to the river, settle ourselves in the dining room tent and wait for news. Everyone had lost interest in the Kumbh Mela. At around tea time the rain stopped and a watery sun appeared in the sky. There was still no sign of Mrs Gandhi and we began to consider the possibility that the rumour was after all just a rumour. All of us were booked on the one and only train back to Delhi that evening but as we were about to leave for the railway station we heard the sound of a helicopter.

Before we knew what was happening the public address system suddenly crackled to life and over it came Mrs Gandhi's thin, girlish voice. We could not see her. We did not know where she spoke from but everyone at this massive gathering of pilgrims from all over India heard her voice. Her speech went something like this. 'Brothers and sisters, beloved countrymen, you know that for some months we have been forced by the behaviour of our opposition leaders and by dark forces from abroad to take emergency measures. We have been forced, against our will, to suspend fundamental rights and other democratic processes. We did this for your good and to save our great country from threats from internal forces and from abroad. But I am happy to tell you today that the nation is now saved and we no longer need those emergency measures. I am happy to tell you that elections will be held in March.'

For a moment we stared at the loudspeaker in shock and then there was a mad frenzy to get to the railway station in time to catch the only train back to Delhi. We nearly did not make it because of the thousands of pilgrims who were as desperate as us to get on to the train to Delhi. When we got to the station we found the platform carpeted with pilgrims and as the train pulled in they rose as if with a single will and swarmed towards it. There was a stampede but somehow we managed to find a coupé and lock the door before a crowd of pilgrims tried to break it down with their sticks. They did not stop until the train started pulling out of the station. I think there were ten of us in that coupé and the only person who seemed not to mind the discomfort of the journey was Raghu Rai. I have a distinct memory of him taking pictures of a waiter with a tray balanced in his hands, swinging from compartment to compartment as the train pulled into Delhi at dawn the next day.

Mrs Gandhi's sudden announcement of fresh elections took everyone by surprise. The country had settled into an Emergency groove. The rage over compulsory sterilizations and forcible 'resettlement' that had caused more than seven lakh citizens of Delhi to be moved had waned. And the opposition parties appeared to have given up the fight. The leader of the Rashtriya Swayamsewak Sangh (RSS), Balasaheb Deoras, had gone so far as to write a conciliatory letter to Mrs Gandhi. The RSS had been among Mrs Gandhi's fiercest critics long before the Emergency was declared and routinely used their English newspaper, *Motherland*, to charge her with all manner of crimes including treason. RSS workers formed a large contingent of the political prisoners in jail during the Emergency. For the RSS chief to seek peace with Mrs Gandhi meant the organization had adjusted to the idea of democracy remaining suspended indefinitely.

Why then had Mrs Gandhi decided that elections were necessary? The consensus in Delhi's newsrooms was that she was deeply hurt that the Western media had taken to calling her a dictator. Mrs Gandhi rarely gave interviews to Indian journalists and treated the Indian press with disdain but was sensitive to what the Western media said about her.

It became clear that Mrs Gandhi wanted to restore her image as a democratic leader and this could only happen if the coming elections were seen to be fair. Within days of the elections being announced most of the opposition leaders who were still in jail were released. They were no longer worth keeping in jail since nobody, not even the opposition leaders themselves, thought in January 1977 that Mrs Gandhi had the slightest chance of losing this election. Every report, even from her own intelligence agencies, indicated that she might lose a few seats but that there was no chance of a total defeat.

When the first posters appeared on Delhi's walls announcing that a rally was to be held at the Ram Lila Maidan that would be addressed by the major opposition leaders all of us thought it was a joke. How could they possibly hope to fill the city's largest public park when the organizational capacities of their disparate political parties had not been tested in months? There were still six weeks to go before the election but the opposition leaders had come out of jail demoralized and defeated. Some were recovering from the ordeal of long months of solitary confinement. Others from ailments caused by age and prison life. Most seemed only to want to spend time with their families and eat home food and none of them had been seen in public. In the *Statesman* reporters' room the feeling was that even if the posters were genuine the rally would be a flop because people would be too scared to attend it. The Emergency was still in effect and the atmosphere of fear that the past eighteen months had created had not dissipated.

On the day of the rally even the elements seemed to be on Mrs Gandhi's side. A thick pall of clouds hung over the city and by late afternoon it started to rain. In the reporters' room we sat huddled gloomily around heaters debating whether there was any chance of the opposition parties being able to hold a successful political rally with so much going against them. Those of us who felt we needed to do our bit to help the opposition parties rang everyone we knew and urged them to go to the Ram Lila grounds to show our solidarity. But Mr Raju, the chief reporter, was his usual pessimistic self and pronounced that since Mrs Gandhi was undefeatable there was no point anyway. 'Even if there's going to be an opposition rally,' he said, as always without looking up from his typewriter, 'it will make no difference. She wouldn't have gone for elections if she had any doubts about winning.'

'Yes, but she could have made a mistake,' I said. 'I've heard that the son and heir was totally opposed to the idea. He told her they could lose.' Rumours about this had been circulating for days. Many years later when Sanjay's best friend Kamal Nath was a cabinet minister in a Congress government in Delhi, I asked him whether it was true that Sanjay had opposed his mother's decision to have elections and he confirmed that it was. He said that Sanjay and he were together in Srinagar when they heard about the elections and Sanjay had been very upset because he believed that it would have been better to first lift the Emergency. He must have had a better sense of the mood of the people than we did on that cold and rainy afternoon as we waited to go to the opposition rally, for we agreed that the chances of Mrs Gandhi losing the election, despite the Emergency, were minimal.

On the short drive from the *Statesman* office to Ram Lila Maidan the only thing that brought some cheer was that the thin drizzle stopped and a weak sun appeared in the sky. Neither my colleagues nor I thought that this would encourage more people to come to the opposition rally. So when we saw large crowds of people walking towards the Ram Lila grounds we were taken aback. Someone said that it could be because there were committed Jana Sangh supporters in Delhi who would have been mobilized.

When we got to the grounds we noticed that people were streaming in from all sides and, beyond Turkman Gate, people were even sitting on rooftops. But not even this prepared us for what we saw when we got inside. There were more people than I had ever seen at a political rally. The crowd stretched all the way to the end of the Ram Lila grounds and beyond. But, unlike at public meetings in normal times, when there is always a carnival atmosphere, there was a seriousness about this rally. People talked to each other softly and sat under umbrellas or in flimsy raincoats in orderly lines on black plastic sheets that covered the wet ground. They looked like they had been waiting a long time.

The press enclosure was bursting with excitement. Noisy reporters were as overwhelmed by the size of the crowd as I was and there were many jokes about Mrs Gandhi's failure to sabotage the rally by showing a super-hit Hindi film on Doordarshan. The usual fare that India's only television channel offered was so dull that its ratings went up only when it showed Hindi films. In the press enclosure that afternoon we laughed about how it must have been some lowly official looking for applause from the prime minister who came up with the idea of telecasting *Bobby* at exactly the time the first opposition rally was being held in Delhi in nearly two years.

At about 6 p.m., the opposition leaders arrived in a convoy of white Ambassadors. They were mostly old men who walked so slowly up the steps of the yellow-washed, faux-Mughal pavilion in which the stage was set that there were jokes in the press enclosure about them being too frail to be out on such a cold winter's day. One by one they rose to make long, boring speeches about their travails in jail. The crowd began to look bored and restless. I said to a colleague from the *Hindustan Times* that I thought people might start to leave unless somebody said something more inspirational. It was past 9 p.m. and the night had got colder although the rain had stopped. 'Don't worry,' he replied with a smile, 'nobody will leave until Atalji speaks. Everyone here has come just to hear him.' He pointed to a small man with steel-grey hair, the last speaker that evening.

'Why?'

'Because he is the best orator in India. Have you never heard him speak?'

'No. I've only been in journalism since he went to jail.'

'Well, you're in for a treat. And to hear him for the first time today will really be something.'

It was well past 9.30 p.m. when Atalji's turn finally came and as he rose to speak the huge crowd stood up and started to clap. Softly, hesitantly at first, then more excitedly, they shouted, 'Indira Gandhi *murdabad*! Atal Behari *zindabad*!' He acknowledged the slogans with hands joined in a namaste and a faint smile. Then, raising both arms to silence the crowd and closing his eyes in the manner of a practiced actor, he said, '*Baad muddat ke mile hain deewane.*' (It has been an age since we whom they call mad have had the courage to meet.) He paused. The crowd went wild.

When the applause died he closed his eyes again and allowed himself another long pause before saying, '*Kehne sunne ko bahut hain afsane.*' (There are tales to tell and tales to hear.) The cheering was more prolonged, and when it stopped he paused again with his eyes closed before delivering the last line of a verse that he told me later he had composed on the spur of the moment. '*Khuli hawa mein zara saans to le lein, kab tak rahegi aazadi kaun jaane.*' (But first let us breathe deeply of the free air for we know not how long our freedom will last.)

The crowd was now hysterical. The clapping and shouting went on for many minutes. Atalji smiled with one hand resting on the podium, the other raised above his head and perfectly still. When he thought the applause had gone on long enough he raised both arms in the air and silence fell over the vast gathering. Yellow bulbs on long, drooping wires provided some light in the front but most of the ground was in darkness. Despite the night being so chilly, and a thin drizzle starting again, nobody left. They listened to Atalji in complete silence.

Eloquently, in simple Hindi, Atalji told them why they must not vote for Indira Gandhi. I no longer have a copy of the speech he made that night, and he spoke extempore, but I paraphrase here what I remember of it. Freedom, he began, democratic rights, the fundamental right to disagree with those who rule us, these things mean nothing until they are taken away. In the past two years they were not just taken away but those who dared to protest were punished... The India that her citizens loved no longer existed, he said, it became a vast prison camp, a prison camp in which human beings were no longer treated as human. They were treated with such contempt that they could be forced against their will to do things that should never be done against a human being's free will. The opposition leaders (he said 'we') knew that something needed to be done about India's expanding population; they did not oppose family planning, but they did not believe that human beings could be bundled into trucks like animals, sterilized against their will and sent back. The clapping this remark evoked went on and on and on and it would be only on election day that I would understand why.

Long after Atalji finished speaking and the opposition leaders got back into their white Ambassadors and drove off the crowds stayed as if they had collectively decided that they needed to do more than applaud a stirring speech. So when party workers appeared carrying soggy sheets in which they collected donations everyone gave something. On that cold January night as I watched rickshaw-wallas and those who lived on a pittance from manual labour on Delhi's streets donate what they could I got my first inkling that there was a chance Indira Gandhi could lose the election.

After the success of their first rally the opposition parties from the extreme left to the extreme right united to form a front against Mrs Gandhi's Congress Party and called this new front the Janata Party. Initially, nobody believed that the Janata Party could stay together because the ideological differences ran so deep. There were Marxists, socialists, Gandhians, former Congress Party leaders, members of the rightist Swatantra Party and people from the Hindu right-wing Jana Sangh. Even when the Janata Party stayed together most political analysts said it had no chance of defeating Mrs Gandhi and would certainly fall apart once the election was over.

As a very junior reporter I was not sent to exotic constituencies to report on the campaign. Newspaper owners in the seventies were notoriously stingy and thought of all travel as 'junkets'. Most newspapers carried the bland reports on the campaign that their stringers sent so nobody in Delhi had a real idea of what was going on beyond the boundaries of the city. As this was the first election campaign I was covering I attended every rally I could in Delhi and spent more time than usual wandering about the streets of the old city. I heard rumblings of big change but every time I returned to the office and reported what I had heard to senior political analysts they laughed at me and said that there was no chance of Mrs Gandhi losing. They said they had heard from 'reliable, high-level sources' that Mrs Gandhi had announced the election only after intelligence reports assured her that their surveys indicated there was no chance of her losing. I conceded that they could be right after attending one of Mrs Gandhi's rallies at the Boat Club in Delhi. The Boat Club is an expanse of manicured lawns that stretches from the square outside Parliament House almost down to India Gate. The size of the crowd was twice the size that had gathered for the first opposition rally on the Ram Lila grounds. As the prime minister, surrounded by all the trappings of power, she looked invincible even though she made a dull speech and got a half-hearted response.

Then about two weeks after the campaign began, some of the Congress Party's senior ministers resigned from Mrs Gandhi's government and joined the opposition. They held a rally along with the opposition leaders at the same Boat Club and this time the crowd was so huge that it disturbed Mrs Gandhi enough for her to send officials to break down the makeshift stage that had been erected for the speakers. But the opposition leaders chose to go ahead with their rally and use the broken stage as a backdrop. Atal Behari Vajpayee used the remains of the platform to mock Mrs Gandhi. He said, using a well-known Urdu phrase, '*Khandar bata raha hai, imaarat bulund thi.*' (You can look at these ruins and see that it must have once been a fine monument.) His audience was delighted because they understood it was as much a reference to Mrs Gandhi and the ruins of her government.

Among the speakers at this rally was Mrs Gandhi's aunt, Vijaya Lakshmi Pandit, who used all the authority of being Jawaharlal Nehru's sister to berate her niece for betraying the democracy that Nehru had worked so hard to leave as his real legacy. The others who made passionate speeches against dictatorship were those who had resigned from Mrs Gandhi's cabinet. They absolved themselves of any responsibility for the Emergency. They had no choice but to go along with it, they said, because they had lived in as much fear as the ordinary Indian but the lesson they had learned was that when the people choose to express their will, the most powerful governments could be blown away like 'cotton in a strong wind'. This particular expression is what I remember most from that rally because it came from Jagjivan Ram who, until he resigned, had been Mrs Gandhi's most powerful minister. He had been in the Government of India since the time of India's first Parliament and was famous for his administrative skills and for having forgotten to pay his taxes in all the years that he was in government. From the first days of the Emergency there were rumours that he had opposed its imposition. From time to time we would hear that the only reason he was not speaking out publicly against Mrs Gandhi was because he was under house arrest. What he said that afternoon in the Boat Club was easily believed by those who gathered to listen to him. And in the press enclosure there were many who predicted that he would be an excellent prime minister if the Janata Party won. As a Dalit he would have been India's first prime minister from the former 'untouchable' caste.

As the campaign proceeded and opposition leaders across north India were greeted by huge crowds the possibility of Mrs Gandhi being defeated began to seem more real. In the reporters' room I consulted as usual with the peons who told me fairly early on that the Congress Party was going to lose in Uttar Pradesh. They understood the mood better than most journalists did. Every 'senior' political correspondent I spoke to scoffed at my suggestion that there may be a wave against Mrs Gandhi and that it had remained an undercurrent because the Emergency had taught ordinary people to keep their political views to themselves.

The possibility of a defeat for Mrs Gandhi began to seem even more real to me after I attended a political meeting on the steps of the Jama Masjid toward the end of the campaign in early March. It was late in the evening and the steps of the mosque were lit so that the thousands who gathered in the narrow streets that led off on all sides of it could see their Imam as he ordered them to vote against the Congress Party.

Syed Ahmed Shah Bukhari was a large, bulky man with a white beard and a preacher's booming voice. That evening he was dressed in his finest robes and when he stood on the steps of the mosque holding hands with RSS leaders the crowd responded with raucous slogans and huge applause. In the tone he used to deliver his Friday sermons he told the largely Muslim crowd that as their Imam he was commanding them to vote against Mrs Gandhi. Then in Urdu he asked them if they agreed to obey. The vast audience that spilled out from every narrow alley around the mosque shouted back, '*Manzur hai.*' Across the road, in the shadow of the Red Fort, a few days later I heard an ancient Gandhian, Acharya Kripalani, who was so feeble he could barely stand, exhort an audience in his quavering voice to remember that the lesson from the Emergency was: 'Don't worship your leaders, they have feet of clay.'

Everything seemed to be going against Mrs Gandhi but even on polling day most people were unconvinced that she could be defeated. In Delhi's drawing rooms and in the circles in which senior bureaucrats moved everyone remained certain that she would win. Rajiv and Sonia Gandhi's friends continued to behave as if 'India is Indira and Indira is India'. The slogan had been invented, in a moment of matchless sycophancy, by the president of the Congress Party, Dev Kant Baruah, at the height of the Emergency.

Summer came early that year and a hot, dusty wind blew through the city on election day. It tossed dead leaves and torn election posters against the windshield of my car as I drove to the office.

I had woken earlier than usual and reached the office before breakfast. Since the old city had by then almost become my permanent beat I had been deputed to cover polling there. I wanted to get going as early as possible because I knew that emotions were running high and there could be trouble if Congress Party workers tried to 'persuade' people to vote in a particular way or played their old game of dividing Hindus and Muslims. On the way to the old city I passed polling booths that were almost empty. Low turnout, I noted sadly, because that meant Mrs Gandhi would win. I had never covered an election before but was told by those who had that a high turnout usually signalled a win for the opposition. In Daryaganj I noticed queues at some polling booths and saw this as a small sign of hope.

But there was very little activity in the bird market and the Urdu Bazaar. By the time I got to a polling booth near Karim's I had talked to several ordinary voters who said rumours were being spread that Mrs Gandhi had arranged for magic ink to be used on ballot papers that would tell her who had voted against her.

Then I heard shouts of '*Jai nasbandi! Jai* bulldozer!' (Long live sterilization! Long live the bulldozer!) The slogan was not so much chanted as sung by a procession of young men that went by with dancing children in its wake. The crowd of slogan shouters stopped at every polling booth to shout '*Jai nasbandi! Jai* bulldozer!' and every time they did people, reminded of the repression of the past two years, seemed to shake off their fear of voting against the Congress Party. Soon voters were repeating the slogans as they stamped their ballot papers. Some waved the ballot papers in the faces of the officials in the polling booths, shouting, 'Look. Look who we are voting for. *Jai nasbandi! Jai* bulldozer!' The election had turned into a carnival. The queues got longer and longer, the mood of the voters increasingly jubilant. By the end of polling they behaved as if Mrs Gandhi had already lost.

At some point Raghu Rai arrived there. He had been driving around the city taking pictures. I hitched a ride with him back to the office. Polling was over and the street that runs along the Zenana Women's Hospital was almost empty except for an old man sweeping torn posters into a jute sack. Raghu stopped the car and for the next half an hour took pictures of the old man and his sack. When I asked him impatiently what he had found so interesting about the old man he said it could be a very important photograph if Mrs Gandhi ended up losing the elections. 'It is a poster of Indira Gandhi being swept into a bag by a man who is obviously very poor, and on the wall behind him is a family planning slogan. It tells the whole story.' Every time I covered a story with Raghu I learned anew that photographers have a way of seeing things that reporters quite simply do not.

On the day of the results I was assigned to a counting centre where votes for three Delhi seats were being counted. It was on the grounds of the Tees Hazari courts. Rough wooden tables stood in a quadrangle under a large tent that provided little shelter from the dust and heat of that warm March morning. At the tables sat the officials in charge of counting the votes, representatives of the different political parties and a supervisor. The arrangements may have been shabby for such an important moment in

India's history but there was a certain order to the proceedings disturbed only by the army of reporters who had been allowed in. There were more foreign correspondents than local journalists and so much conviviality and chit-chat that when the big metal ballot boxes arrived with their red seals the senior supervisor ordered us to be silent or leave.

The boxes were placed on the tables and their seals broken amid silence and solemnity. Counting began. The officials had two trays on either side of them. On their left was the tray for ballots that Mrs Gandhi's Congress Party had polled and on their right the tray for the opposition. From the first round it was the tray on the right in which the ballots piled up. By the time they got to the second round of counting it was clear that the Congress Party was losing. We reporters had watched silently until then but when we saw what was happening we were gripped by an insane elation. We rushed from table to table examining the trays and by the time the third round of counting began even the officials began to smile. The supervisors tried their best to enforce solemnity but failed completely. By late afternoon, when all the votes were counted and the Congress Party had lost all three Delhi seats we heard the sound of drums from outside the counting centre. Bhangra dancers appeared out of nowhere and along with them came huge crowds who cheered and danced.

When I got back to the *Statesman* office late that evening there were lights on in the whole building. Nobody went home that night. From the canteen came endless cups of tea and greasy snacks and the peons who brought them lingered in the reporters' room to get the latest news to carry back to those who worked in the canteen. Later, a whole lot of us, reporters from the *Statesman* and the *Hindustan Times*, the only other newspaper with offices in Connaught Place, drove in a convoy of Ambassadors to Bahadur Shah Zafar Marg where thousands of people had gathered outside the *Times of India* building to follow the results coming in from all over the country. The latest results were displayed on billboards suspended high so they could be seen from a distance. There were so many people there that night that traffic had to be halted at both ends. When in the early hours of the morning the news finally came that Mrs Gandhi and Sanjay Gandhi had lost, Mrs Gandhi to her old tormentor, Raj Narain, and Sanjay to an unknown Bharatiya Lok Dal candidate called Ravindra Pratap Singh, a huge roar of approval went up. And the sounds of drums, cheering and people dancing continued to reverberate in the old city right through the night.

It was 5 a.m. by the time I went home. My parents were awake and listening to the BBC. 'She lost,' my mother said with a bewildered smile, 'and her son lost. I never thought it would happen. We have to salute the Indian voter.'

Later, when a new government came to power in Delhi, there were rumours that Mrs Gandhi had tried to get the Army Chief to impose martial law on the country rather than surrender power. These rumours were never confirmed, nor were rumours that Rajiv and Sonia Gandhi's first reaction after hearing of the defeat was to seek refuge in the Italian embassy. Sonia was still an Italian citizen at the time and there was so much uncertainty about what might happen to Mrs Gandhi and her family that if she did seek help from her embassy it would have been a sensible thing to do. What I did hear from one of the members of the inner circle was that the children, Rahul and Priyanka, were sent away from Delhi to take shelter in the home of Arun Singh's mother in Mussoorie. Again, they can hardly be blamed for wanting their children safe in such uncertain times.

It was just after Mrs Gandhi's defeat, while a jubilant Janata Party government was taking over in Delhi, under Morarji Desai, that I met Akbar Ahmed. He was better known by his nickname Dumpy though I have always called him Akbar. He was introduced to me at a dinner party in the Oberoi Hotel as 'Sanjay Gandhi's best friend'. I took an instant liking to Akbar because of his ability to laugh at the most serious things and because he admitted without hesitation that he did not know how he had wound up in politics. At our first meeting he told me he had been studying chartered accountancy in London throughout the Emergency and had returned just before the elections were announced. He ended up helping Sanjay Gandhi with his campaign to win his first Lok Sabha election from Amethi at the behest of a senior politician in the Congress Party. 'Weren't you friends in the Doon School? Shouldn't you be helping him?' He was in Lucknow, he said, not doing very much and with Amethi so close by he just drove down and offered his help.

When I got to know Akbar better I discovered that his best quality was his ability to give unstinting loyalty and friendship. After the defeat in 1977 when many of the sycophants around the Gandhi family vanished quietly into the Delhi night Akbar felt it was his duty to be as much of a friend to them in every possible way. Even if he had no work with Sanjay he went and saw him nearly every day. He told me that after they moved to 12 Willingdon Crescent, the house Mrs Gandhi was allotted after her defeat, the family lived in considerably reduced circumstances. Mrs Gandhi was not known to have made any money for herself when she was prime minister and the party funds vanished with as much speed as the sycophants.

From Akbar I learned that after the defeat Mrs Gandhi was so shaken that she had seriously considered retiring to a cottage in the hills to write her memoirs. She thought this would be a good way to escape any political retribution that the Janata government may have been contemplating. According to Akbar it was because Sanjay Gandhi insisted that they stay to fight another day that Mrs Gandhi did not leave Delhi. Sanjay became her pillar of support and consolidated what remained of the Congress Party. Mrs Gandhi seemed lost and defeated. I remember running into her at obscure diplomatic parties and once even at some non-event in Sapru House. Her presence was often an embarrassment at these events because it meant that the host or hostess would have to be in permanent attendance. Ordinary socialites were too overwhelmed to chat to her and diplomats and bureaucrats too intimidated. The occasional journalist would go up and ask a question or two but she did not like journalists and made this clear by responding to most questions in curt monosyllables.

It was Akbar who first told me that there were serious domestic tensions in Mrs Gandhi's household. Since 12 Willingdon Crescent was not very far from my parents' home he would drop by often full of stories and gossip. One evening when he settled down with his glass of Scotch whisky on my veranda he told me that Rajiv and Sonia blamed Sanjay for everything that had gone wrong and that they never tried to hide their feelings about this. Tensions ran so high that the smallest trigger could set Sonia off, Akbar said. There was a particular story about a fight over dog biscuits that I remember well.

This is how Akbar told the story. 'Yaar, can you imagine anyone getting upset because some dog biscuits got eaten by the wrong dog? What happened was that Maneka saw these biscuits in the fridge and fed them to her dogs and Sonia had a screaming fit. Then Rajiv started screaming too and it was all very unpleasant. Apparently they were imported dog biscuits or something. But, they were just dog biscuits, yaar.'

My first real conversation with Rajiv Gandhi took place some weeks after the Janata government came to power. It was around the time of the first anniversary of the Turkman Gate incident so this would have been April 1977. I had spent the whole day in the old city trying to piece together what had happened at Turkman Gate the year before, for a commemorative piece I was writing, now that press censorship had been lifted. Drained by the stories I heard in the old city and from trying not to be overwhelmed by the raw pain of people who had lost homes and loved ones I was happy to be in the salubrious setting of a dinner party at Vicky Bharat Ram's home.

It was a warm evening and the long windows of the drawing room were open allowing in a soft breeze that scattered cigarette smoke and the scent of French perfume. After dinner, when most of the guests had left, I must have got a little reckless from drinking an extra glass of white wine, because when I spotted Rajiv Gandhi sitting on the beige carpet with his back against a wall and with only Romi Chopra for company I sat down next to him and asked him a question that I would not otherwise have asked. The conversation I recount here is from memory as I was off duty and not carrying a notebook. It was the sort of conversation that remains vividly etched in one's mind and I described it in the column I wrote the week after Rajiv was killed.

'I've been meaning to ask you this for many months,' I said, 'but have never been able to summon up the courage... I've always wondered what you knew about the Emergency and what you thought about it.'

To my surprise, instead of being annoyed, a look of relief passed over Rajiv's face. 'Thank God someone has finally asked me that question,' he said with a big smile. 'I've been waiting so long for someone to mention the subject and nobody has. Now that you ask let me tell you that I totally disapproved of it and tried telling Mummy that she had become very unpopular because of the Emergency. I would tell her all the stories I heard.' He added that despite his lack of interest in politics it was hard for him to be oblivious to what was going on.

'And?'

'She didn't believe me,' he said with a self-deprecatory laugh. 'She said I couldn't possibly know what real people were thinking because I moved in "elitist" circles. What would your elite friends know, she said. These are people who have never voted in their lives.'

'That may be true. But it wasn't the elite who were upset with the Emergency. It was ordinary people, people whose homes had been demolished, who had been victims of the sterilization squads.'

'That was all nonsense and exaggeration,' interjected Romi.

'No. It wasn't nonsense,' said Rajiv quietly. 'The numbers may have been exaggerated but we knew that this was happening. I heard stories, too, from people who live in the old city and I told Mummy about them but she discussed them with my brother who said they were rubbish, and that was that.'

'Do you see yourself in politics one day?' I asked eagerly, getting in as many questions as I could like reporters do at press conferences.

'Me? No. Never. My wife hates politics and politicians, so the question does not arise. Besides, it's my brother who has become the family politician.'

'But you have political views, don't you? On the country's problems, the issues before us?'

'Not really, no. My mother has a rule that we never talk about politics at the family dinner table and so there is never any discussion at home about such things. So, no, I don't have any views.'

'It's such a dirty business,' I remember Romi saying with what looked to me like an angry flounce, 'that nobody with any decency can survive.'

'His family has,' I said, and Romi glowered ferociously at me. He seemed displeased that I should have had such a long conversation with Rajiv.

It took me a few moments to notice that silence had fallen over the room and everyone was staring at us. Sonia and the other ladies were seated on a sofa nearby and when she saw that the conversation was getting too intense she came over and stood beside Rajiv with her hand outstretched, indicating that it was time for them to leave.

My relationship with Rajiv and Sonia changed after that night. I admit that my perception of Rajiv changed as well. It was the first glimpse I had of what I was to later discover was his enormous charm. It may have been something that Rajiv told them afterwards but it seemed to become obvious to the inner circle that not only did he not mind talking about politics but he actually enjoyed it. But since none of his close friends had ever taken any interest in politics they had no idea what to talk about. I found myself in unusual demand at parties that Rajiv and Sonia were attending. The same people who had discouraged me from talking to him about politics earlier started to use me as a party trick. It would be arranged in such a way that when I got to ask him something about politics or current events everyone would join the discussion.

Rajiv usually had an opinion on the political issue or event being discussed but now that such conversations were openly had it became evident how little any of the others knew about what was going on in India or the world. I have met illiterate people in desperately poor villages who had a better understanding of political issues. They were, at the least, able to identify what their problems were in clear terms. In the most remote villages I met people who talked about schools without classrooms. Teachers who never came to teach. Hospitals and primary health centres that had neither doctors nor medicines. Roads that got washed away as soon as they were built. Electricity poles that stood for years without delivering any electricity. In the drawing rooms in which Rajiv and Sonia spent their evenings, it would have been next to impossible to find two people who could explain why the vast majority of Indians, including all of us, were denied such basic things as electricity and clean water.

Besides there were a lot of political topics to talk about once Mrs Gandhi was no longer prime minister because Morarji Desai and his government seemed to make it their mission to become very unpopular in the shortest possible time.

6 THE ALTERNATIVE

By the time he was sworn in as prime minister Morarji Desai was already famous for his austerity. He had survived solitary confinement during the Emergency without the smallest trauma, people said, while other political leaders had been driven to despair. Those who spread this story invariably added that this was because he had no taste for cooked food or other people's company. He lived on nuts and, as all of India was to soon find out, his own urine. He apparently refrigerated supplies at night and drank a glass without fail every morning. The new prime minister's peculiar choice of beverage rapidly became a subject of discussion every time he was mentioned in any conversation. Not just in India but almost everywhere I went. In London, during that first summer of his rule in 1977, everyone I met asked if it was true that the prime minister of India drank his own urine.

In India many ordinary, apolitical people were horrified by this habit and the prime minister's office went to great lengths to spread the word that drinking one's own urine led to the cure of otherwise incurable diseases like cancer. Most people remained unconvinced of the healing properties of auto-urine therapy and found the new prime minister's drinking habits both repugnant and amusing. In those first few months after the new government came to power, the prime minister's taste in beverages became the source of much ribaldry and 'political' chit-chat. Where did he keep it? Did it have to be drunk chilled? Was it all right to just pee into a glass and then knock it back? What happened if you drank too many whiskies the night before?

Almost the first announcement the new government made was the imposition of prohibition in Delhi. The new prime minister, a dedicated

Gandhian, meant this as a tribute to Mahatma Gandhi who was a passionate prohibitionist. But the Janata government appeared not to have paid sufficient attention to the ground realities of prohibition in India. Every attempt to impose prohibition, since the days when Jawaharlal Nehru was prime minister, had failed hopelessly. Since Gandhiji was from Gujarat, it became the only state where the law was kept alive to honour the Mahatma but bootleggers and the illicit liquor trade have thrived as a consequence.

Delhi's drawing rooms did not suffer when Morarji Desai's new rules came into force because it was usually foreign liquor that we drank and this came from bootleggers. It was the ordinary citizens of Delhi who were most affected. Or not, because those determined enough would drive across the border and bring back supplies from Haryana where there was no prohibition. For those who could not afford the drive the services of cross-border smugglers quickly became available. If these smugglers were checked at the border a small bribe could ease logistical problems and policemen were in any case inclined to look the other way. In the time that prohibition remained in force in Delhi, I watched Pappu the bootlegger go from strength to strength. Before prohibition he used to bring me my supplies of cheap French wine and dodgy Scotch whisky in an autorickshaw but business improved so dramatically for him after Morarji Desai became prime minister that he soon managed to buy himself a car. Friends who continued to use his services reported some years later that they had seen him driving a Mercedes. Thanks to the laws imposed by the Janata government Pappu rose from being a shady bootlegger to a respectable businessman in no time.

The Janata government seemed to develop an unhealthy obsession with beverages. After news of the prime minister's urine drinking and the imposition of prohibition in Delhi news came that Coca-Cola was going to be thrown out of India. For this last policy change in the beverage department we had the minister of industry George Fernandes to thank.

Until he became a cabinet minister in Morarji Desai's government, Fernandes had spent his political career as a trade union leader. His singular achievement had been to organize a massive railway strike in the summer of 1974. He was the president of the All India Railwaymen's Federation and led seventy million railway workers in a strike that lasted twenty days. Mrs Gandhi broke the strike by arresting thousands of railway workers and leaving them in prison much longer than they expected.

Fernandes's real moment of glory came later and was also brought about by Mrs Gandhi. When the Emergency was declared he became the only well-known political leader who managed to remain underground for a year. In June 1976 he was finally arrested on charges of being involved in what came to be known as the Baroda dynamite case. Fernandes and his comrades were accused of attempting to blow up railway tracks and government buildings. He remained in jail during the 1977 general election and contested from Muzaffarpur in Bihar with campaign posters that showed him in fetters, raising clenched fists behind the bars of a jail cell. This made him India's most famous political prisoner.

Fernandes was an attractive, erudite man but with very rigid views that were founded on the principle that the Americans were imposing a new kind of colonization through their multinational corporations. So one of the first things he did after becoming the minister of industry was to throw Coca-Cola out of India. I happened to be present, quite by accident, when he announced this decision. I had been assigned to cover a meeting he was having with trade union leaders and it was at this meeting that he casually made his announcement. Eager-beaver reporter that I was I remember racing back to the *Statesman* office and telling my news editor that Coca-Cola had been thrown out of India. Sadly, he was unable to understand the importance of the story, and I was only a junior reporter, not yet eligible to argue my case, so he carried my scoop on page three. It was only when other newspapers picked it up the next day and ran the story with huge headlines on their front pages that he realized its significance. It was the beginning of my disenchantment with the *Statesman*.

After the Emergency ended it did not take long for me to realize especially after despondently casting my eye over my colleagues in the reporters' room and calculating how many years they had spent there that if I continued working for this newspaper I could remain in the reporters' room until I was very old. My dream of becoming a major political reporter with a famous byline was likely to die in that small, windowless room.

Most English-language newspapers of the time modelled their ideas of probity and their usage of English on the Victorian era, when they had first started their lives. But the *Statesman* was the most conservative of them all. It was said that this was because it had been edited by a British editor for many years after Independence. This editor, whose name I no longer remember, appears to have taken the old-fashioned view that journalism should be treated as a higher calling and not just a career, or so we were told in the reporters' room.

After Coca-Cola was thrown out, the Janata government continued its beverage obsession by ordering one of its public sector factories to produce a copycat Coca-Cola that was christened '77' in honour of the year that saw the end of the Emergency. It had a strange aftertaste that made it quite undrinkable and it is no surprise that it soon disappeared altogether. There are those who believe that Coca-Cola's eviction eventually laid the foundations of the Indian soft drinks industry, so perhaps Fernandes did well for the beverage business, but he did not do well by computers because he banished IBM at the same time delaying, according to experts, the arrival of computers in India by at least a decade.

Within months of the Janata government coming to power a deep disenchantment began to set in. The new ministers seemed to spend most of their time publicly fighting with each other, which was inevitable since they came from disparate ideological backgrounds, or fighting Mrs Gandhi. They found so many ways to harass her and her family that she was never allowed to step off the national political stage.

If this had been accompanied by serious changes in governance making it less colonial and more attuned to the aspirations of ordinary Indians it may not have been viewed as a mistake. But this did not happen. The new ministers simply stepped into the shoes of their predecessors to do exactly as they had done without being able to fill their place adequately. Most of the information about what was going wrong came from senior bureaucrats who, with their Oxford accents and Western refinements, found it hard to deal with the rustic ways of the new ministers. Indian bureaucrats in the seventies were nearly all upper middle class, Western-educated, and more fluent in English than Indian languages. Their disdain for the Janata ministers came from silly snobbishness more than anything else. But they liked to regale the denizens of Delhi's drawing rooms with stories of ministers slurping their tea from saucers, eating with their mouths open and picking their noses.

Soon even Vasundhara Raje and Naveen Patnaik, whose parents were part of the Janata government, were beginning to worry about its ability to last a full term. Naveen tried weakly, on occasion, to defend the new ministers when some bureaucrat mocked them for their rusticity and lack of refinement. I remember him telling a story that he thought was a good example of the 'native intelligence' of the man who became Mrs Gandhi's nemesis by first charging her with electoral malpractices and then defeating her in Rae Bareli. Raj Narain was appointed minister of health and family welfare in the Janata government. So it was his task to investigate allegations of compulsory sterilization during the Emergency. When his officials told him that there were no records because the orders had been 'verbal', he ordered one of them to go into the next room and kill the clerks sitting there. When the official looked alarmed he said, 'I'm giving you a verbal order. Why aren't you following it?'

It was a good story but it was easier to attack the new government than to defend it. Had the Janata government been more cohesive and more capable of coherent changes in policy, there was much that it could have achieved. India had been ruled for nearly all of its years as an independent nation by Jawaharlal Nehru and Indira Gandhi and the failures of their rule were abundantly obvious. Nehru was prime minister for fifteen years and at the end of his rule Indians were neither more literate nor less mired in poverty than when he became prime minister. In his long tenure as the first prime minister of independent India he failed to build the schools, village roads, sanitation and rural health services that would have provided the tools for India's poorest citizens to better their lives.

This brought the responsibility for removing poverty so squarely on Mrs Gandhi that her campaign slogan in the election of 1971 was '*Garibi hatao*'. She failed to find ways to do this, and it led to the political disquiet before the Emergency. A wiser prime minister than Morarji Desai would have concentrated on improving governance and on changing the policies that had failed. Instead, his government decided to put all its energies into prosecuting Mrs Gandhi and her family and on 'rectifying' what came to be called the 'excesses' of the Emergency.

Sanjay Gandhi was the first person they went after. During the Emergency, he was responsible for banning a Bollywood film called *Kissa Kursi Ka*, which, literally translated is 'The Story of a Chair' but less literally means the story of power. The film annoyed Sanjay because it contained disparaging references to an unnamed politician who was given a licence to produce India's first small car. In the film, the unnamed politician declares that he deserves a licence to set up an automobile factory because, 'I learned about making cars when I was still in the womb.' Sanjay correctly saw this as a reference to himself and not only banned the film but also destroyed every copy of it.

The Janata government decided to prosecute him for this. The problem was that it was a little like doing him the one favour he really wanted. A chance to waltz back into the national spotlight. No sooner did the Desai government announce that it would be prosecuting Sanjay for stealing and destroying *Kissa Kursi Ka*, than he sent his Youth Congress supporters on to the streets of Delhi to defend him and wreak havoc. It was the summer of 1978 and I was covering a rally by his supporters on Janpath, which at the time was one of Delhi's main thoroughfares. The procession started peacefully enough as it wandered past the row of small shops that lined one side of the street. Sanjay Gandhi, unsmiling and bespectacled, was at the head of it. Like the protesters, he was dressed in a white kurta–pyjama, and I was walking beside him in the front. Ahead of us were policemen, in charge of controlling things if they got out of hand.

It was when we got to one of the gates of the Imperial Hotel that from behind us came the sounds of slogans and cars screeching to a halt. When I turned around to see what was happening I saw that the 'peaceful protesters' were stopping traffic and forcing shopkeepers to pull down their shutters. At this point the senior police officer present, a distant cousin of mine, appealed to Sanjay to stop the violence. 'Please, sir,' he said, 'if you don't stop your supporters from disrupting traffic I will be forced to arrest them.' When, instead of cooperating with the police, Sanjay and his supporters began to taunt them with cries of 'Arrest us first' they were arrested and driven away in police vans.

Sanjay spent a few days in jail and this caused much melodrama but the courtroom scenes that followed were even more melodramatic. When Sanjay was brought to the Tees Hazari courts for a bail hearing there was the sort of chaos and mayhem that is usually forbidden in courtrooms. Someone snatched the pen out of his hand and threw it in the air. This acted as a signal for Sanjay's supporters in the courtroom to start shouting slogans and creating a general nuisance. Eventually, as far as I know, the *Kissa Kursi Ka* case was quietly buried in some government file and the question of punishing Sanjay was buried with it.

In everything they did, the new government appeared ham-fisted and confused and it did not help that the prime minister himself was personally very unpopular. His advisors must have noticed that his real problem was that he lacked the common touch. They advised him to rectify this flaw by meeting ordinary people every day in a public audience. A durbar. He consented reluctantly, or so we heard, but no sooner was this decision announced than the deputy prime minister, Chaudhury Charan Singh, who by then was known to have his eyes on Morarji's job, decided he would have a morning durbar of his own. And, when Mrs Gandhi heard rumours of daily public audiences she must have decided that this was a game she could play better than anyone else so she announced that she would have a morning durbar as well.

Other newspapers carried desultory accounts of the morning audiences but the *Statesman,* famous for its quirky feature articles that appeared regularly on page three, decided that the story was worth a full feature article. As the resident expert on 'colour' stories I was picked to write it. So it was that I rose early one morning to get to the prime minister's house before he was scheduled to meet 'the people'. It was a beautiful, early, summer morning with a crisp coolness in the air and the roundabouts of Lutyens's Delhi were covered in flowers. The prime minister had not moved into Mrs Gandhi's house yet and continued to live in what was still called Dupleix Lane in a decrepit bungalow that had not been painted in years.

By the time I arrived a small group of people had gathered outside the closed gates. There was a young girl of about eight who had come with her blind father, an old lady who hobbled on rickety crutches, a man in a wheelchair who looked as if he had once been a soldier and a group of schoolgirls in blue frocks with red ribbons in their hair. They were with a teacher who wore a bright blue and gold sari and confided to me in a happy whisper that they had an appointment with the prime minister.

'And you?' she asked me.

'I am a reporter.'

'You people are writing such mean things about the prime minister. Why don't you write about the good things he is doing instead of writing only, and only, about his urine drinking? And you know it works. It cures many diseases and is a prevention against cancer...' her voice trailed off and a bemused expression crept into her eyes as she looked over my shoulder and joined her hands in greeting. '*Namaskar, pradhan mantriji.*'

'*Namaskar pradhan mantriji,*' her flock echoed. The schoolgirls pushed forward with their neatly oiled plaits and their red ribbons, leaving me among the derelicts and the handicapped, who were less sure of how to approach the prime minister. The man they had come to see looked clean and starched and so upper-caste with his long, thin face, his wide forehead and thin, austere lips. His skin shone and the hands he joined together to greet us were long and manicured.

After the schoolgirls had been greeted and photographed with the prime minister, a flunkey from his office pushed us forward, with the little girl and her blind father just ahead of me and the old lady with crutches just behind. The blind man was the first to speak.

'*Aadarniya pradhan mantriji,*' he said, 'I lost my eyesight in an industrial accident and now there is nobody to pay for my little girl's education. I have come all the way from Bhopal. Can you please help me?'

'All the way from Bhopal?' the prime minister said, unable to keep the irritation out of his voice. 'Why have you come all the way from Bhopal? Why didn't you go to your chief minister for help?'

'I did, *pradhan mantriji*, but they told me there was no chief minister's relief fund and that I should come here because there is a prime minister's relief fund.'

'Yes, there is. And it is not meant for charity but to be used when there is a natural disaster like a drought or a flood. I cannot help you.'

The old woman was next. '*Pradhan mantriji*, my husband died in the 1965 war and they've stopped the pension I was getting since last year. Please, sir, it's the only money I have to live on, please help me.'

'How can I help you? I am the prime minister not god. How can I possibly help you?'

'The pension, sir, if you could just instruct them to restore the pension I was getting. It is only Rs 100 a month.'

'It's not my business. Go to the defence minister.'

He did not notice me lurking in the background taking notes. One of the sentences I wrote about my experience was, 'exercise in reaching out to the people not working'. The impression he left on me was a bad one. In my notes I described him as a nasty old man who reeked of expensive cologne. Later, my colleagues in the reporters' room told me that the cologne was necessary to disguise the smell that he had acquired from all the urine drinking. This may only have been journalistic speculation but it did in a way explain why someone as punishingly austere as Desai would allow himself this peculiar indulgence.

On another elegant tree-lined avenue in that part of Delhi which since Independence has been reserved almost exclusively for our socialist rulers was the house of the deputy prime minister. This was my next stop. Chaudhury Charan Singh wore his peasant origins like a badge of honour and made it a point to be as rustic as possible. That morning he seemed to have made a special effort to look like an ordinary farmer by wearing a rough dhoti–kurta and sitting on a charpai. The gates were open to allow a steady stream of peasants to enter. At first they seemed perturbed by the manicured lawns and elegant pergola that the last occupant had left behind in this once-beautiful house. But when they saw their leader sitting on his charpai under the shade of a tree they relaxed and joined the group of men seated on their haunches at his feet. Charan Singh had slanted eyes and a receding chin. He sat cross-legged on the charpai and greeted new arrivals with his hands joined together and a loud 'Ram, Ram'.

The audience began with the villagers praising 'Chaudhury Sahib' to the skies. They told him how wonderful he had been as the chief minister of Uttar Pradesh and how they remembered his rule as a time when electricity had been available twenty-four hours a day and how they never had any problems getting water for their fields. Once they felt the deputy prime minister had been sufficiently softened by their flattery they presented him with a list of the things that they were unhappy about. They told him how in their villages the electricity always went off just when they were preparing to irrigate their fields so their tubewells became useless. They told him of failed crops and desperate shortages of water, and they told him how shocked they had been to see that power and water meant for farmers was being used in the cities.

The deputy prime minister was sympathetic and ordered his assistants, who stood around with notebooks in their hands, to take down the names of the villages that had power and water problems. Then a new group of peasants arrived and the gathering of men squatting on their haunches got bigger and the litany of complaints louder. The deputy prime minister listened to everyone. Those who had come to Delhi for the first time told him they had been stunned by the wide roads and the sight of decorative fountains everywhere while their fields were starved of water.

It surprised me that they did not mention problems such as how bad the schools were in their villages, how abysmal the standards of primary health care, basic hygiene and sanitation. But I was new to journalism and did not understand that farmers concern themselves primarily with what goes into making their crops grow well. And this was before the time of cell phones and colour television when the average Indian peasant knew very little about how people lived in the cities and had almost no aspirations to a higher standard of living.

At some point during the deputy prime minister's peasant durbar I needed to go to the bathroom and was directed into the house. The vast drawing room had been stripped of all furniture except for a few shabby cane sofas that had 'P.W.D.' (Public Works Department) written on their sides in black paint. There were no curtains and the long French windows that led on to an elegant garden in the back looked as if they had not been cleaned in weeks. The door to Chaudhury Sahib's bedroom was open and I noticed that it had been stripped of furniture as well. A mattress on the floor, covered in a white sheet, was presumably his bed and in a bay window, on another mattress covered in white, stood a low wooden desk of the kind Indian accountants used in older times. It was here that he sat every morning to write his books on agriculture and the peasantry. His books were translated into English around this time and later when he fulfilled his dream of becoming India's prime minister, albeit for a fleeting moment, I think he managed a certain celebrity as an author.

By the time I got to Mrs Gandhi's durbar the blind man and his daughter and the lame old lady were already there, seated on plastic chairs with glasses of steaming tea in their hands. Mrs Gandhi, sprightly and glowing in a white sari, flitted briskly about the garden stopping to talk to every visitor individually and making them feel for that moment that her thoughts were only of them. The visitors were mostly from southern India and they told her how sad they were that she had been defeated and how certain that she would be back. 'You are India, madam, and India is you,' said a fat, white-haired man. With him was a large group of party workers from Tamil Nadu in shiny white kurtas and dhotis. In the election she lost to the Janata Party most of the seats she won had been from the four southern states so Mrs Gandhi had reason to be especially nice to her supporters from that part of India. She smiled her warmest smile, allowed the leader of the group to hold her hand, blessed some of the younger members of the group by placing her hand on their heads as they plunged for her feet, and then moved on to the next group, who were people from her own constituency.

As she approached them they began to wail as if at a funeral before telling her they were certain that the polls had been rigged. 'Look, Indiraji, these are ballot papers,' a young man said angrily, waving some papers before her face, 'we found them in a polling booth. We know there was a plot by the collector.'

'You mustn't talk like that,' she said with a sweet smile, 'you mustn't talk of cheating. We lost the election but this doesn't mean that I am not here for you any time you want.'

'Oh, madam, already our party workers are being harassed. The Janata Party workers come late at night to our houses and threaten us for continuing to support you. Your leader is never coming back, they say, so you better learn to behave yourself or we will fix you.'

'Who are these people who come to your houses?'

'Ruling party workers, or that's who they say they are. They are strangers.'

'Well, you must find out who they are and I can take the matter up with the prime minister.'

At this the group chanted in unison, '*Desh ka neta kaisa ho*, Indira Gandhi *jaisa ho*...' (What should the country's leader be like? He should be like Indira Gandhi.) It sounds funny in English but rhymes so well in Hindi that it remains among the most popular political slogans in India with only the name of the leader changed.

Mrs Gandhi noticed me and another reporter from some Hindi newspaper following in her wake and stopped and smiled at us. Since she had never in my limited experience of journalism done such a thing before it rendered me momentarily speechless but my more experienced colleague was quick to seize the moment.

'Would you like to tell us what, if anything, you regret about the Emergency?' he asked.

'Censorship,' she said with a sweet smile, 'if there had not been press censorship, I would have known from you people what my officials were doing.'

'Would you have held elections if you had known that you might lose?' my colleague persisted.

'Yes. I would have. I believe in democracy and never intended to suspend it forever. It was a temporary measure because there were internal and external threats to the country.'

'Have they now abated?' I asked, finally finding my voice.

'Well, I leave that for you to judge,' she said with another sweet smile. 'After all, you can see what this government is doing and what it is not doing. India cannot survive if we allow fissiparous tendencies to grow. The new government has within it representatives of these tendencies.' I was as stupefied by the word 'fissiparous' (which she pronounced as 'fissiparious') as I was by the way she spoke English. It was the first time I had a personal conversation with her. She had the sort of accent Indian girls get when they are what we call 'convent-educated'. She rounded her vowels and modulated her thin voice and one of her eyes twitched as she gave us one last sweet smile and skittered off to the next group of visitors.

She was quickly surrounded by yet another ardent group of supporters and I found myself once more beside the blind man and the old lady.

Why were they still here I asked the blind man's daughter. Had madam promised them help?

Oh yes she had, the girl said, she had promised to speak to the prime minister and had asked them to wait while she did so. There was more than enough money in the prime minister's relief fund she had told them so there was no reason why needy people like them should not benefit from it.

After an hour at Mrs Gandhi's durbar I knew with a terrible certainty that it would not be long before she became prime minister again. When I returned to the office and wrote my story comparing the three durbars I did not say this in so many words. I wrote that Mrs Gandhi had lost none of her charisma or charm and there was a dearth of these qualities in the new leaders.

My story on the three durbars had unexpected consequences. The day after it appeared, on page three of the *Statesman*, a high official arrived in the reporters' room and asked for me. 'I am from the prime minister's office,' he said politely, 'and I am here to ask you to come and meet the prime minister tomorrow at 5 p.m.'

'The prime minister? For an interview?'

'Well, let's put it this way...he would like to see you.'

Taken aback, I asked him why.

'He read your article and thinks that you misunderstood him so he would like to explain some things to you.'

'I don't know what to say. I've never been summoned by a prime minister before.'

He smiled cryptically, told me he would pick me up from the *Statesman* office at 4.45 p.m. the following day, and left.

It was my first visit ever to the prime minister's office and I was both excited and awestruck to be entering one of the most magnificent buildings in Delhi. The prime minister's office was originally built as the Viceroy's office. It is of the same pale red sandstone that was used to build the Viceroy's Palace, now Rashtrapati Bhavan, the official residence of the President of India. It sits at the top of Raisina Hill, and has an imperial air and an architectural beauty that government buildings built in more socialist times hopelessly lack. From the outside it continues to retain its aura of colonial grandeur so it came as a shock to see how decrepit it had become on the inside. We entered a dank hall that smelt of damp carpets, mildew and hair oil. A shabby reception area had been created beneath the magnificent stone staircase that led up to the prime minister's office. Two officials sat there at desks with grimy ledgers open before them. They had oily hair, towels on the backs of their chairs, with which they wiped their faces from time to time, and the haughty expressions of clerks who have more power than they deserve.

We waited in this disappointingly bleak reception area while one of the clerks dialled a three-digit number on an ancient black telephone on his table. It was so old and dirty that it creaked with every digit that was dialled. The clerk seemed aware of how filthy the receiver was because he held it with his towel. He also held a bit of the towel over the mouthpiece whose holes were thick with greasy dirt. After several attempts when he finally managed to get through and discovered that we were expected he looked resentful.

We walked up the grand sandstone staircase that looked as if it should lead to some particularly splendid ballroom but led instead to a veranda on which pigeon droppings had made indelible patterns and monkeys played. A wire mesh covered the courtyard that the veranda overlooked, with the ostensible purpose of keeping monkeys and pigeons out, but there was a monkey-sized hole in one corner that nobody had bothered to fix. The monkeys sat on the sandstone ledge of the veranda and made threatening faces at the prime minister's visitors. My escort told me they amused themselves by stealing papers from people's offices if they did not manage to steal food. 'It is a big menace,' he said as a monkey made a face at him, 'but nobody can do anything about it.'

Leading off from the veranda were cubbyholes crowded with officials seated at desks covered in dusty files. We walked to the end of the veranda where in big brass letters on the sandstone wall was written 'PRIME MINISTER'. When my escort pushed open the door I expected to find myself in a splendid high-ceilinged room with the prime minister seated at an imposing desk. Instead we entered a small ante-room in which more officials sat at small desks stacked with files. One of them stood up when he saw us and said, 'The prime minister is expecting you, but I'll just go in and check if he has got busy with something else.' He disappeared through a door and returned a minute later. 'Yes, yes. You can go in,' he whispered.

I entered an enormous room. Gilded specks of dust danced in the beams of sunlight that came in through two high ventilators. The windows were closed and the curtains drawn. My first glimpse of the prime minister was through a carved Kashmiri screen of painted walnut wood. He was indeed seated at an imposing wooden desk that looked as if it could have been inherited from a Viceroy but had been given a socialist touch. The green embossed leather that would have once covered it had been ripped off and replaced by thick glass. Beneath it was a film of dust that nobody had bothered to clean in a long time. The prime minister looked up and when he saw me he greeted me with a polite namaste. He went back to examining his files. I sat down on one of the chairs in front of the desk waiting for him to finish.

He worked. I watched. He would take a pink or yellow cardboard file from the tray on his left that said 'IN', examine it closely for a few seconds, sign it and place it in the tray on his right that said 'OUT'. He did this without any movement of his facial muscles and seemingly without breathing. I wondered whether along with his strange nutritional habits he practised yoga of the kind that enables yogis to hold their breath for a long time. While he proceeded with his yogic file clearance I glanced around and noticed how majestic the room was and how shoddily it was furnished. The furniture was new and badly made and the curtains and upholstery were the wrong colour, clearly chosen by an interior designer without any respect for the period in which the room had been built. At the end of fifteen minutes or so the prime minister looked up and said, 'Yes?'

'You sent for me.'

'Did I?'

'I am...from the *Statesman*...newspaper.'

'Oh. Yes. Yes. I was expecting a man.'

'Sorry about that,' I smiled. The prime minister did not. He had recently given an interview in which he said (thinking, perhaps, of his predecessor) that women should not be allowed to rule countries.

'I have nothing against women,' he said, looking irritated. 'I never said that women were not as capable as men. Only that women, when they enter politics, need to be careful because they tend to be of a more emotional nature than men.'

'Margaret Thatcher? Golda Meir?' I asked with feigned innocence. He realized I was being insolent and looked more irritated.

'Anyway, I didn't say that women should not be allowed in politics only that they should try to be less emotional if they went into it. But you journalists, you can distort anything. Now, look how you wrote about the three durbars.'

'I wrote what I saw.'

'You saw what you wanted to see. You wanted to make me look bad compared to Mrs Gandhi. Have you people forgotten the Emergency already? Have you forgotten censorship?'

'No, prime minister. I just described what I saw.'

'Well, next time maybe you should think before you write. Do you know the stress I am under? Do you know how difficult it is to be prime minister? The number of things I have to think about all day? And you people come along and write that I am heartless. What could I do for those people? Nothing. Why don't you people write about the mess that Mrs Gandhi has left behind, about the fact that she was in power for so many years and did nothing for the people? Nothing at all. India would not be a poor country if we had followed better economic policies. Why don't you write about those things?'

'In this story I was just asked to compare the three durbars...'

'What a stupid idea. And calling them durbars like that. Durbars are what kings and emperors have. We are ordinary people trying to do a very difficult job after a very difficult time. Do you know that I spent eighteen months in solitary confinement without newspapers or the radio? Do you know that others who were treated like this by Mrs Gandhi nearly went mad? They had to be hospitalized. Do any of you write about what we went through for the country? Did you people fight censorship? No. None of you fought. When she asked you to bend, you crawled, and you think you can just come along afterwards and attack us for everything.'

When his monologue was done the prime minister fell silent and went back to examining his files. It was a cue for his aide to tiptoe into the room and indicate with a silent gesture that it was time for me to go.

7 DISAPPOINTMENT

When I look back on that brief period when the Janata Party ruled India, two factors strike me as the main reasons why the Janata government failed to survive a full term in office.

The first and most obvious is that it was a coalition of different parties pretending to be a single party. This led to contradictions that quickly became impossible to reconcile. The Janata government may have lasted longer had it been an honest coalition. The second was their choice of prime minister. If by some lucky twist of fate Atal Behari Vajpayee had been made prime minister in 1977, instead of foreign minister, the political history of modern India might well have been very different. Vajpayee was not just the most charismatic Indian politician in the Janata Party's motley team but as he was to prove when he finally became India's prime minister, two decades later, he had a real talent for managing the disparate needs of a coalition. And he had an idea of India that had not been defined, as in Morarji Desai's case, by long years in the Congress Party. As foreign minister, Vajpayee showed that even his ideas of foreign policy were different. In two years he did more to improve relations with Pakistan than anyone had done before. On the larger canvas of international relations he saw the need for India to move away from being an undeclared satellite of the Soviet Union (under the guise of non-alignment) and evolve a foreign policy that was more balanced. He took the first steps in this new direction.

It is even possible that, unlike his party colleagues, he may have had the wisdom to deny Mrs Gandhi the spotlight the Janata government continued to focus on her by persecuting her personally. A commission of inquiry, the Shah Commission, was set up to investigate the Emergency but instead of allowing it to do its job quietly, the government took it upon itself to repeatedly attempt to throw Mrs Gandhi and Sanjay into jail on every charge it could fling at them. The charges brought against her ranged from misuse of power to breach of parliamentary privilege. Had Mrs Gandhi and her son been summoned before the Shah Commission and made to explain why they acted as they did during the Emergency, it would have been far more useful than sending them to Tihar Jail in the harsh glare of publicity. It was as if the Janata government had forgotten that Mrs Gandhi was voted out only because of the Emergency but remained a popular leader. And in the eyes of millions of poor and illiterate Indians she was almost a goddess. Or perhaps the new leaders remembered this too well and understood the need to destroy her. If this was so they went about it the wrong way.

By 1978 Mrs Gandhi was back in the Lok Sabha as the member of Parliament from Chikmagalur in Karnataka and was in the Lok Sabha on the evening of 19 December when a resolution was passed demanding that she be 'committed to jail until the prorogation of the House and also expelled from membership of the House for serious breach of privilege and contempt'. She had been found guilty by the Privileges Committee of obstructing four officials investigating Maruti Limited.

Later on that cold December night I waited amid a small army of reporters outside the main entrance of Parliament House for Mrs Gandhi to appear and be escorted to jail. But since my newspaper already had a reporter inside Parliament, and Mrs Gandhi seemed to be taking a very long time to emerge, I was asked by the news editor to go to her residence to get details about the family that might add some colour to the story. So I arrived at 12 Willingdon Crescent to find the house in total darkness. There were no cars in the drive and apparently nobody there. I was about to leave when out of the darkness I heard the sort of 'pssst' you read about in comic books. I stopped and looked in the direction of the sound and discovered that it came from Romi Chopra who was peering out of the doorway of an unlit bathroom. 'There's nobody here but the children and me,' he whispered dramatically. 'Everyone left before the police arrived. We were forewarned, you know.'

'Where did they go?'

'Rajiv and Sonia have gone to Parliament House and I don't know where the others are, but isn't it thrilling? What a stupid mistake for this stupid government to make.'

I agreed with him but did not want to get into a discussion so I said, 'I have to go. I have a deadline. I better get back to Parliament.'

As I left I heard a child shouting, 'Romi Chopra, come here at once.' He went off with a happy smile on his face.

The army of journalists gathered in the porch of Parliament House had swollen by the time I got back. But nobody seemed to have noticed Sonia Gandhi standing in the shadows in a long skirt, boots and an elegant coat, carrying a picnic basket in her hands. She smiled when she saw me and said, explaining the picnic basket, that it contained sandwiches and coffee in case Mrs Gandhi was forced to spend the night in jail.

As I remember it, this is the conversation we had that night.

'Where's Rajiv?'

'He is waiting in the car over there, he doesn't want to attract attention. If they don't arrest her then we will just go home.'

'And if they arrest her?'

'We'll go to the jail to make sure that she is all right.'

'Are you even more horrified by Indian politics now than before?'

'Oh, I am getting quite used to the way things work,' she said, smiling. 'I think I am getting to understand it better. My real concern is for the children. I would hate for them to be hurt by all this.'

'I just saw them at the house. Romi was with them. They seemed all right...there were no policemen or anything...'

A sudden commotion caused us to stop talking as a large group of people rushed out of Parliament House. Police vans screeched up minutes later. Sonia said a quick goodbye and hurried towards the blue Matador van in which Rajiv was waiting. I moved towards the main entrance of Parliament and, in the melee, noticed my newspaper's Lok Sabha correspondent. 'What happened inside the House?' I asked.

'First Mrs Gandhi said her arrest was illegal since she was a member of Parliament and could not be arrested without the Speaker's permission. Then she came out of the House and held a press conference.' His eyes took on a bewildered expression and he stopped.

'Then?' I urged.

'She said she was not afraid of going to jail...then she recited a poem.'

'Which one?'

'I didn't know it, but it sounded like "Row, row, row your boat gently down the stream".'

'No!'

'Well, maybe not but it sounded like one of those nursery rhymes you learn in kindergarten.'

I discovered later that it was a line from a poem by Gracie Fields that Mrs Gandhi had recited. I think it was, 'Wish me luck as you wave me goodbye; Cheerio, here I go, on my way.' It served mostly to confuse her audience.

As an eyewitness to the drama of a former prime minister being arrested in Parliament, I found myself wondering why the Janata government did not see how their attempts to prosecute Mrs Gandhi were working so wonderfully in her favour. After the incident, she spent a week in Tihar Jail and emerged from it a heroine in the eyes of most ordinary Indians. Memories of the Emergency and its 'excesses' were beginning to fade.

In a column I wrote after Rajiv Gandhi was assassinated I took credit for having advised him in the summer of 1978 to give his first interview to the media.

At the dinner parties where I would run into Rajiv and Sonia we now talked only about politics. For me this was a pleasant change from those endless conversations about children and holidays. There was at this time a lot of bad publicity surrounding Sanjay and it came up in these discussions, which is when I think I suggested the interview, mainly in the hope that Rajiv might let me do it. This was not to be. I was too junior a reporter and whoever Rajiv may have talked to about my suggestion must have said that he should give it to a more important journalist. This was how M.J. Akbar was chosen and I was asked to be the go-between.

I was, at this time, beginning to lose interest in the *Statesman*. So when I met Akbar, then editor of a weekly news magazine called *Sunday*, I considered his suggestion of writing for the magazine under a pseudonym on a freelance basis. *Sunday* magazine had begun publication in the early months of the Emergency but, like *India Today*, it came into its own after press censorship was lifted in 1977. Both magazines did more to seriously analyse the Emergency than the newspapers did. While *India Today* was relatively conservative, *Sunday* magazine soon became famous for its radical political views and Akbar for being India's rebel editor.

In any case, Romi rang me one day and said that Rajiv was happy to do an interview with M.J. Akbar and since I knew him, could I please make the arrangements. When I asked Akbar if he would like to interview Rajiv Gandhi, he thought at first that I was joking. When he realized I was serious he wanted to know how I was in a position to arrange an interview with Mrs Gandhi's son. I said I knew him a bit. Akbar said he would love to do an interview with Rajiv Gandhi and added that it was worthy of being a cover story. Rajiv asked me to warn Akbar that he would not say anything that sounded like criticism of his family and Akbar said he had no problem with this.

The interview was arranged on an especially hot Sunday in April or May in the summer of 1978. The plan was for me to collect Akbar from his office and take him to 12 Willingdon Crescent. Akbar seemed both nervous and excited about the interview and asked me all sorts of questions about Rajiv on the short drive to Mrs Gandhi's house.

Tall trees line Willingdon Crescent and it has rows of colonial bungalows of monotonous uniformity. The walls that half conceal the bungalows from passing traffic are of unpainted brick and have bamboo fences that are painted military green. Some are so high you cannot see the bungalows that lie beyond, some are lower and reveal squat white- or yellow-washed bungalows. In the seventies the PWD was too poor to keep them in good condition so, often, there were dark patches on the walls where there had been seepage. Since all the bungalows were built in the 1920s when there was no air-conditioning, to keep out the terrible heat of Delhi summers they had large porches to shade entrances. And dingy rooms with high ventilators and small windows to allow the passage of light and fresh air but not so much as to heat up the interior. Mrs Gandhi had been allotted one of the smaller bungalows, which at the time had a circular entrance hall with a corridor that led from it to living rooms on either side and bedrooms beyond.

Rajiv was waiting in what seemed to be the study, seated beside a window that offered a view of the garden. He was reading a magazine but stood up when he saw us, held out his hand to Akbar and said something like, 'Hello, nice to meet you...Let me tell you, I'm very nervous. I've never given an interview, ever.'

The sincerity of the remark disarmed Akbar. A look of wonder came into his eyes as he held Rajiv's hand and it took me a few moments to realize that Akbar was overawed to be in the presence of Mrs Gandhi's son. Rajiv made a gesture that indicated that he would like me to stay during the interview so I sat down and pretended to be looking out of the window and at the Tanjore paintings on the wall. Mrs Gandhi was careful about keeping her socialist image intact and the room was not air-conditioned. A slow, dusty fan grumbled creakily overhead, birds chattered in the garden and ribbons of sunlight came in through the ventilators.

As I remember it, Akbar started by asking soft, easy questions about Rajiv's childhood and what it had been like to grow up as the son of one prime minister and the grandson of another. And, Rajiv gradually relaxed and became chattier. I could see from Akbar's expression that he would prefer it if I left so I slipped quietly back into the circular entrance hall and was about to go into the garden when Sonia appeared from a door at the end of the corridor, a hairdryer in her hand. She asked me to come into her room. It was the first time I had been inside her bedroom and I was struck by its austerity. I had expected elegance, charm, some effort at luxury and was surprised to find a nondescript bed, a couple of old carpets strewn across the floor and some unremarkable armchairs. It could have been furnished by the PWD for its charmless severity but those were socialist times and most rooms in government bungalows were unattractive and bare.

Sonia quickly explained what she wanted to talk to me about. She reminded me that we had a plan to go on to lunch at Romi's house after the interview and wanted to know whether we should take Akbar with us. I said that it might seem rude if we did not and saw no harm in taking him along. He was usually good company, I remember thinking, and besides it would have seemed very odd for me to stay on while he left after the interview ended. So he came with us.

We arrived at Romi's house in Vasant Vihar to find him and Vasundhara Raje ensconced in the drawing room. They looked momentarily surprised to see Akbar but greeted him as if they knew he was coming. Akbar looked uncomfortable. He had seemed slightly dazed from the moment he got into Rajiv's car. Rajiv drove with Akbar sitting beside him, and Sonia and me in the back. There were efforts at polite conversation, but Akbar seemed too overcome to do more than respond in monosyllables. Now he seemed bemused by the intimacy of Romi's small lunch party. Rajiv noticed that Akbar was unsure of himself and went out of his way to make him feel at home. He joked about the interview and said he was sure he was going to sound like a fool when people read it, but added that it had been painless because Akbar had been so gentle with him.

After the usual pleasantries, I think we got into a conversation over lunch about the merits of dictatorship, and someone expressed a commonly held view in Delhi at the time that what India needed was a period of 'benign dictatorship'. It could have been because we had gone from the totalitarianism of the Emergency to the indiscipline and confusion of the Janata government, but there was much talk in those days of the need for a benign dictator and even some debate over whether a period of military rule would be best for the country. With democracy now considered one of India's greatest assets, it seems absurd that people thought this way in 1978. But they did.

Whatever the political conversation over lunch, and I remember that almost all the talk was about politics, it was a pleasant enough afternoon. The food was delicious. Sonia had brought with her some lasagna that she had cooked and it was as good lasagna as I have ever eaten. By the time we got to whatever the pudding was, I remember that Akbar was the centre of attention as he regaled us with political gossip about the flaws and foibles of the Janata government.

This lunch at Romi's was to later become the cause of a problem between Akbar and me after Rajiv became prime minister. But I am getting ahead of my story. Years ahead of it. Akbar's interview with Rajiv appeared on the cover of *Sunday* magazine and although it may have made no difference to improving Mrs Gandhi's image, it was much discussed in the drawing rooms of Delhi with most people agreeing that Rajiv sounded like a very good man and that it was a shame that he was not in politics. This was meant as a comparison with his younger brother who, because of his role during the Emergency, was not seen as a 'good' man.

By the summer of 1978, when Rajiv gave that first interview, the Janata government was already beginning to fall apart. The smallest disagreement could turn into a crisis, and at the crux of it all was the uncontrollable ambition of Chaudhury Charan Singh.

It was knowledge of this that made Sanjay and his friends use the services of a skilled 'holy man' called Chandraswami to bring down the Janata government in a political manouevre that could have come straight out of a Bollywood film. Chandraswami was persuaded to use his legendary fortune-telling skills to tell Charan Singh that he had seen in the lines of his hand the possibility of him becoming prime minister. I first heard the story from Akbar Ahmed, and confirmed it years later with Chandraswami himself.

Ironically, the man Sanjay's friends used as a go-between to introduce Chandraswami to Charan Singh was Mrs Gandhi's old opponent from Rae Bareli, Raj Narain, who was known to be very close to Chaudhury Sahib. Raj Narain was also well known by then for his rustic peculiarities. He lived in his large ministerial bungalow just as he must have done in his village. On the few occasions that I went to meet him there were always masseurs in attendance while Raj Narain reclined against bolsters having a limb massaged. When he went out in public, he often wore a green or red bandana and this along with his greasy white beard and thick spectacles gave him the appearance of a weather-beaten garden gnome.

Chandraswami was a tall and dark-skinned man with thick lips who looked like the quintessential 'holy man' from a Bollywood film. Years later when I met him in his house in south Delhi that he had converted into an ashram I noticed that his room looked like a film set. It had powder-blue walls and ornate furniture in gaudy colours and on the mantelpiece were pictures of Chandraswami with important American politicians and, of all people, Elizabeth Taylor. Chandraswami's chair was designed to look like a throne and was covered with a tiger skin. Around his neck he wore a heavy gold necklace strung with sacred rudraksh beads. Those who knew him well said that if he had a gift at all it was in the area of astrology. Apparently, his predictions were rarely wrong.

It is possible that knowledge of Chandraswami's gift and his prediction persuaded Charan Singh to bring down his own government, or it may have been Charan Singh's ambition, or even real political considerations. But the Janata government had become, within a year of being in power, such a bundle of contradictions and absurdities that I find it entirely credible that in the end it was brought down by the chicanery of Chandraswami.

8 JANATA FALLS

Dynastic democracy in India began when Mrs Gandhi made Sanjay her political heir. When analysing why the Nehru–Gandhi dynasty continues to endure even serious political analysts say it is because of their charisma, their ability to win votes. This is only partly true. It is my conviction that the dynasty's real power comes from the support they get from the bureaucracy in Delhi. High officials in India are famous for the disdain with which they treat the representatives of the people but put almost any of them in the presence of a member of the Gandhi family and they behave like humble employees. This is something I have observed in long years of covering politics and governance.

If they ever make it to the inner circles of the court around the family their obsequiousness knows no bounds but they have not usually been admitted to this inner court. Indira Gandhi trusted her former stenographers Yashpal Kapoor and his nephew R.K. Dhawan more than she did any senior bureaucrat. Sanjay preferred to surround himself with his close friends, as did Rajiv. This tradition has been continued by both Sonia and Rahul Gandhi, but on the edge of their courts have always lurked senior bureaucrats dripping with a servility they rarely show anyone else. The most sycophantic are those who went to Oxford and Cambridge and who appear to have developed from this British experience a genetic memory of serving colonial masters.

Towards the end of 1978, when it became clear to the bureaucracy that Morarji Desai's government was not going to last a full term, they began to court people who they thought were close to the Gandhi family. Not just people around Mrs Gandhi but those close to Sanjay Gandhi as well.

I discovered this accidentally when I took Akbar Ahmed to dinner at the house of a senior bureaucrat who shall remain nameless. He was far from being the only civil servant who behaved this way once the winds started to blow against the Janata government but I remember this dinner party more vividly because it happened to be the first time I saw a senior bureaucrat demean himself before someone he believed was close to the Gandhi family.

The bureaucrat lived in a particularly beautiful colonial bungalow on Aurangzeb Road. The rooms had high ceilings and long French windows that opened on to wide verandas. Akbar and I arrived late and the drawing room and verandas were already filled with people. The scent of summer flowers wafted in from the garden and Indian classical music played discreetly in the background. Since officials were not allowed to serve foreign liquor, and the Indian liquor available then was undrinkable, we were served a rum punch with enough fruit juice in it to disguise the coarse taste of Indian rum.

Akbar looked around nervously when he saw that the gathering consisted mostly of what he called 'intellectual types'. This made him so uncomfortable that we were about to do a quiet disappearing act when our host came up to us with an obsequious smile on his face, and bowed deeply before Akbar, who looked embarrassed and unsure of how to react. The bureaucrat wasted no time in telling him that he had seen his pictures in the newspapers and knew that he was a close friend of Sanjay Gandhi. This is how I remember the conversation that followed.

'How long have you known him?' the bureaucrat asked with a look almost of wonder in his eyes. Sanjay at this point, it is important to remember, was being painted as a criminal by the Janata government for whom the bureaucrat worked in a senior position.

'Since we were in the Doon School together,' Akbar said, looking like he thought he should make a run for it.

'Well, let me tell you,' the bureaucrat continued, 'that I think Sanjay Gandhi is what this country needs. He has a vision for this country.'

'Yes,' Akbar said uncertainly.

'Let me tell you that the incident in the court the other day, when he refused to sit in the dock and you threw a pen at the judge... I think it was justified. I know there is no case against him. It's a witch hunt.'

'Yes. But we'll get our revenge when the time comes.'

'Yes. There is no doubt that Mrs Gandhi will soon be back in power. This government cannot last because it has no idea how to govern.'

'Right. Well, I know nothing about governance,' Akbar said with a laugh and a wink at me.

'Ah, but the country waits for the moment when we will be ruled once more by a strong leader instead of by these people, who should not have been in politics, leave alone government. Look at my minister. He is an absurdity, he understands nothing of the job he is supposed to be doing.'

'And Mrs Gandhi's ministers did?' This question came from me.

'Oh, much, much better. They came from the right class, which is why they will be back for sure.'

'Yes,' said Akbar with a wicked grin, 'we must all get our chance to fuck this mother-fucking country.'

He made this last remark in Hindi, making it sound cruder, and I thought our host would be embarrassed, but he laughed happily.

'Come on, Akbar, let's see if Naveen is here,' I said, before Akbar could make another informed comment on governance.

'Yes, yes. Please go ahead,' the bureaucrat said with another low bow. 'I just wanted to tell you that I think that your friend's 5-Point Programme was the most visionary programme I have seen in my long years in government.'

Even as the Janata government was in the process of finding all sorts of cases to file against Sanjay Gandhi, he and his circle of friends seemed to become more powerful by the day.

At the edge of this circle of friends was a group of Doon School boys who wanted to get closer to him by showing him how important they were in the political circles of Punjab. They were mostly from Sikh feudal families with little to do other than manage the affairs of their rundown estates. One of them, Anant Bir Singh Attari, was an old friend of my brother-in-law, and I had met him at parties in Delhi without knowing until much later that he had dabbled in Sikh politics in his student days. Anant Bir had a famous ancestor called Sham Singh Attariwala, who had for a brief period been Maharaja Ranjit Singh's governor in Kashmir and had married one of his daughters to Ranjit Singh's son. Sham Singh Attariwala went on to become a great Sikh hero for his skills on the battlefield. His estates lay in Attari, between Lahore and Amritsar, and it was there that Anant Bir spent most of his time. Since he had been in the Doon School around the same time that Sanjay was briefly a student there, he hovered on the outer circle of his friends when he came to Delhi.

By 1978 there were clear signs that Sanjay was more important politically in the Congress Party than Mrs Gandhi herself. While she amused herself with organizing such events as a Save India Day in Delhi, or travelling to the remote village of Belchi in Bihar on an elephant to meet Dalit victims of a hate crime, Sanjay concentrated on a comeback strategy for the Congress. A small part of his political master plan was to find a way to defeat the Akali Dal in Punjab. And this is where Anant Bir and his friends came in.

When the Punjab problem began in the eighties many believed that its roots lay in the support that Sant Jarnail Singh Bhindranwale got from Sanjay Gandhi and the Congress Party. Rumours of this were so widely believed that when I first interviewed Bhindranwale in the Golden Temple in 1982, I asked him if he had ever been paid by the Congress Party to create trouble for the Akali Dal. He was furious that I had dared to ask him such a question and brought the interview to a quick end by virtually ordering me out of the room.

It was many years later that I discovered that Bhindranwale had not been paid by the Congress Party but had certainly been lured into politics by Anant Bir and his friends who hoped to impress Sanjay. By then Operation Blue Star, which led to the assassination of Indira Gandhi and a decade of terrorism in Punjab, had already happened. But the story of what happened remains important if only as a footnote. Anant Bir's story as he told it to me is that, having been head of the Akali Dal's student wing, the All India Sikh Students' Federation, he knew that the best way to beat the Akalis was by beating them at their own dangerous game of mixing politics with religion. It was with this idea in mind that they began looking for a religious figure to use against the Akalis.

Sant Bhindranwale was at the time making a name for himself as an itinerant preacher. He was head of an important Sikh seminary, the Damdami Taksal, and spent his time wandering from village to village urging Sikhs to follow his simple ideas of faith. Do not cut your hair. And stay away from drugs and alcohol. This was what he understood as the fundamental message of Sikhism. When Anant Bir and his friends first approached him, in 1978, to play a more political role he refused. He told them he did not want to divide the Sikh community.

They persevered. When they next went to see Bhindranwale they took with them a *khanda* (a double-edged sword) that had once belonged to Sham Singh Attariwala and had come to be in Anant Bir's possession by way of inheritance. According to Anant Bir, Bhindranwale was so overwhelmed to be in such close proximity to a weapon that had belonged to the great Sikh hero that he was moved to tears. He bowed before it reverentially and saw the weapon as a sign that he should play a more active role in politics in order to save the Sikh community. What he wanted to save the Sikh community from was something he never explained to the end of his days, but his desire to save it was sincere.

Punjab was going through a bad time economically. Decades of land reforms had reduced the size of Punjab's farms to very small holdings that did not need every son in a farmer's family to work fulltime. So the villages were full of idle, unemployed young men who whiled away their time drinking and experimenting with drugs. Bhindranwale's message to them to give up intoxicants and become baptized Sikhs fell upon receptive ears and his following among young Sikhs grew and grew. Bhindranwale was sincere in his faith that the Sikh religion's tenets be followed to the letter and remain unpolluted and it was this that made him see the Nirankari sect as his first enemy.

The tenth Sikh guru, Guru Govind Singh, had ordained that after him there would be no more living gurus and that the Granth Sahib, the holy book, was to be the only guru for people of the Sikh faith. Bhindranwale had little understanding of the deep Sufi philosophy that is the basis of the Sikh religion, but he adhered with passionate fanaticism to the tenets that the tenth Sikh guru had put in place to create the Khalsa army. Finding it hard to create an armed struggle against Mughal repression because every time his soldiers were arrested they would say they were Hindu and not Sikh, Guru Govind Singh found the need to create an identity they could not deny. He ordered his soldiers to stop cutting their hair, to wear a steel bangle on their wrist and always carry a dagger called a kirpan. It was these tenets that Bhindranwale believed were the fundamental tenets of Sikhism. He carried his devotion to Guru Govind Singh to the bizarre degree of ordering his followers to dress in medieval attire. He and the young men who followed him started wearing blue turbans and long kurtas over loose shorts that stopped just above their calves.

The Nirankaris were Sikhs who had disobeyed the tenet that there should be no more living gurus. The sect was founded in 1929 by a man called Baba Buta Singh and although he started by refining the Sufi philosophy of the Sikh religion to make it more spiritual, by the sixties the sect was headed by Baba Gurbachan Singh who projected himself as a living guru. He published a text called *Avtar Bani* in which he described himself as a new *avtar* with divine powers. In the eyes of Bhindranwale, this was apostasy and all Nirankaris apostates. He fought them publicly every chance he got. It did not help that whenever there was a public clash that turned violent, the police and administration usually sided with the Nirankaris because their guru was a man with powerful connections.

Other than the publicity he got from fighting the Nirankaris, since Bhindranwale had acquired a significant following in the villages of Punjab, he was in a good position to take on the Akali Dal which, as a semi-religious Sikh party, had a small army of preachers in their employ. Anant Bir and his friends persuaded Bhindranwale to contest in the elections for the committee that controls Sikh temples and other religious institutions, the Shiromani Gurudwara Prabandhak Committee, in 1978. His candidates lost all the seats they contested and he retired briefly from politics. Later he was persuaded once more to play a political role, this time by more senior Congress leaders like Zail Singh, who went on to become President of India. It is hard to believe in retrospect that the wooing of this man, who would go on to create one of India's most serious political problems, started as a sideshow. A game played by amateurs with no real understanding of politics or religion.

While Sanjay and his friends were working on their comeback strategy Rajiv and Sonia continued to live in apolitical obscurity. I saw them regularly at those same dinner parties and came to know them quite well. I discovered that Rajiv had enormous charm and now that we had broken the barrier on political discussions, he was happy to talk about anything with quite remarkable frankness. He never commented on his brother's politics and it was clear that although they got on reasonably well their paths were quite different as were their friends. Sonia was more difficult to get to know because of her reserve but I discovered, quite by accident, that she would go out of her way to help people whom she considered her friends.

She had absolutely no interest in politics. The only comment on politics I remember her making was on a night when Rajiv and she were dropping me home after a dinner party. I asked her if she would like her children to be in politics some day, and she said, 'I would rather my children begged in the streets than went into politics.'

This conversation remains vivid in my mind not just because of how much changed afterwards but also because the words she used to describe her disdain for politics were so fervent when she spoke them. We were driving past Race Course Road, where she moved when Rajiv became prime minister and where the prime minister of India continues to live, when she made the remark. She was sitting beside Rajiv who was driving, and I was in the back seat, and she turned around to look at me when she said she would rather her children begged in the streets than enter politics. There was something about the look on her face that made me wonder for the first time if she was not a stronger person than she gave the impression of being.

But, to come back to how I discovered that she could be a good friend. Madhu Jain, a colleague who had asked me to collaborate with her to write a book on the growing influence of Hindi cinema, called me one day to say that Khushwant Singh had become editor of a new magazine called *New Delhi* and wanted us to do a story on Bollywood. The only problem was that he wanted an important section of the story to be on a day in the life of Amitabh Bachchan. This was when Bachchan was at the height of his stardom and so much in demand that he was being described as a one-man film industry. Madhu said it would be impossible to get to spend a whole day with him unless we had the right introduction.

I told her that I knew nobody who knew him and she pointed out that I did. Sonia Gandhi. Amitabh Bachchan's family was from Allahabad, like the Nehrus, and he and his brother had grown up with Rajiv and Sanjay. In 1968, when Rajiv and Sonia were married, Mrs Gandhi was prime minister and since it would have been inappropriate for her son to get married to a foreigner in Italy the wedding had to be held in Delhi. In searching for a bridal home for Sonia, the automatic choice seems to have been the

Bachchan home and the Bachchans became Sonia's Indian family. I knew that she treated Amitabh and his brother Ajitabh as her brothers.

When Madhu suggested I ask Sonia to introduce us to Amitabh Bachchan, I hesitated because I had never asked her for a favour. But since it was our only hope of getting an interview with him I called Sonia. When I asked if she could introduce Madhu and me to Amitabh Bachchan she was more than ready to help. She said that 'Amit' was going to be in town soon and she would take us to meet him. One morning soon after, she rang to say that we should come to Amitabh's parents' house, next door to the Gandhis', in 13 Willingdon Crescent.

Madhu and I reached the Bachchan home, more than a little overwhelmed to be meeting the biggest star in Bollywood. I think we may have stared speechlessly like villagers when we went into the drawing room and saw him sitting there with Sonia. We were so starstruck, at least I was, that it took us a few moments before we explained that we needed to spend a whole day with him for an article on the film industry. Amitabh was charm itself. He said there would be no problem at all. All we would need to do when we got to Bombay was call his secretary, Rosy, and she would set it up.

After I had wiped the stardust out of my eyes, I remember thinking how odd it was that the Bachchan family should remain so close to Indira Gandhi and her family even after he became Bollywood's 'angry young man'. India's symbol of rage against the government, the political system and the injustice of the established order of things. Because if there was injustice in the established order it was entirely due to the Nehru–Gandhi family.

But I remember this meeting in the Bachchan drawing room mostly because it was the first time I saw Sonia's ability to go out of her way to help a friend. I was to see it again, many times, and must record that this was her finest quality.

Madhu and I arrived in Bombay some weeks later and I became instantly fascinated by the illusions and unreality of Bollywood. This world filled with beautiful people and artificial light was so different to the real India that the people who lived in it seemed to belong to another planet. After long days spent wandering from studio to studio, we would find ourselves invited in the evenings to a Bollywood dinner or event, or we would just sit in a Juhu cafe and watch the sunset. To my eyes, unused to the changing colours of the sea, these gaudy orange sunsets were so perfect over the dark grey waters of the Arabian Sea that they seemed as much the creation of a Bollywood art director as the effects we saw when the lights went on in dark studios.

There were very few stars in the Indian firmament at the time. Politics had only Mrs Gandhi and her family and sports only a handful of cricketers so those that shone in Bollywood glittered so brightly that they tended to become obsessed with their own celebrity. They behaved as if they lived in the stratosphere, high above the dark realities of poverty, misery and repression that were the defining characteristics of India at the time. One night we found ourselves in the house of Rajesh Khanna who, until Bachchan burst upon Bollywood in his 'angry young man' persona, was the biggest star of the Hindi film industry. Rajesh Khanna lived in a house by the sea decorated in the hues of a Bollywood film set. That night we could well have been part of some bizarre Bollywood plot because the first thing we were introduced to in his living room was his mother's gallstones. They drifted in a murky liquid in a jar. The jar had been placed on the bar next to bottles of liquor and was the centre of all conversation, since among the guests that evening were the doctors who had extracted the stones. Rajesh Khanna gazed at the jar lovingly and, between sips of his Scotch and soda, told us how much he loved his mother and how he had brought her all the way from Amritsar so she could be operated on by the finest doctors in India.

There were just 12,000 cinema halls in India in the seventies but cinema was the only entertainment for the masses, the only brief escape into a fantasy world of dream sequences and happy endings. At least that is how it was until two young script writers, Salim Khan and Javed Akhtar, collaborated to invent the character of Amitabh Bachchan as the eternal rebel who could take on the richest, most powerful men and always win. To understand how Bollywood films had turned political with the invention of Amitabh as India's angry, young man we went to meet Javed Akhtar. Javed had come to Bollywood as an impoverished aspiring poet who hoped that his father, Jan Nisar Akhtar, a successful lyricist for Hindi films, would introduce him to Bollywood. But his father had struggled hard to climb the ladder of success and believed his son should do the same. He offered him no help, and Javed spent years struggling to find work, sometimes sleeping on park benches, and sometimes, because of the kindness of a watchman in Mehboob Studios, in a dressing room filled with costumes and props from films of yore. It was the invention of Amitabh Bachchan as India's symbol of protest that finally brought him fame and fortune.

We met Javed in his sparsely furnished apartment that offered a magnificent view of the Arabian Sea. He sat on a low, white diwan that looked like mattresses piled on the floor. With a head of thick, wavy hair and his brooding, romantic look, he was every inch the poet. I remember him as being very political and quite an angry young man himself. He was by then as successful as Bachchan and although it was never certain how much anyone got paid in Bollywood, it was rumoured that Salim–Javed made as much money for a script as Bachchan did for playing the lead role in a film. What was certain was that they earned more than scriptwriters had ever been paid before.

Javed had agreed to meet us for an interview through the good offices of a mutual friend, but treated us as Bollywood stars in those days treated film journalists. With disdain. I remember asking him an innocent question like what he attributed his fame to and him saying, 'It is because I am brilliant. I am the most brilliant person I know.' Many years later, when I got to know him as a friend, I asked him whether he had invented Bachchan's character as a response to the Emergency and the general anger in the country against our political leaders. He said he had not done this consciously. The character he created for Bachchan was not political but that of an ordinary man fighting everyday repression by corrupt officials, politicians and other people in power.

Everything went well for us in Bollywood except for one thing. My day with Bachchan nearly did not happen. I called Rosy, as he had asked me to, soon after arriving in Bombay, and I continued to call her every day for more than a week before a date was finally set for our day together. Bachchan was so busy at the time that I am certain it was only because the introduction had come through Sonia that he agreed to see me at all. But when Rosy finally set up the appointment and told me to be at his home in Juhu at 6 a.m., I arrived to find quite a different man to the one I had met in Delhi. He treated me to an icy stare and barely said hello while his Mercedes was loaded with pillows, cold drinks, water and food. His wife, Jaya Bachchan, a star in her own right, stood in the doorway of their house with his lunch box in her hand and she made up for his unexpected coldness by smiling and making friendly conversation.

Then we got into his dark blue Mercedes and set off for the first 'shift' of the day. When I tried to ask him the sort of questions that interviews usually begin with, he replied with either a 'yes' or a 'no' and made it clear that he would rather read his newspaper than talk to me. So I shut up. When we stopped at traffic lights on the long drive to the studio, street children recognized him and swarmed all over the car gleefully shouting his name. He became, for that moment, cheerful and friendly. Then it was back to long, uncomfortable silences.

When we got to Film City, where his first shoot was, I tried to follow him to his dressing room but he stopped me and said he would prefer it if I waited in the studio canteen. So I did. The canteen smelled of fried snacks and instant coffee and its plastic chairs were occupied by young actors and extras who chatted noisily over 'masala' omelettes and glasses of tea. When I introduced myself as a reporter from Delhi, they were eager to tell me their stories of struggle and failure and the elusiveness of success in Bollywood. There was a 95 per cent failure rate, they said, but once you came into the 'industry' you became addicted to it and unable to work elsewhere. They could not explain what it was that stopped them from finding ordinary jobs and living more regular lives. But said it could be because the fantasy world that exists inside the studios was so seductive.

When Mr Bachchan next appeared, he was in full make-up and went straight for 'his shot' with Shashi Kapoor who was the other star in the film. A man held a clapper-board before the camera that said, 'Dewar Films – *Do Aur Do Paanch*. Scene 108B – shot 1 – 8.9.79'. In a shot that had taken all morning to set up, Bachchan had a single line of dialogue, '*Kahan ho Faquirchand Khachramal?*' Once the shot was over I was summoned back to the blue Mercedes and we drove in another uncomfortable silence to Vasant Studio, to shoot for a film called *Naseeb*, which went on to become a huge hit.

It was late afternoon by the time we got to the studio and the crew, who included the actor Rishi Kapoor and the director Manmohan Desai, were gathered in the shade of a garden pavilion eating together in convivial, chatty harmony. In their company Bachchan became a different person. He was full of stories and jokes and very much the soul of the party. He did not touch the food we ate and restricted himself to eating the simple vegetarian fare that was in the lunch box he brought from home. It took an endless amount of time for the shot to be readied but Bachchan seemed used to this. He joked about how in Hollywood actors 'put their meter down' from the minute they arrived on set.

Finally, when the director was satisfied that his shot was ready, the star was asked to wander down a street lined with fake shop fronts and lit by fake streetlights, drunkenly singing a song. Rishi Kapoor, his younger brother in the film, followed in his wake and helped him up each time he fell. By the time this 'shift' was over, dusk was falling and I had given up all hope of interviewing Bachchan, so I said goodbye and told him that I would take a taxi back. He asked where I was staying. 'Colaba,' I said. He told me that I should go with him since his next 'shift' was in town and he would be driving to the Oberoi Hotel. So I stayed more for the convenience of the ride home than from any expectation of an interview.

On the drive to the Oberoi darkness fell and when it was too dark for me to take notes or turn on my fat tape-recorder, Bachchan started to talk about his life as an actor and its difficulties in the most spellbinding way. He talked of how, when you spent your whole time playing different roles, the lines between reality and fantasy blurred, and how there were times when he was not sure if the emotions he felt in real life were any more real than what he felt when he was acting. It was the sort of stuff that journalists dream about when they interview famous people and all I could do was make notes in my head on the long, smoggy drive into the centre of the city.

It took us an hour to get to the Oberoi during which he talked endlessly and I listened, as carefully as I could, too frightened to put on my tape-recorder in case it broke the spell. When we got to the Oberoi we went up to the suite that was reserved for him and collapsed on the bed looking as if he would be happy for the day to end there and then. But, although he had worked for more than twelve hours, he still had another shoot to do. His last 'shift' was for a film called *Dostana*. The producer sent up a home-cooked, vegetarian meal and a message that they would be ready to shoot at 10 p.m. This gave us an hour to talk and Bachchan talked tiredly about the difficulties of being India's only superstar. When I asked him why he needed to work such long hours day after day despite being the biggest star in Bollywood, he said, 'Why do we do it? I don't know. It's just the system. If only the film press were interested in more than bedrooms and champagne they would see the other side, the blood and sweat. It's hot and sticky in the studios and you have to fight with a guy three times your size, and then you go to the next studio and you have to sing a song in the rain and you get all wet. By this time you're physically drained and you're working on sheer willpower – all this switching on and off characters and roles – and there is this heaviness in the head, and after all this you finish work at 11 p.m. and someone comes up and asks for an autograph and you say "I'm tired", and they think you're being snobbish and uppity.'

It was after 10.30 p.m. that Bachchan, in dark trousers and a grey leather jacket, began his last shift of the day. It involved shooting an 'action shot' in a dark Bombay back street. This sequence had the star dodging a speeding car and finally being thrown on to the bonnet on his chest. It took five takes to satisfy the director. And the small crowd of spectators who had gathered to watch taunted the star with comments like, 'If you can't do it, Amit, then let me take a shot at it.' It was 2 a.m. before the shift ended and when the producer still wanted 'a few more shots', he finally said he could do no more. Bollywood's superstar had worked for nearly twenty-four hours by then.

By the time he dropped me home at 4 a.m. we had become friends. As for me, I had fallen in love. When I did try to ask a couple of political questions, in between shots, I asked mostly silly ones. I asked if it was true that he had influenced Mrs Gandhi to censor certain Bollywood films, a widely believed rumour during the Emergency. He laughed and said, 'Didn't they also tell you that I was responsible for declaring the Emergency?' The questions I should have asked, about his being the most important symbol of opposition to the established political order while remaining so close to the Gandhi family, I have to sadly confess I never did. On the train back to Delhi Madhu, heavily pregnant and not very sympathetic, said she did not think I was fit to write about a day in Amitabh Bachchan's life since I seemed to have developed a 'silly crush' on him.

It was not one of the finest moments of my journalistic career.

9 THE RETURN OF INDIRA GANDHI

Charan Singh's dream of becoming India's prime minister came true but only for twenty-three days though he remained caretaker prime minister from August 1979 to January 1980. Having engineered the collapse of Morarji Desai's government on account of silly prophecies and uncontainable ambition, and deluded about how much support he really had, Charan Singh set off for Rashtrapati Bhavan to declare that he was in a position to form a new government. He was invited by the President to do so, on 28 July 1979, on the condition that he establish in Parliament within a month that he did indeed have the support of a majority of the Lok Sabha. He would not have made it even as far as the gates of Rashtrapati Bhavan if he had not been assured by Indira Gandhi that he could rely on the 'outside support' of her MPs. But, in the days that followed, Mrs Gandhi discovered that the new prime minister had no intention of doing away with the special courts that had been set up by Morarji Desai's government to try Sanjay for his 'excesses' during the Emergency. Realizing that she had no need of him she withdrew her party's support to Charan Singh's government a day before Parliament was due to meet on 20 August.

When the government fell and an early general election was announced it caused unexpected problems for Vasundhara Raje. Her mother, the Rajmata of Gwalior, decided to contest personally against Mrs Gandhi in Rae Bareli, which led to Vasundhara Raje's brother protesting angrily against what he called their mother's reckless determination to destroy the family. Madhavrao Scindia had joined the Congress Party after returning from self-imposed exile during the Emergency. This political decision was probably influenced by the fear that Mrs Gandhi would find ways to deprive him of what was left of his inheritance. Much had been lost, many palaces surrendered to the state and vast sums paid in taxes, but enough property and wealth remained for him to be nervous about the government's future actions against him as a member of the Jana Sangh. It was not paranoia that made Madhavrao Scindia react this way but his understanding of the reality that the Indian state had immense power and that Mrs Gandhi had grown accustomed to using that power against her opponents. The Rajmata had chosen, instead, to spend the Emergency in Tihar Jail where she was put in a room reserved for prisoners facing execution. Through the iron bars of her cell she had a view of the jail's execution chamber but it did not seem to frighten her in the least.

The Rajmata was a woman of cheerful, indomitable courage. The sort of courage that comes effortlessly to those who believe they are fighting on the side of right. I had got to know her a little because of my friendship with her daughter, and every time we met she talked to me of nationalism and the glory of India as if there was nothing else in the world worth talking about. She told me that when she was a few days old she had lost her mother and as she grew older and felt the loss, in those heady times of the freedom movement when nationalism permeated the air, she was comforted by the idea that Bharat Mata was her real mother. Her mother was of royal Nepalese blood and her father from an ordinary Rajput family in Uttar Pradesh. He worked as a provincial official in the British Raj.

The Rajmata had become a maharani by a romantic accident. An uncle worked in the palace of the Maharaja of Gwalior and when the young maharaja started searching for a bride he slipped a photograph of his beautiful niece among those of Maratha princesses and other suitably high-born girls. The maharaja fell in love with her photograph and announced that he would marry only her. Black-and-white photographs of the royal wedding show her as a tall, beautiful bride gazing adoringly at her fairy-tale maharaja. But life measured in small doses the happiness that it gave Rajmata Sahib and she became a widow in her thirties. So it was again Bharat Mata and her service to which she turned for solace. She joined the Jana Sangh and donated vast sums to build schools and spread the cause of Hindu nationalism, and she allowed the palaces of Gwalior to be used for what she considered noble causes. When I asked her why she had chosen to contest against Mrs Gandhi in an election she was bound to lose, she said simply, 'I am a loyal soldier of the party and the party asked me to do this. How could I refuse?' Many people admired the Rajmata for her decision but her son was not one of them. Vasundhara found herself torn between her brother and mother and resolved the problem by not taking sides. She did not campaign for either of them.

For my part, I saw in the situation a great election story and when Rajmata Sahib went on her first election tour I went along with a group of reporters from Delhi. We travelled by train to Lucknow and then followed her cavalcade to Rae Bareli by road, although 'road' might be too grand a word to describe the broken strip of tarmac that led to Mrs Gandhi's constituency. In some stretches the tarmac had completely disappeared and our Ambassador lurched from one rubble-filled ditch to the next, raising such large clouds of dust that we had to roll up the windows. Dusty trees lined the road and beyond lay villages of the most primitive kind.

We passed village after village of windowless hovels huddled together haphazardly with roofs so flimsy the first rain would have washed them away. In front of the mud huts skinny buffaloes stood chained to their feeding troughs staring listlessly into the distance and naked children with protruding bellies and hair bleached from malnutrition played beside them. They gazed at the Rajmata's motorcade of white Ambassadors with the same expression as the buffaloes. Snot dribbled from their noses and mingled with the dust to become a paste that spread across their faces. They looked as if they had never been washed. Their mothers stood beside them in tattered saris with one end of which they half covered their faces. The men sat apathetically on string beds. All of rural India looked pretty much like this, I remember thinking, but surely Mrs Gandhi's constituency should have looked better.

When the Rajmata stopped in the first village and rolled down her window to greet a group of villagers, we jumped out of our car and raced up to her to listen.

'Ram, Ram,' said the Rajmata.

'Ram, Ram,' replied an old man with a grimy turban and a wizened face who appointed himself spokesman for the group.

'I have come because the fight we fought two years ago against Mrs Gandhi's *taanashahi* (dictatorship) is not over. We're still fighting that fight and I'm relying on you people to help me fight it. Can I rely on you?'

'Yes,' said the old man uncertainly.

'We cannot allow Mrs Gandhi to win again because once more the country will be ruled by a dictator. Once more poor people will be bundled into trucks and taken away to be sterilized as if they were animals. Once more they will come and tear down your houses and tell you that you have to move elsewhere because that is the government's wish. Are we going to let this happen?'

'No.'

'Do you have electricity in this village?'

'No.'

'Do you have drinking water?'

'No.'

'Water for your fields?'

'No.'

'Whose fault is this? Ours? We have been ruling for less than two years. It is the Congress Party who is to blame for this state of affairs. Thirty years after Independence, if Indira Gandhi has been unable to provide electricity and drinking water to people in her own constituency, can you believe that she will do it now?'

The old man looked around at the group of men who had gathered around him, waiting for one of them to speak. They stared silently at the Rajmata. When nobody spoke, she rolled up her window, joined her hands together in farewell and drove off.

We lingered to ask the villagers if they knew who she was. They responded with suspicious stares and silence.

'We are reporters from Delhi,' I said, 'we are not from any political party.'

The only person prepared to speak was the old man. He said, 'We don't know her name, but we think it is the Maharani who has come to stand against Indiraji.'

'Can she win?'

'We will not know till the election is over,' said the old man, with a crafty glint in his eyes.

We hurried on behind the Rajmata's convoy past more dusty trees and mud-hut villages. There were many more roadside stops. Sometimes she talked to people without getting out of her car. Sometimes, if there were enough people, she got out and held impromptu roadside meetings. In every speech she reminded people that Mrs Gandhi was a dictator and that there would be another Emergency if she was voted back to power.

By late evening we were in some unrecognizable rural part of Mrs Gandhi's constituency. Through the smoky darkness came the occasional gleam of a village identifiable only by the lanterns of street vendors selling roasted peanuts. Not one of the villages we had passed in the gathering dusk showed signs of electricity. We stopped finally in a bazaar and the Rajmata's staff jumped out to ask for directions. This appeared to be the town we were to use for our 'night halt'. It was lit by dusty streetlights and lined on both sides with rows of small shops in which electricity manifested itself in dim, yellow bulbs dangling on long wires. It was late in the evening so when we passed a dhaba that smelled of freshly baked rotis we resolved unanimously to return after we had found our lodgings for the night.

The Rajmata's party had made arrangements for us in the local dak bungalow. In the days of the Raj these rural dak bungalows were used as rest houses for postmen travelling to deliver mail. From my childhood travels I remembered them as lovely old colonial bungalows with wide verandas and gardens filled with flowers. After Independence, they were allowed to decay while independent India's officials made small fortunes from the construction of ugly, new government guest houses.

The bungalow we were staying in that night looked quite charming from the outside but no sooner did we enter than harsh reality dawned. There was no electricity. The only light came from kerosene lanterns held up by two barefoot old men in khaki uniforms who stood in a dark entrance hall that smelled of stale food and something else that we could not identify till we saw bats flying out of the eaves of the veranda. I was among those who shrieked and ran out into the garden. The Rajmata was unperturbed and told us, with a sweet smile, that it was better than Tihar Jail. In her own case it certainly was because as a frequent traveller in rural India she knew what needed to be done. So an advance party of maids had arrived ahead of us and from the glimpse we caught of the Rajmata's candle-lit bedroom, we could see that it had been transformed. There were clean sheets on the bed, fresh flowers in vases and a spotlessly clean mosquito net.

Our room was what hers must have looked like before her maids arrived. It was large, musty and lit by a single kerosene lantern. Its feeble light did not penetrate the room's dark corners that seemed to hide all sorts of moving creatures. There were two narrow beds in the centre of the room covered with dusty green mosquito nets. Desperate to use the bathroom, I fought my terror of creepy-crawlies and, torch in hand, headed towards a rickety door at one end of our nocturnal cavern. When I pushed it open, an enormous cloud of mosquitoes rose out of the Indian-style WC and a rat as big as a kitten started racing around the room in panic.

I decided that I would be better off using a dark corner of the garden instead and more comfortable sleeping on the veranda. So did my colleagues. Like me they were young reporters but our limited experience of travels in what Gandhiji liked to call the 'real' India had taught us basic survival techniques. We asked for a bottle of water from the kitchen, washed up as well as we could in a corner of the unkempt garden, and used a darker corner in it as the toilet, keeping our fingers crossed that there were no snakes or scorpions. Then we drove back to the bazaar for dinner. We discovered from a man we met on the way that we were in one of the larger towns in Mrs Gandhi's constituency. I no longer remember its name but to this day they all look the same: neither town nor village and with an absence of municipal amenities so stark they seem untouched by governance.

On the drive back to the dhaba we discussed the primitive living conditions we had seen in the villages and wondered why Mrs Gandhi had done so little to improve standards in her own constituency. As prime minister it would have been easy for her to insist on at least basic things like electricity and clean water. The roads could have been better. Lesser political leaders like Sharad Pawar had so transformed their constituencies that we heard tales of them in newspaper offices in Delhi, so why had she done so little? We concluded that it must have been a deliberate policy not to allow development because people living in extreme poverty tend to vote unquestioningly for whoever they are told to by religious and caste leaders even today.

The dhaba's rickety wooden tables were laid out on a mud pavement that stank of the clogged drain running alongside it. Chicken feathers and onion skins lay around and in one corner there was a dark patch where chickens seemed recently to have been beheaded. Mingled with the stench of the drain came the distinct smell of human excrement. When I looked around to detect its source, I noticed three small children squatting by the drain over piles of shit. They were half naked but must have been from the dhaba owner's brood because they looked well fed. There were two girls and a boy, and they grinned and waved when they noticed us looking at them. Inside the dhaba was a mud oven for making rotis and a gas cooker on which stood three metal cooking pots. There was rice in one, dal in another and a mixed vegetable stew in the third. A comforting scent of spices wafted up when the skinny, bare-chested cook lifted the lids to show us what was on offer. We ordered a bit of everything.

We must have made a curious spectacle with our urban clothes and manners because before our food arrived dark figures started emerging from the shadows. Soon a crowd of male spectators gathered around us. The first to arrive was an elderly Muslim man with a white beard and a dark prayer mark on his forehead. Behind him came three tall, well-built young men wearing kurtas and lungis. They looked like his sons. Behind these men came a caboodle of boys of various ages and sizes.

'*Aadaab arz hai*,' the old man said in a courteous, educated tone.

'*Aadaab*.'

'My name is Aazim Ali Khan, I am the village headman. These are my sons.'

'We have come from Delhi.'

'Ah.'

'We are travelling with the Rajmata of Gwalior.'

'Ah.'

'Well? Can the Rajmata win?' one of us asked, getting straight to the point.

'Who knows,' the old man replied with a cryptic smile. It was a typical answer and we knew that we would only get more information if we persisted with our questions.

'Oh, come on. You always know. At least tell us which way the wind is blowing.'

The old man smiled even more enigmatically and stroked his beard.

'All right, *can* the Rajmata win?' I asked. The directness of the question seemed for a moment to confuse him but by now his sons, who had been listening impatiently, decided to intervene.

'Never,' said the older bearded one emphatically, 'never. Nobody associated with the Jana Sangh can win here – this is a constituency in which more than 35 per cent of the voters are Muslim.'

'But what about the Emergency? What about compulsory sterilization?'

'Oh, that is all in the past. We know that it cannot happen again. At least when Mrs Gandhi was in power there was some development, some progress...in the past two years nothing has happened. Nothing at all. They haven't even put in a new hand pump anywhere in this district. As for things like electricity and clean water, we have stopped hoping that we will get them.'

'What about your new MP?' I asked. 'Did you not tell him your grievances? What did he do?' Surely, I remember thinking, the proudly rural Raj Narain must have spent more time in Rae Bareli than Mrs Gandhi had.

'We haven't seen him since he became a minister in Delhi. Mrs Gandhi has come many times. But he hasn't come here once, not even to his own village.'

'So Indiraji is completely forgiven for the excesses of the Emergency?'

'What is there to forgive? It wasn't her fault. She had some bad people around her who did some bad things and she didn't find out in time. She is a great leader. Everyone knows it.'

Our food arrived, and it was delicious. The spicy dal and hot, freshly made rotis made us momentarily forget the squalor of our surroundings. The villagers stared silently as we ate and when they noticed that we were not paying them any more attention they slipped away quietly into the night. We drove back to the dak bungalow and made ourselves as comfortable as we could on the wicker chairs and benches on the veranda. Nobody wanted to go back into the dark room with its creatures and its smell of dirty clothes. Besides, there were only a few hours left of the night.

Nervous about not finding a secluded place to perform my morning ablutions, I woke earlier than the others and wandered off into the garden with my bottle of water and my toilet bag. Luckily, one of the bungalow's cooks spotted me and guided me to an outhouse in which there was a relatively clean toilet. Next door to it was a wet, dark bathing area, which looked completely uninviting, but the old man brought me hot water in a plastic bucket and I managed to have a sort-of bath. By the time the others woke I was dressed and drinking my first cup of tea, and happy to be their consultant on the local amenities.

We were in the middle of ordering breakfast when the Rajmata's cavalcade of white Ambassadors pulled up in the porch ready for departure. The cars were filled with party workers and the roof of her car was covered in marigold garlands. She emerged from her room, greeted us with a smile and a namaste and the cavalcade set off amid the sound of screeching tyres and slogans. We abandoned all hope of breakfast and raced after it.

The first meeting was in a small town; its main architectural feature was a Hanuman temple with a giant Hanuman statue painted in gaudy shades of saffron and red standing at the entrance. The meeting was in a small field near the temple. Four tables had been pushed together and covered with a dusty red rug to make a stage. A ragged shamiana provided a measure of shade. But the crowd was small and the party workers looked nervous. While the Rajmata was paying obeisance in the Hanuman temple they rushed about trying to get more people to gather around the stage, and by the time she came out of the temple with a large red tika on her forehead they had managed to rustle up a satisfactory gathering.

From where I stood near the stage, not far from her, it was easy to see that she was disappointed with the size of the crowd but she did not let this deter her. She joined her hands in prayer and recited something in Sanskrit with her eyes closed. After the prayer was over, she spent a long time standing with her hands joined together and her eyes closed. Then she greeted the crowd, which consisted mostly of party workers, and began to speak in highly Sanskritized Hindi. She spoke of democracy and dictatorship, and the importance of this particular election. She spoke of her time in jail and how the danger of India being turned into 'one vast prison camp' still remained.

'This is why I am standing for election against Indira Gandhi. I believe that she has done grievous harm to this country, to our beloved Bharat Mata, and I am here to defeat her with your support,' she said.

The small crowd listened quietly to everything but there was no enthusiasm, no excitement and hardly any response (except from her party workers) when she asked everyone to shout '*Bharat Mata ki jai*' three times.

Then we were off again, down dusty trails and broken roads to the next meeting, and the next. She addressed many roadside meetings before lunch but there were no signs of enthusiasm or spontaneity, not even at the one that was organized in a village square. The crowds were sometimes large but they seemed to have come out of idle curiosity rather than for political reasons. By the time we stopped for lunch in an inspection bungalow in a nondescript town, my four colleagues and I agreed that we had seen enough and would be better off driving back to Lucknow to board the night train to Delhi. We were discussing this over lunch with the party workers when one of them said, 'Don't go by the meetings we've seen so far. They were unusually small only because Mrs Gandhi is holding a meeting not far from here. People have been taken there in buses. Money power...they have money power.'

'Where is Mrs Gandhi's meeting?' we asked in one voice.

The party worker, a skinny man with long oily hair and big red tika in the centre of his forehead, stopped eating his rice and dal and gave us a puzzled and slightly irritated look. 'You aren't going to her meeting, are you?'

'Why not? We are here to report on the atmosphere in the constituency. We aren't committed to any particular party. So where is it?'

'About 40 kilometres from here.'

Before he could finish speaking we were on our way. The road to the town in which the meeting was being held was unusually smooth so we reached there well in time but once we were within five kilometres of the town, we found ourselves stuck in a massive traffic jam. Tractors, bullock carts, trucks and all manner of other vehicles clogged the entrance to the town. We decided to get out of the car and walk in the direction of the loudspeakers. Patriotic songs from the freedom movement blared from them.

When we got to the school where the meeting was being held, we saw there was such a huge crowd that people were perched on trees and sitting on rooftops and walls. We had barely got to the press enclosure beside the stage when we saw Mrs Gandhi's chopper. It landed in a massive cloud of dust behind the school wall.

'Our beloved leader, sisters and brothers, will soon be among us,' a voice shrieked over the loudspeakers. 'She will be here at any moment, so I urge you to please remain seated. Your long wait is now over. I know some of you have come from distant villages and have been waiting all day without food or water but she is now here so have just a little more patience.' The crowd that had stood up en masse and started moving forward to catch a glimpse of the helicopter slowly settled down, but when Mrs Gandhi appeared on the stage people started pushing forward again. The hysterical shrieks of the party workers to 'sit down, please sit down' did nothing to stop a surge towards the stage.

The surge forward seemed to please Mrs Gandhi. She smiled and waved, then she stepped off the stage and into the crowd until she disappeared in a swirl of dark skeletal arms and wrinkled faces. She wore a simple cotton sari, a shawl of rough wool, a big watch of Indian make on her wrist and a string of the holy rudraksh beads around her neck. After mingling with the people for a few minutes, she climbed back on the stage and stood with her hands joined together as the crowd roared, 'Indira Gandhi *zindabad!*'

The audience consisted mostly of men with faces that had poverty written into every wrinkle of their ravaged faces. But it was in the women and children that desperate poverty was most visible. The women were unnaturally skinny and small. They had faces that were old before their time. Their children had dull eyes, scrawny limbs and the sad, whiny faces children get when they have not had enough to eat. Their distended bellies and discoloured hair were signs that they had never had such things as milk and fresh vegetables. Our inquiries in the villages we had stopped in revealed that the average child lived on one meal a day of watery gruel made from seasonal grain.

This was Mrs Gandhi's constituency and had been for years so if there was desperate poverty it was her fault. But they did not blame her. They loved her.

When she began her speech, Mrs Gandhi spoke in colloquial Hindi. And, her message was simple. She blamed all the problems of India on 'the two years of misrule in Delhi'. Unlike her opponent, the Rajmata, she made not the slightest effort to explain big political issues or use big complicated words to explain her case. What she seemed to understand better than any of her political rivals was that destitute, illiterate people do not care about big political issues. If they opposed the Emergency, it was not because they understood the difference between democracy and dictatorship but because they understood that it was wrong to break down the houses of the poor and to compulsorily sterilize people. Besides, two years of the Janata government had caused memories of the Emergency to fade from public memory.

Mrs Gandhi sensed this and in her speech concentrated on stirring up the general feeling of anger and disappointment over the Janata government's failures. They have emptied the treasury, she said, so there is no money left to build new roads and schools. The country has suffered for two years because of 'these people' and their 'misrule' and this is why prices of such necessities as rice and dal had gone up. She said she had met women in the villages who told her that they had stopped feeding their children dal because it had become too expensive and added that she herself could no longer afford to buy onions more than twice a week.

They cheered her on with shouts of 'Indira Gandhi *zindabad!*', and when her speech ended people surged forward once more despite the entreaties of her party workers. Once more, she descended from the stage and mingled with them. And then, as suddenly as she had come, she vanished into the clear blue skies in her helicopter.

Most people had never seen a helicopter. Most of them had never travelled outside their villages and had only an idea of India that existed from tales told to them by political workers. Long after the helicopter disappeared, Indira Gandhi's emaciated, wretchedly poor supporters continued to stare up at the sky. If they had seen an alien from another planet, they could not have been more filled with wonder.

Afterwards, we wandered among them asking the sort of questions urban reporters ask when they travel to rural areas.

'Is there electricity in your village?'

'No.'

'Is there water?'

'No.'

'How far do you walk to get it?'

'It takes long, the whole morning.'

'Is there a school in the village?'

'No.'

'Is there a primary health care centre?'

'No.'

'Will you vote for Indiraji?'

'Yes,' they said in unison, and laughed happily.

Indira Gandhi was sworn in as prime minister for the fourth time on a January morning in 1980. According to a BBC report, at the end of a sixty-three-day election campaign she had travelled through 384 constituencies, making more than twenty speeches a day. When the 196 million votes were counted, the Congress Party had won 351 seats and neither the Janata Party, nor the Lok Dal, which Charan Singh had formed when he had broken away, qualified with enough seats to be declared the official opposition party in Parliament. In Rae Bareli, the Rajmata won only 13.1

per cent of the votes. And in nearby Amethi Sanjay Gandhi won a seat in the Lok Sabha for the first time.

When Mrs Gandhi returned as prime minister it was as if she had never been away. The bureaucrats who had so hated working with the 'uncouth' ministers of the last government breathed a collective sigh of relief and things went back to what they had always been. There was not much governance, few new ideas, and little acknowledgement of the economic and political changes that were sweeping across Southeast Asia and China. But here was a prime minister whom our officials liked to call 'a real leader'. It was not just officials who were relieved to see Mrs Gandhi back at the helm, ordinary Indians felt the same way. Polls taken decades after Mrs Gandhi passed into history reveal that most Indians continue to believe that she was the best prime minister India ever had. Whenever I have tried asking why I have received the same answer. She was strong, and India needs strong leaders.

Soon after the new government took office Akbar Ahmed dropped in to see me. It was late in the evening and I teased him about his becoming the second-most important man in India. He laughed and said, 'Look I've come to say that whatever our political differences, I am your friend and I think we should keep our friendship out of politics.' All these years later I can say truthfully that whenever I have needed Akbar's friendship he has been there despite the vicissitudes of his political career and his changing political loyalties. That evening on my parents' veranda in Southend Lane when we talked of politics and the campaign, Akbar admitted without hesitation that Sanjay Gandhi was India's de facto prime minister.

It would have been pointless for him to deny it because the first thing that became clear after Mrs Gandhi's new term in office began was that she had anointed Sanjay as her heir and that many of her new ministers were young men who owed their political careers and their allegiance to Sanjay. He did not go to the prime minister's office at all, unless it was to see his mother, but everyone knew that it was he who was running the country. And this time nobody seemed to mind.

From being the villain of the Emergency, Sanjay was now, suddenly, India's new hero. Everyone from political analysts and high-ranking officials to important businessmen and ordinary voters seemed to think that India's future was safe in his hands because he was young, determined and tough. In newspaper offices we accepted the new political realities that the election had thrown up and made it a point to find out what we could about the man now widely acknowledged as India's future prime minister. We heard that he was very different from his mother, not just in his ideas about governance (he liked instant results) but ideologically as well. Reporters with investigative instincts and access to Sanjay's friends found out that not only was he not of socialist disposition but that he had contempt for the Marxist parties, although they had always been Mrs Gandhi's most devoted allies. Businessmen from Bombay started appearing in Delhi's drawing rooms and singing Sanjay's praises. They talked of how he was going to 'open up the economy'. Nobody had any idea what they meant, not even in the newsrooms of Delhi's newspapers, because the idea of the licence-quota-permit raj as a hurdle in the effective functioning of the government was something that not even the finest political analysts in Delhi had thought about.

The Indian economy was not even described as a 'licence raj' in 1980. Judging by the articles that appeared on the opinion pages of newspapers at the time most political observers seemed to accept that it was normal for businessmen to need a licence to do business and for factories to be governed by quotas and permits. It had been that way since the time of Jawaharlal Nehru who was deeply influenced by the Soviet Union's model of economic growth and was at heart a passionate socialist. He had a contempt for profit and the creation of wealth. He expressed this so often that he was very unpopular with Indian businessmen. In his time major business houses that had flourished under the British were reduced to ruin. Those who survived did so by begging for licences and concessions from the officials who controlled the 'commanding heights' of the Indian economy in Delhi.

The controls were so punishing that the economy languished in deep stagnation. For decades it grew annually at an average of 3 per cent reducing rich Indians to genteel poverty and poor Indians to subsistence. Sanjay never actually said that he would like the economy to take a new direction but because of his rumoured contempt for Marxists he was seen as someone who might be on the side of free enterprise. It helped his image that he was credited with being directly responsible for giving the Tata group permission to set up their first Taj Hotel in Delhi. It helped his image that he surrounded himself with young businessmen like Kamal

Nath and princes like Madhavrao Scindia. He seemed to prefer them to the khadi-clad 'socialists' who surrounded his mother.

When I try to remember if Rajiv and Sonia said anything about Sanjay's rise to iconic status I cannot think of a single conversation in which either of them said anything derogatory about him. Sonia often hinted that she did not like Maneka but even this would come out in oblique ways. I remember a conversation with her about a film called *Network* in which Faye Dunaway used her television network as a tool of power. The Gandhi family went, en famille, to see this film and Sonia was horrified that Maneka thought well of Dunaway's character and said she would like to be that kind of person.

The conversation made a special impression on me because in newspaper offices stories were already circulating about Maneka Gandhi's propensity to throw her weight around. According to these stories Maneka, in the last months of the Emergency, had taken to threatening journalists who did not please her. There were rumours of her marching into the offices of senior editors and telling them what she thought about them. I cannot vouch for any of these stories since the *Times of India* and the *Hindustan Times* never defied censorship during the Emergency and one of the stories of Maneka's arrogant ways emerged from the *Times of India* office. What I can report are my own unexpected problems with Maneka.

Soon after the Janata government came to power in 1977, the facsimile of a cheque from a Swiss Bank account mysteriously appeared in the offices of the *Statesman* and circulated among senior correspondents before being passed down to us in the reporters' room. It was for a very large amount of money and was in Maneka Gandhi's name. It seemed authentic enough to us, who had no idea what cheques from Swiss Bank accounts looked like, so I, ever the diligent reporter, called Maneka to inform her about the cheque and ask her opinion of it. She was polite and friendly on the telephone and I duly recorded what she said, but when the *Statesman*'s news editor, S. Sahay, heard that I had tried to verify the authenticity of the cheque he had a fit and accused me of 'alerting' the Gandhi family. So I rang Maneka back and told her that I would not be able to use her comments on the cheque. I thought I had behaved quite correctly until I heard from Sonia and Akbar that she had told them awful things about me on account of this incident. From what they told me, it became clear that Maneka blamed me for not publishing her comments on the cheque, which, as it happens, turned out to be fake, and accused me of being a dishonest journalist. I never got a chance to explain what really happened.

Meanwhile, in newspaper offices, reactions to Sanjay's increasing political authority were mixed. While there were those who worried about his thuggish side and his lack of education, there were many journalists who admired him as a 'doer'. What India needed in order to achieve better standards of governance, they said, was someone who could get government officials to do their job properly. Sanjay was seen as someone who could demand results and get them even from the slothful clerks who manned the creaking machinery of government. In retrospect, it needs to be said, he was completely acceptable to the majority of Indians as their future leader.

Mrs Gandhi seemed to involve herself fully in only those aspects of governance that Sanjay either did not understand or that did not interest him. Like foreign policy. South Asia was going through a problematic, turbulent time, and Sanjay would not have known what to say had he been asked what India's policies should be towards our immediate neighbours.

Pakistan was in the middle of one of the most difficult moments in its short, difficult history. Zulfikar Ali Bhutto had been executed in April 1979 and General Zia-ul-Haq, who was responsible for this, calmed political dissent by invoking and strictly enforcing Pakistan's raison d'etre: Islam. He imposed an early version of radical Islam on his country with shariat laws controlling the rights of women and men being publicly flogged for Islamic misdemeanours. Mrs Gandhi knew Bhutto well from the time of the Bangladesh war and the Simla agreement she signed with him to end hostilities and enable the return of the more than 90,000 prisoners of war who were still in India. Like most Indians she had been appalled by the execution of a democratically elected prime minister. She had tried to get Morarji Desai to make a statement against it on behalf of India and had publicly expressed her disapproval that the Government of India said nothing. She took a dim view of the military dictator who replaced Bhutto and relations between her and the General next door were frosty.

If radical Islamism in Pakistan was not disturbing enough for India more instability came with the Soviet Union's invasion of Afghanistan just weeks before Mrs Gandhi became prime minister again. India needed to make its position clear on whether or not it supported the invasion of a friendly country. Sanjay Gandhi would probably not have had the slightest idea what India's stand should be so it was left to Mrs Gandhi to deal with Leonid Brezhnev when he came to Delhi seeking India's support. On the political grapevine I heard that she treated Brezhnev with unusual coldness. The story told to me by an official who was present at the meeting was that she continued to doodle on a little pad on her desk while Brezhnev made his case, and when he finished she got up and left the room without a single word. But she had a complicated relationship with the Soviet Union. As we were to find out decades later through the memoirs of a KGB spymaster, Vasili Mitrokhin, many senior members of Mrs Gandhi's government were compromised by the KGB. In the end India backed the Soviet invasion of Afghanistan.

None of the turmoil in Pakistan and Afghanistan concerned the average Indian or even most Indian journalists much. India is such a huge country with so many problems of her own that the problems of other countries rarely cause concern. So even as the seeds of radical Islam were being sown next door and even as the Soviet Union, with its invasion of Afghanistan was hastening its own collapse and the end of the Cold War, in Delhi domestic political changes mattered more. Winter turned quickly to spring in Delhi that year, more quickly it seemed than usual, because of the excitement of a new government and the rise of a new young leader. Not a day seemed to go by when Sanjay Gandhi was not on the front pages of national newspapers. Sometimes addressing a public meeting somewhere, or meeting people at his morning audiences, sometimes driving himself to the flying club for his flying lessons, and often just seated beside Mrs Gandhi as she gazed proudly at him.

He surrounded himself with young men who talked loudly and had about them a reckless air. Their very presence indicated a new order but there were other changes as well. Sanjay's men still wore white khadi kurta–pyjamas but it was now more a fashion statement than a tribute to Gandhiji's use of handspun cloth as a weapon against the British Empire. His friends had no interest in paying lip service to any of the things that the Congress Party had treated as sacrosanct. Not for them the pseudo-socialist rules that made Indian politicians look scruffy in the interest of showing humility, nor the pretence of meeting their political associates in cheap coffee houses in Connaught Place. Instead, it was in the faux-Mughal lobby of the glamorous new Taj Mahal Hotel, or its fashionable coffee shop, Machan, that Sanjay's friends had their political meetings.

Sanjay was good to his friends. Some he made ministers, others like Akbar he made his personal aides. They were more powerful than any of Mrs Gandhi's colleagues including her once powerful stenographers. Bureaucrats kowtowed to them, businessmen fawned over them and before winter had time to change to spring there was a new court in Delhi with a new set of court favourites.

Among Sanjay Gandhi's new favourites was Vasundhara Raje's brother, Madhavrao Scindia. I cannot remember exactly when I started seeing him in political and social circles in Delhi but it would have been after Sanjay became India's de facto prime minister. It was either through Vasundhara or at some Delhi party that I first met him and took an instant liking to him. He was intelligent, funny and a maharaja in the nicest sense of the word. Since we met mostly at social events I cannot remember discussing politics with him till much later. But I remember conversations with him about his mother and the 'evil influence' he thought his uncle, Sardar Angre, had on her political beliefs. He was convinced that it was because of this uncle that his mother had said during the election campaign that had she lived in older, feudal times she would have had her son's head crushed under an elephant's foot, as a ruler of Indore, Ahilya Bai Holkar, had done. The remark harmed her more than it did him.

By the time summer came that year, my interest in politics and journalism had waned on account of my having met and fallen madly in love with a Pakistani called Salmaan Taseer. He came to Delhi to promote a book he had written on Zulfikar Ali Bhutto and what was meant to be a short interlude turned into a much longer relationship when I discovered that I was pregnant and he was married. It was a relationship that was doomed from the start but I was in love and I followed him to Pakistan, Dubai and London.

We were in London in the last week of June when Sanjay Gandhi was killed but I was in Delhi soon afterwards and pieced together the story of what had happened from talking to friends and reporters. The first thing I heard, from either Vasundhara or Madhavrao himself, was that the only reason the young Maharaja of Gwalior had not been on the plane with Sanjay was that he was late that morning. So Sanjay took off in his little aircraft with only a pilot for company and, as usual, flew in a most reckless way. It is one of life's macabre ironies that Madhavrao Scindia died in another plane crash twenty-one years later.

Those who saw Sanjay's aeroplane come down on the morning of 23 June 1980 said they had seen the aircraft performing somersaults and flying dangerously low before it crashed. The crash occurred not far from Safdarjang Airport from where it had taken off minutes earlier. Reporters who went to the site of the crash came back with stories of how Mrs Gandhi had arrived shortly afterwards and searched Sanjay's pockets for something, and then driven away. Political gossips in Delhi spread rumours that the prime minister had come looking for the keys to a bank locker. It was the sort of story that was easily believed as were the conspiracy theories that he had been killed by a foreign intelligence agency that did not want India to have a strong leader. Since Mrs Gandhi was very cosy with the Soviet Union this could only mean the CIA. Another equally implausible theory was that he had been killed by Mumbai's gangsters.

From Akbar I heard of the thousands and thousands of ordinary people who lined the streets of Delhi on a day of searing heat when they took Sanjay's body to be cremated on the banks of the Yamuna. Akbar had been sitting on the gun carriage that bore his body and admitted that even he had not realized how popular Sanjay was till he saw the crowds waiting in the burning heat. From colleagues who attended his funeral, I heard that Mrs Gandhi proved that she was a 'real leader' by displaying no emotion at all during the cremation. Pictures in the newspapers show her wearing big dark glasses that half covered her face but did not conceal the expression of deep sadness about her mouth.

Sanjay Gandhi's untimely and tragic death caused even his political opponents to become unusually emotional. Atal Behari Vajpayee memorably commented that it had brought 'darkness at noon', and journalists who had not liked him much when he was alive became quite poetic about his death. I remember a report in one of the newspapers in which the reporter used this verse in Urdu to express his feelings: '*Ai gulcheen-e-ajal tujh se nadani hui, phool voh tora ke gulshan mein veeranee hui.*' He translated it as, 'O gardener of Death, what a mistake you made. You plucked that one flower and turned the garden into a wilderness.'

Sanjay's death affected Mrs Gandhi profoundly. It was as if something inside her died. I met her a few months later in Abu Dhabi where my travels with Salmaan had taken me. I was quite bored of just hanging about in situations of domesticity when I heard that Mrs Gandhi was coming on a state visit. A few quick inquiries revealed that R.K. Dhawan, her ever faithful factotum, was on the trip as well so I called him and asked if I could meet her or at least join the press party for the events she was attending. He seemed happy that I had called and explained why before I could ask.

'Yes. Yes. Good, good,' he said. 'You see, she is going to be visiting the Sheikha Fatima for tea this afternoon and only women are allowed in the palace. There is only one woman journalist from a Hindi paper travelling with us so I can arrange for you to go as well.'

So it was that I found myself in the Sheikha Fatima's palace by the sea. Never having had any experience of purdah in India I was fascinated by this purdah palace in which only women could enter. Young women veiled in black robes led me through smoky verandas that smelled of frankincense and had the most magnificent view of white beaches and the Arabian Sea. I remember thinking what a waste the private beaches were since it was hard to imagine the black-beaked young women (the beaks are the severest form of a burqa) frolicking in bikinis by the sea.

They led me and the other woman journalist to a drawing room with gilded cornices and gaudy furniture. The chandeliers were so enormous and so bright that instead of just lighting the room they seemed to take it over. We were led to a corner of the room where there were two gilded thrones, on one of which sat the Sheikha Fatima, as befitted her status as the wife of the emir of Abu Dhabi. She wore a beak and black robes underneath which glistened a surprisingly low-cut silk gown in pistachio green. The Sheikha's décolletage was decorated with a diamond necklace that glittered as brightly as the chandeliers. All the women were veiled except two ladies in Western clothes who explained to me that they were from Kuwait and did not follow the same traditions as women in Abu Dhabi.

After the other Indian woman journalist and I seated ourselves in the circle of women around the Sheikha, Mrs Gandhi arrived in a sombre black sari. She was still in mourning and I remember thinking that she looked as if someone had drained her of her life force. Her eyes were dull and her smile more sad than happy. In the hour that she spent in the Sheikha's palace I did not hear her say one thing that sounded as if she were really participating in the conversations she had. She smiled politely when someone read a poem about women, and she spoke to the Sheikha and everyone who talked to her, but as if she were only half present. I think it was the other woman journalist, although it may well have been me, who asked her views on the practice of veiling women in Arabia and she said, 'People have different traditions and cultures, and we must respect them.'

Afterwards, we were led to a dining room, larger and more glittering than the drawing room, where there were long tables covered with food. Kebabs, curries, rice, bread, smoked salmon, caviar, eggs, everything. It reminded me so much of a very grand supermarket that I remember wondering if the Sheikh had asked his architect to copy the food hall at Harrods. There was so much food and so many women buzzing around it that I lost my appetite and noticed that Mrs Gandhi, seated beside the Sheikha, seemed to have lost hers as well.

10 TROUBLED STATES

The announcement that Rajiv would be standing for election from his brother's constituency came soon enough.

Rajiv and Sonia went off to Amethi so that he could file his nomination papers and the friends he left behind in Delhi, who had now started making political predictions, talked about his political future. They said they were certain he would be prime minister one day and that it would be wonderful for India. Nobody seemed to notice that Mrs Gandhi was instituting a form of dynastic succession that so far had not existed in our proud democracy. In our little set this could have been because Rajiv was so loved. Acceptance within the Congress Party was understandable since Mrs Gandhi had already divided the party twice and now had her own Congress (I), the 'I' standing for Indira. But, either because of Sanjay's untimely death or because political dynasties did not exist at the time, nobody seemed to find it strange that Sanjay's constituency should pass on to his apolitical brother.

The first time I met Rajiv after he became a politician was at a dinner party in one of the usual drawing rooms. I cannot remember where it was or who else was there but it was a small enough gathering for Rajiv and Sonia to be able to talk freely about what they had seen in Amethi. He looked both elated and a little confused, and she seemed quite overwhelmed. I report the following conversation from memory. My recollection remains vivid enough for me to be able to recount it almost verbatim.

'The real shock is the poverty,' Rajiv said. 'I know I should have realized that we are a poor country and that means there would be poverty. And it's not that I haven't seen it in the faces of beggars and street children in

Delhi. But in the villages it really is something else...beyond anything I had imagined.'

Sonia was appalled by the filth she had seen in the villages. It made her unusually eloquent. 'In one hut we saw a small baby crawling around right next to this large pile of cow dung. He was playing with it and putting it in his mouth. It was awful and I wanted to tell his mother to stop him from doing this, but I thought she would mind so I said nothing.'

'It's better not to interfere in local customs,' said one of the ladies, sipping delicately at her Campari-soda.

'We heard from a health worker in one village that the main reason why newborn babies die from tetanus is because midwives put cow dung on their belly buttons to dry up the cord. Can you imagine?'

'Well, that is the practice...' someone said.

'They have nothing,' Rajiv continued. 'The women have never seen the inside of a hospital. The men depend on what they can earn from the land, and that isn't much. I can't believe that they live without something so basic as clean water.'

'Indians believe in karma,' one of the men said, 'and that makes them believe it is their fate to be poor, that they must have done something bad in their last life to suffer in this one.'

Rajiv's political career began at almost exactly the same time as the violence began in Punjab. Before he had time to understand the complexities of poverty and its connections to caste and social barriers in his constituency, before he had time to think about the flawed policies that may have been at the root of India's economic problems, there began a bigger problem that would concentrate the attention of the whole country for more than a decade.

In Punjab violence had lain under the surface for a while but revealed itself without warning on a hot September day in 1981 when Lala Jagat Narain, a newspaper baron from Jalandhar, who owned the three most influential newspapers in the state and was a well-known public figure in Punjab, was killed while he was driving home. Jalandhar, like other Punjabi cities has a large army presence because of its proximity to the border with Pakistan. Whole areas of the city are reserved exclusively for regiments garrisoned there. They have their own hospitals and clinics for out-patients called Medical Inspection Rooms (MIRs), their own cinemas and shopping centres, parade grounds and playing fields. The soldiers live in barracks of tedious uniformity, with sloping roofs, narrow verandas and small rooms with barred windows, which make them look like prison cells. For the officers there are fine colonial bungalows set in gardens so large that their wives plant vegetables and often grow their own wheat and rice so that their kitchen gardens resemble small farms.

By the eighties some of the traditional boundaries between the civil and military areas of cities like Jalandhar had blurred. Senior civilian officials had moved quietly into the more salubrious surroundings of the cantonment. The best residential areas in the civilian half of the city could not match the cleanliness, order and immaculate standards of the cantonment, where even trees had their lower halves painted white to add to the sense of military order. The officials who moved to the cantonments from the civilian side were the most important ones. The district magistrate, the collector, the chief of police, leading to a dangerous disengagement between them and ordinary citizens. This is, perhaps, one of the reasons why nobody at the higher levels of administration in Jalandhar appears to have noticed the growing divisions between Hindus and Sikhs.

Simmerings of these divisions had existed since Partition. For reasons that remain puzzling even today, while other Indian states were created on a linguistic basis Punjabi was not declared the official language of what was left of Punjab after Pakistan took most of it away. With Punjabi becoming unusable for competitive examinations for public service, the Sikhs were officially disqualified from participation since they neither spoke Hindi nor read the Devnagari script. The Hindus in Punjab spoke Punjabi at home but were familiar with the Devnagari script because their scriptures were written in it. At this time a small group of influential Sikhs started to demand that Sikhs be given their own *suba* or state, with Punjabi as its language, in the tiny piece of Punjab that remained in India.

Eventually, when Mrs Gandhi became prime minister, she conceded the need to divide Punjab once more on a linguistic basis and the state of Haryana came into being. But most Sikhs continued to resent Hindus for having betrayed Punjab, because during a census ordered after the Punjabi *suba* agitation, they had declared that their mother tongue was Hindi (and not Punjabi). One of the men who had led the campaign to urge Hindus to declare that their mother tongue was Hindi and not Punjabi was Lala Jagat Narain. He used his newspapers, *Hind Samachar*, *Jagbani* and *Punjab Kesari*, to persuade Hindus to disown Punjabi as their mother tongue.

As someone who grew up in a Sikh family I remember hearing often about the 'betrayal' of Punjab by the Hindus. It was this sentiment that Bhindranwale tapped into when he revived the demand for a separate country for the Sikhs. When Bhindranwale started to preach militant Sikhism one of the first issues he raised was the Hindu 'betrayal' of Punjabi and one of the first men he targeted was Lalaji. Without realizing the terrible consequences of criticizing Bhindranwale's violent ideology, Lalaji had been openly hostile in his newspapers towards him and his political activities. Bhindranwale was quick to respond. In a speech he made at Guru Nanak Dev University in Amritsar, in a hall filled with Sikh students, he openly targeted Lala Jagat Narain. A university official later gave this report of the speech: 'On that day in a great fury he [Bhindranwale] called upon someone to read aloud what Narain had said. [After the passage was read ...]...there was silence. "Our turban has been torn from our heads!" he proclaimed. Then one of his followers asked, "What are your orders?" Again in anger, he said, "Orders? You need orders? What orders? Are you blind?"'

On 9 September 1981, Lalaji was on his way from Patiala to Jalandhar when he was shot dead by unidentified Sikh gunmen on the highway near Jalandhar. Bhindranwale's open threats against Lala Jagat Narain were taken seriously enough by India's home minister, Zail Singh, for him to link Bhindranwale to the assassination. He was taken into custody from the gurudwara in the village of Mehta Chowk, which he used as his headquarters, and put under arrest for a month. His imprisonment served only to make Bhindranwale a bigger hero.

At the end of the summer of 1982 I returned to India with a young son to bring up and desperately in need of a job. M.J. Akbar, who had just become editor of a new newspaper, the *Telegraph*, was happy to give me one. The newspaper was only a few months old but by the time I joined the *Telegraph*'s Delhi bureau, it consisted almost entirely of women who had taken charge of covering all the important ministries and were fiercely possessive about them. I was the joker in this female pack with not a lot left to do except tread on other people's toes and so it was that I suggested

I go to Amritsar and take a look at what was going on in the Golden Temple. I think I may have argued that as a Sikh I might find access to Bhindranwale easier and, besides, the only language he spoke was Punjabi so this gave me a natural advantage.

Bhindranwale had recently moved into the Guru Nanak Niwas, a rest house for pilgrims within the temple's boundaries. He and his men had occupied it completely. Nobody asked any questions about why he had moved into the Golden Temple, how long he planned to stay there, or whether he intended to pay for the rooms he and his men occupied. He was too powerful by then. More powerful than the men elected to the committee that controlled Sikh religious affairs, more powerful than any other Sikh religious leader.

The bureau chief at the *Telegraph*, Kewal Verma, happened to be a fellow Punjabi with a deep understanding of Sikh politics. He was a stocky, rotund man with a shock of white hair who saw the world through the Marxist prism that had defined his life. His view of Bhindranwale was almost sympathetic. In the briefing he gave me before my first visit to Amritsar, he explained that it was not a Hindu–Sikh problem yet, but a problem that Bhindranwale seemed to have with the police. 'Notice that in all his speeches the only people he attacks are the police.'

'Why would he have killed Lalaji then?'

'Ah, that's different. You see Lalaji's newspapers have always taken an aggressively anti-Sikh line. In the time of the Punjabi *suba* agitation the group openly encouraged Hindus to say that Punjabi was not their mother tongue. I remember personally asking my own Hindu family why they were doing it...imagine, the census man asks them in Punjabi what their mother tongue is and they reply in Punjabi that he should write down Hindi. It was wrong to do that and it upset the Sikhs.' The violence and Bhindranwale's power had been growing for months before Lalaji's murder but neither Mrs Gandhi nor anyone in her government appeared to notice what was happening. Remembering her as I did from Sheikha Fatima's purdah palace I concluded that this must be because she had lost interest in government and politics after Sanjay's death.

She was so removed from what was going on in Punjab that while Bhindranwale wandered about making hate speeches and inciting violence in village gurudwaras she was busy supervising the Asian Games. Delhi was not usually chosen as a venue for major sporting events so for the Games to be held there in 1982 was a big thing, but not so much that political violence in a border state should have been considered less important. Yet, this is what happened. The Asian Games were considered such a triumph for India that the first political assignment Mrs Gandhi gave Rajiv after he won his election from Amethi, with a stunning majority (84 per cent of the vote), was the organization of the games. Delhi had never hosted a major international sporting event before so it had neither enough stadiums nor suitable accommodation for visiting athletes. This infrastructure had to be built very quickly. The PWD, with its slothful ways and shabby record, could not be trusted with providing either speed or quality and Rajiv was given charge of making sure things happened on time.

After becoming a politician one of the first things that Rajiv did was select from his small circle of close friends those whom he thought should assist him in his new career. This could have been because he was politically unsure and it could have been because he wanted to bring a new kind of person into politics. Whatever the reasons, one of his first decisions was to ask his oldest and closest friend, Arun Singh, to give up his job in Calcutta and come to Delhi to help him. The other friends he enlisted were Satish Sharma and Vijay Dhar, whose father, D.P. Dhar, had been one of Mrs Gandhi's advisors at an earlier stage of her career. He was remembered in Delhi's political circles more for his passionate leftist beliefs than for his administrative skills.

Arun Singh, despite a dour exterior that could deter the friendliest human being from starting a conversation, was intelligent, refined and educated. He read books, thought deeply about the issues of the moment and had a serious interest in matters of security. He read *Jane's Defence Weekly* as a hobby. And would have been one of only a handful of Indians who had even heard of the British magazine that caters to the arms trade and a niche group of weapons aficionados. I heard from those who knew him well that one way to break through his formidable reserve was to begin a discussion on the latest weapons in the international arms bazaar.

Vijay Dhar was a very tall, very thin Kashmiri Hindu who had no political or administrative experience but it was possible to have an intelligent conversation with him about political issues. I learned a great deal about what was going on in the Kashmir Valley from talking to him. So he was a good choice for Rajiv to have made as an advisor in those early days of his political career. But the choice of Satish Sharma has continued to baffle me all these years later. It is hard to think of a man less likely to be chosen as a political advisor. When I asked Rajiv's close friends what they thought about Satish being recruited as a political aide they admitted that they were mystified but suggested that it could have something to do with the cockpit camaraderie that develops among pilots when they fly together.

Rajiv and his small coterie treated the task of organizing the Asian Games as if it were the most momentous event in the history of India. They spent all their time wandering in and out of high-level meetings at which they discussed matters of infrastructure, accommodation and security, and personally supervised the building of the stadiums and the Games Village, in which athletes from abroad were going to stay. Had India been planning to invade Pakistan the planners could not have been more committed or diligent. They reminded me of the sort of earnest schoolboys that end up being popular with their teachers and hated by their peers.

For middle class Indians the best part of the Asian Games was that Mrs Gandhi relaxed her socialist principles enough to graciously allow colour television sets to be imported into India so that the Games could be watched in full colour. For the suffering people of socialist India television until then had meant the grainy, black-and-white images that Doordarshan's state-controlled channels telecast across the land. If that was not bad enough we had the misfortune of being subjected to the bleakest programming outside the communist world.

Mrs Gandhi believed that Doordarshan's only purpose was as a vehicle of government propaganda and during the Emergency, when she became a dictator, this reached unimaginable heights. If the Emergency had continued longer it is possible that Indian television would have become entirely a forum to project the Great Leader and the Little Leader in North Korean style. The Janata government had considered allowing private investment in television but it did not last long enough to take the idea forward so we remained stuck with Doordarshan, which to this day continues to produce unwatchable and amateurish programmes despite competition from hundreds of private channels. In the early eighties it was much worse.

As an ambitious young journalist eager to enhance my career by working for television, I tried from time to time to suggest new ideas to Doordarshan but was thwarted at every step by officials drunk on their petty power. I was not the only one. Other journalists I knew complained that whenever they went to Doordarshan with new ideas for programmes they were treated with disdain. Almost the only way to get a programme on one of Doordarshan's channels was if you had a hefty string or two to pull. Then you would find doors opening magically and perhaps even end up getting twice as much money for a programme than you needed. I did not know any high officials and had to often wait outside in the corridors with the peons until the Doordarshan potentate I had come to see thought it was time to grant me an audience. Then I would usually find myself treated to a long lecture on how little I knew about the differences between print and television journalism. The assumption being that someone trained in the Indian Administrative Service automatically knew more.

I remember, in particular, a woman official to whom I suggested we do a series called *Interview with History* in which we could interview political leaders who had been witnesses to the important events that had formed modern India. I mentioned Sheikh Abdullah and Jayaprakash Narayan as possible interviewees. The official looked at me over the tip of her protruding nose and said, 'Why do you think ordinary Indians would want to watch a programme like that? Don't you see that they would much prefer to see a long interview with a rickshaw-walla?' I never tried making programmes for Doordarshan again, comforting myself with the thought that in any case it was pointless making good programmes that would be telecast in snowy, black-and-white images when the whole world was watching colour television. In 1982, thanks to the Asian Games, Indians finally discovered the joys of colour television even if Doordarshan's offerings continued to be as dreary as ever.

The only cloud over the Games was Bhindranwale. He saw them as an opportunity to draw attention to himself, something he excelled at in the worst of times. In those weeks, when Rajiv and his friends were working long hours to make the Games a success, the Sant spent his time making menacing speeches. He warned of disruptions and disaster in such clear terms that he had to be taken seriously, so once the Games were ready to begin Delhi's borders were sealed. Instructions to the policemen who manned the borders were to search all Sikhs coming into the city. The policemen, who were mostly peasants from Haryana and unskilled in detecting terrorists, did their job in the clumsiest, crudest way. They stopped all buses coming in from Punjab and searched every Sikh.

War heroes and retired bureaucrats were treated like common criminals. Dignified old soldiers who had helped India win its wars against Pakistan and China were pulled off buses and trains, stripped and ordered to take their turbans off in a manner so humiliating that many turned around and went home instead of coming to Delhi to watch the Games. They took back tales of humiliation and shame, and when their stories reached the ears of the Sant he was delighted. This was just what he needed to inject life into his movement for Khalistan. He called a press conference to declare that Sikhs could not live in a country in which they were treated like second-class citizens. It was a signal for the violence to grow and it did. Horribly.

But first we saw the Asian Games on our new colour television sets. Everyone I knew from socialites and politicians to journalists and people who could not afford their own television sets found some way to watch the opening ceremony. It was not just the Games they were interested in but the drama of seeing them in colour. It was the first time that Indians got a chance to see the first family of the country in full colour. Mrs Gandhi sat proudly with Rajiv beside her, a handsome prince, and Sonia, so beautiful with her perfectly made-up face and her blow-dried hair. Behind them, in the VIP enclosure, sat friends from the inner circle in carefully pressed clothes and expensive sunglasses.

Once Rajiv joined politics he no longer came to the usual dinner parties and I saw him less and less. If I wanted to see him I would have to call in advance and set up an interview. I saw Sonia more at cosy lunches in Nina Singh's elegant farmhouse where, often, it was Sonia who would go into the kitchen and make something delicious for us to eat. She was a very good cook. Sometimes we would meet for coffee and talk of this and that though never about politics.

What puzzled me about Sonia in those early days was her complete lack of interest in doing something worthwhile as a response to the dreadful poverty she saw every day of her life in her husband's country. Sometimes she would go with Nina to one of Mother Teresa's homes for abandoned children but for someone married to the Indian prime minister's son she had a remarkable indifference to social causes and to India in general. It is true that none of the people in the circle in which the Gandhis moved had much interest in India's problems either but I expected, perhaps wrongly, that having spent all her time in India in the prime minister's home Sonia would have developed a deeper sense of social consciousness. Especially because her mother-in-law liked to flaunt her concern for 'the poor' so much that it virtually defined her politics.

It was around the time of the Asian Games that I went to the Golden Temple to meet Bhindranwale.

The Guru Nanak Niwas where he was staying was a bleak, ugly building full of dank corridors and small, smelly rooms. It was in one of these rooms that I first met him. He wore long underpants covered by a long dark blue kurta, with a kirpan dangling from a strap over it and a blue turban. He had a silver arrow lying beside him in brazen imitation of Guru Govind Singh. In one corner of the room, two foreign women, converts to Sikhism judging from the white veils and turbans that covered their heads, were boiling milk on a small kerosene stove.

To establish my Sikh credentials, I had worn as many emblems of the religion as I could lay my hands on, including a steel bangle on my right wrist and a big gold *khanda* on a chain around my neck. When Sandeep Shankar, the photographer who was doing the story with me, started to take pictures I noticed that Bhindranwale liked having his picture taken. Without appearing to be posing, he posed and kept a close watch on where the camera was. It was not vanity but narcissism, as I was to discover when I got to know him better.

Pilgrims came in small groups to pay obeisance by kneeling before him and bowing so that their foreheads touched the floor. Sikhs are supposed to do this only before the Guru Granth Sahib but he did not stop them. He accepted their obeisance in the manner of a practised guru. When the interview began, I asked him to explain what he thought his problems were with the Indian state. It was a bad first question because it set him off into a tirade that lasted several minutes. As my bureau chief, Kewal Sahib, had predicted, Bhindranwale's complaints were mostly about the police and their 'atrocities'. He summoned one of his followers, who he claimed had been beaten up by a policeman, and asked him to lift up his shirt to show me the bruises. He then asked the bruised man to name the policeman who had done this to him and repeated the name loudly for everyone to hear. 'Govind Ram.' When some weeks later I heard that a policeman by that name had been killed by Sikh gunmen I realized I had witnessed the Sant ordering an execution.

It was at the very end of this first interview with Bhindranwale, that I asked him if it was true that the Congress Party had paid him a large amount of money to make trouble for the Akali Dal. The question angered him and he ended the interview.

I wandered out of the Guru Nanak Niwas and ran into the two white women who had been boiling milk in the Sant's room. They wore black turbans under their white veils, which only fanatical Sikh women do in some kind of bizarre imitation of Islam's injunctions for women to cover their hair. When the white women noticed me staring at them with undisguised curiosity, one of them asked me what I had thought of their Sant. I replied truthfully that I did not believe he had understood the Sikh religion at all. This annoyed the new converts and we got into a discussion about what Sikhism meant. At some point, slightly fed up with their limited knowledge, I may have said something provocative because one of the women turned on me angrily and said, 'What would you know about Sikhism, you who pluck your eyebrows?' I told her that I had been brought up steeped in the Sikh religion and knew for certain that there was nothing about plucking eyebrows in it. There is not a single word in the Granth Sahib about not cutting your hair either. It was the tenth Sikh guru who had instructed Sikhs to not cut their hair and he had meant it for a limited period. I reminded them that no injunctions relating to the creation of Guru Govind Singh's Khalsa army had been put into the Guru Granth Sahib and that this was deliberate.

I was still instructing the ladies in the finer details of the Sikh religion when Sandeep came racing down the stairs and said, 'I think we should get out of here fast. The Sant didn't like your last question and is asking who you are and all sorts of other things.' Sandeep, who had stayed on to take more pictures after I left, had heard him ask one of his followers who I was and how I had dared to ask him about receiving money from the Congress Party.

'So?'

'So we should go. A journalist who annoyed the Sant was stabbed in the thigh not long ago and we don't want any trouble.'

It was the first of many unpleasant encounters with Sant Bhindranwale. They became more frequent as the violence in Punjab grew.

The first incident in which Bhindranwale's men targeted Hindus, came a few months after I met him. It was in October 1983. A night bus was stopped by masked gunmen late one night. They boarded it, surveyed the passengers, and asked the travellers to identify themselves by religion. Men who said they were Hindu were ordered to get off the bus. Then, in full view of the women and children they were lined up in a field and shot in the back of their heads.

Kewal Sahib woke me up at 4 a.m. that morning and ordered me to leave immediately for Punjab. 'Sandeep has already left for your house. He should be there in half an hour,' he said.

'What happened? What exactly do we know so far?'

'We know only that the killers were Sikhs and the victims Hindu. And that it was a night bus that was going from Kapurthala to Jalandhar. I am not even sure of the name of the village where this happened, but it's closer to Kapurthala, I think.'

'Anything else? Like if there were any indications that they were connected to Bhindranwale?'

'They apparently shouted "Long live Khalistan" but I don't know this for sure.'

It took us four hours to get to the village of Dhilwan, where the massacre had occurred. It was a cold, early winter morning and a wet mist hung over the countryside. The bus still stood on the highway with frightened survivors huddled inside. The relatives of the dead sat beside the bodies in a farmer's field. A boy of about eleven was sitting beside the body of his father. He seemed to be waiting for someone to tell him what he should do next. When I asked him what happened he said in a whisper, 'I was sleeping. Then these men with their faces covered came on the bus and asked my father if he was Hindu. When he said yes they told him to go with them. I tried to go too but they didn't let me. Then we heard shooting and someone told me my father was dead.'

We drove on to Amritsar. In the Golden Temple Bhindranwale was addressing a meeting in a large hall when we arrived. He wore a white kurta and a blue turban and around him stood a group of young men carrying Kalashnikovs. Next to Bhindranwale and his bodyguards stood two young Sikh boys in white turbans and white kurtas with beatific expressions on their faces. When the audience of Sikh pilgrims settled down and a hush fell over the gathering, the two boys in white started to sing a Punjabi song.

'It is a time for sacrifice,' they sang with their eyes closed, 'it is a time for sacrifice. The community is troubled and needs healing. Only sacrifice will heal...' I was reminded absurdly of a scene from the film *Cabaret* in which a blond Nazi youth sings 'Tomorrow belongs to me'.

When the song ended, Bhindranwale rose to address the congregation. He spoke in abstractions. 'These are troubled times for the Sikh community. There is violence everywhere and nobody knows how to control it. We do not believe in violence but our Gurus have taught us that when rulers resort to repression and injustice then it is the duty of every true Sikh to fight. It is better to die fighting for justice than to leave the field of battle like a coward. Only that man can be called a hero who has the courage to let himself be cut to pieces in the field of battle rather than abandon the cause of righteousness. *Sura so pehchaniye jo lare deen ke heth, purza, purza kat mare, kabhi na chhade khet.*'

When he finished speaking, Sandeep and I went up to the stage to try and speak to him. He saw us and stood up abruptly, saying, 'I am not giving any interviews today.'

'Please. Just a comment on the bus massacre,' I said as Sandeep took his pictures.

'Why should I comment?'

'They say the killers were Sikhs.'

'So? What does it have to do with me?'

'Do you think they did the right thing? Do you think it is right to kill people just because they are Hindu?'

'I don't want to say anything because you will twist what I say. If I say something you people write that I am encouraging violence. But Bal Thackeray can say that Sikhs and Muslims must be killed and you people never write anything against him.'

I tried once more to ask my question. 'Do you condemn what happened?'

'Why should I condemn it? Who am I to condemn it?'

A month later there was another massacre on a bus travelling from Amritsar to Chandigarh.

After this, the Punjab government stopped buses from travelling at night and police cars started patrolling the highways. But the violence did not stop. It spread. The killers began to target Hindus living in villages. They would arrive at night on foot, kill and disappear into the fields. Because they always seemed to know which house belonged to Hindus the police suspected that they had local support, and were probably local youths, but nobody dared identify them. Everyone knew that the killers were Bhindranwale's men and that they took shelter in the Golden Temple and other Sikh temples but nobody was ever caught.

My trips to Punjab became weekly events as the violence grew. Hindu families left their villages for the relative safety of towns, so masked killers started to visit the crowded bazaars of Jalandhar, Amritsar and Patiala. People stopped going out in the evenings, and in the countryside it was as if the rule of law no longer existed. Nobody dared drive on the highways after dark because you never knew when armed men would appear and surround your car and perhaps kill you. Everyone knew that Bhindranwale was behind the violence. He talked openly about Khalistan from his pulpit in the Golden Temple. Nobody stopped him.

By the end of 1983, violence in Punjab had become almost routine and every time I went to cover the latest incident, someone or the other, from officials to ordinary people, asked me why Delhi was doing nothing to control the violence. Many said they thought it must be because Mrs Gandhi wanted the Sikhs and Hindus divided so that she could 'consolidate' the Hindu vote. Conspiracy theories, rumours and fear turned Punjab quickly from India's most prosperous state to its most dangerous.

I was among those who did not understand why nobody in Delhi was doing anything to stop Bhindranwale, and when I came back from one of my trips to Amritsar I asked Rajiv if I could see him. We met in the new office he shared with Arun Singh on Motilal Nehru Marg. It was a crumbling, old colonial bungalow that had been spruced up. Big glass windows had been added, new Kashmiri carpets covered broken terrazzo floors and pretty pictures had appeared on freshly painted walls. What must have once been a drawing room was converted into a large office crammed with desks and Godrej cupboards. It was here that Rajiv's secretaries worked. The man in charge was V. George, a man from Kerala, who eventually rose to great heights of political power but at the time seemed to be just a gofer.

Rajiv's office was in a large room with a lovely view of the garden. Arun had a similar office on the other side of the corridor. Rajiv was by now general secretary of the Congress Party and acknowledged as his mother's heir. I remember thinking when I saw him in his new office that politics had made him more assured and confident.

He was charming, as always, and quite keen to hear about what I had seen in Punjab. I told him that what seemed to be worrying a lot of people was the government's refusal to act against Bhindranwale despite his involvement in the violence being quite obvious. 'People are beginning to say that this refusal to control Bhindranwale is quite deliberate,' I remember saying, and a look of exasperation crossed his face.

'I've told Mummy so many times that we should do something,' he said, 'but she listens to her senior advisors and they tell her that she shouldn't do anything that would upset the Sikhs.'

'But the Sikhs are even more upset that they are being blamed for the violence.'

I took the chance to do a full interview with him on various political issues. When I came back to the office, I told Akbar excitedly that I had an interview with Rajiv Gandhi, thinking that he would be pleased. He was not. He looked quite irritated that I had managed to get an interview and wanted to know how it had come about. I told him that I had actually just dropped in for a chat about Punjab and had taken the opportunity to ask questions on other issues. Later, I discovered through the office grapevine that Akbar had been trying to get an interview with Rajiv for many months and had not succeeded. My interview was not used on the cover but buried obscurely inside the magazine in an issue published some weeks later. Rajiv gave very few interviews, so it was something of a scoop for *Sunday* magazine but Akbar, who was editor of both *Sunday* magazine and the *Telegraph*, did not think so.

In the interview Rajiv said some things that remain interesting even from the perspective of history. On the economic policies of his mother's government he said, 'I think we have drifted a little too far to the right today. I also feel that where we're making a mistake is that we have too many taxes...in the sense that a substantial amount of the taxes that the government levies are paid by the government itself. For example, if you tax copper and if you see where it is used – it is used by the telephones, by power and by defence. For example, we tax fuel, petrol, but I'm sure 80 per cent of the petrol is consumed by the government or by companies where the expenditure is tax-deductible, so we're putting up a lot of machinery to transfer money from our left pocket to our right pocket.'

When I asked him what he thought should be India's priorities, this was his answer: 'I think the biggest priority is population control. Without that there's no question of survival. On a long-term basis, I think the second priority is education, where I think our system has…I wouldn't say it has failed, but I don't think it is standing up to the pressures that it is being put under. Third, I think we need a major breakthrough in agriculture. We've been on a sort of plateau of agricultural production. We need a strong push. The development of energy is another vital sector but population and education are much more important because without these two we're not going to last more than twenty or thirty years.'

India did not move economically to the right until after Rajiv's death and it may not have done so even then if Rajiv had lived to become prime minister again, since, judging from this interview, his economic views were similar to those of his mother. And, when Sonia Gandhi became India's de facto prime minister in 2004, she presided over two governments that stopped the process of economic liberalization and brought back the leftist economic policies that Mrs Gandhi had followed in the name of 'the poor'. But Rajiv's acolytes and the sycophants that the Congress Party breeds in huge numbers continue to credit Rajiv with ending the licence-permit raj that debilitated India for so many decades. As for population control being at the top of his list of political priorities for India, it shows Rajiv's naivety in political matters. Today, India's vast population of young people is considered one of its greatest assets. Education remains of utmost importance and needs radical changes, but no government has dared to make them. It remains dragged down by the red tape of the licence raj and is one of the last bastions of government control.

In the summer of 1983 there were elections in Kashmir. The first elections to the legislative assembly after the death of Sheikh Abdullah. The election campaign was at its height when I accidentally ran into Rajiv in Srinagar. I was walking out of Nedou's Hotel and he was driving by and stopped. In the short time we chatted I tried to warn him that reports he would have read in Delhi newspapers about a possible Congress victory in Kashmir were wrong. I told him Farooq Abdullah would win because this was something the people of Kashmir felt they owed the old Sheikh.

Sheikh Abdullah spent almost all his life in and out of jail and became for ordinary Kashmiris a symbol of Kashmir. I met him only once, a year before he died, when Farooq invited me to Srinagar to cover his anointment as the Sheikh's heir. It remains in my mind one of the most extraordinary political events I have ever covered because of the effect that the Sheikh had on the hundreds of thousands of Kashmiris who poured into Srinagar to hear him speak at the rally where he declared Farooq his heir. He did it with these words, 'The crown that I put on your head, Farooq Abdullah, is a crown of thorns.' The Sheikh died in September 1982 and I never met him again.

Since this was the first election I was covering on my own I worked harder than I ever had, travelling to every constituency in the Valley, other than the border district of Uri, which somehow I never managed to get to. Wherever I went people said that this was the first election that they were participating in as Indians and secession was not an issue. They felt that as far as they were concerned the historical Kashmir problem was over.

The trouble was that most of the journalists who had come from Delhi to cover the election were determined to keep history alive. They treated press conferences with Kashmir's leaders like inquisitions at which they demanded from people like Mirwaiz Mohammed Farooq, one of Kashmir's most important religious leaders, that he condemn secession. When he did not, they spread rumours that there was a secret secessionist agenda that lay hidden beneath the surface calm of the campaign and hinted that Farooq Abdullah was part of it. These journalists worked closely with Congress Party leaders in Srinagar, so they managed to convince themselves and the Congress Party leaders that the party had a real chance of winning. They travelled to cover mostly Congress rallies and in Srinagar's Nedou's Hotel, where most of them stayed, I saw them being regularly entertained by local Congress leaders.

Mrs Gandhi continued to believe the lies she was told as much by the newspapers as her own party. When Farooq's National Conference won with a full majority, the misreporting of the election became a story in itself. It was the first time I saw journalists behave as if they were representatives of the Government of India and not just reporters. They did this for reasons of 'nationalism'. The correspondents of the main national newspapers in Srinagar even joked about their role in the Valley being that of 'India's viceroys'. It was only later, when Kashmir started producing its own reporters, that things changed.

When I returned to Delhi after three weeks in Kashmir I met Rajiv at some social event and tried to persuade him that Farooq Abdullah had won the election fairly and it would be a terrible mistake for the Congress Party to create trouble. Sadly, we had this conversation surrounded by his newly 'political' friends and they convinced him that I was talking rubbish. The clinching argument they offered came from someone who shall remain nameless, who said, 'I know for sure that the elections were rigged by Farooq because my servants in Kashmir voted three times each.'

It is one of the great tragedies of Kashmir's tragic history that this kind of foolish argument was considered credible not just by Rajiv but even by his mother, who should have known better. Mrs Gandhi had campaigned energetically in Kashmir, wearing Kashmiri clothes and speaking her best Urdu, convinced that she would win at least 15 seats from the Valley for her party in the legislature. She sent all her Muslim MPs from Uttar Pradesh and Bihar to campaign on behalf of the party without noticing that outside the towns the ordinary Kashmiri understood very little Urdu at the time. When the results gave Farooq Abdullah's National Conference a full majority, she convinced herself that he had led a secret, secessionist campaign, and tried to bring his government down almost before it could take office. Rajiv and his friends, apolitical novices that they were, went along with this new and dangerous political game and a new Kashmir problem was created. A problem that had nothing to do with the historical one.

11 1984

It may seem like an odd thing to say, with the perspective of history, but Kashmir was so peaceful in 1983 that it was easy to ignore the bad seeds being sown by Mrs Gandhi's policies. There were tourists in the houseboats and hotels of Srinagar, music in the air, nightclubs that stayed open all night, trekkers in the mountains and anglers in the government rest houses along Kashmir's rivers, where in the summer you can catch the best trout in the world.

Farooq as the new chief minister contributed to the atmosphere of fun and frolic by behaving like a chief minister without a care in the world. He developed a passion for motorcycles and took to racing about on them, often with Bollywood actresses riding pillion so that he became the delight of news photographers. On summer evenings he could be seen everywhere. At Kashmiri wazwan feasts on boats that glittered with fairy lights on the Dal Lake, at weddings and dinner parties, concerts and intimate social events in the chief minister's official residence. He continued to live in his own house on Gupkar Road but used the official residence for concerts by young singers who sometimes came from as far away as Delhi to sing romantic Hindi film songs and Urdu ghazals.

It was Punjab that was India's biggest political problem. Bhindranwale's ragtag band of angry young Sikhs had created so much violence and terror that by the end of 1983 I can remember meeting senior police officers who admitted they were losing the fight because in the villages ordinary Sikhs were too frightened to speak out against the violent young men who lived among them. Those who did dare to raise their voices against the violence ended up dead.

Months went by and still Mrs Gandhi continued to do nothing to stop Bhindranwale from conducting his ugly war against the Indian state from the sacrosanct cocoon of the Golden Temple. Years later, Arun Nehru, Mrs Gandhi's cousin, and one of her close aides at the time, said it was because she was so deeply religious that she was afraid of attacking the Golden Temple. 'She had prayers said in all the temples,' he told me, 'and said that she didn't want to attack the Golden Temple because she didn't want to send soldiers into the house of god.' This is probably true. It was well known that Mrs Gandhi was deeply religious. She wore around her neck at all times a string of sacred rudraksha beads, believed to have been given to her by a woman guru she was a devotee of, called Anandamayi Ma. And, until Rajiv and Sonia began to put their foot down one of the most frequent visitors to the prime minister's house used to be an ascetic called Dhirendra Brahmachari, a most irregular sort of yoga teacher who ended up owning one of India's first private aeroplanes and a gun factory in Jammu. Mrs Gandhi's belief in Hindu rituals was encouraged by Dhirendra Brahmachari and her visits to temples and other places of worship when she travelled around India were never hidden from the general public.

Bhindranwale ranted daily against that 'Brahmin woman who rules Delhi' and against Hindus in general. His speeches poisoned the air of Punjab and the number of executions that were carried out at his behest were so many that we stopped counting. One of the victims was Lala Jagat Narain's eldest son who had taken over the newspaper group after him. Many were innocent Hindus killed at random. But mostly he targeted policemen, many of whom were Sikhs. The Punjab government seemed hopelessly unable to control the violence and the state slid into a state of ominous lawlessness.

By the summer of 1984 things got so bad that not a single policeman or government official dared set foot inside the Golden Temple. Anyone suspected of being a police informant was brutally killed and his body thrown into the drains of the temple in small pieces. Bhindranwale seemed to realize that the Government of India would have to act against him at some point, so overnight he moved from his pilgrims' lodge into the Akal Takht in the inner perimeter of the Golden Temple.

As a Sikh he understood well the political significance of the Akal Takht and its unique position among the sacred monuments of the Sikhs.

It was then a beautiful sixteenth-century building, with painted frescoes on its ceilings, and golden domes, and was built by the sixth of the Sikh gurus as a symbol of political resistance to the Mughal emperor. The Sikhs remained in permanent conflict with the Mughal emperors and at the root of this conflict was the imperial mission to impose Islam on those communities who had refused to become Muslim. 'Akal Takht' literally means 'Throne of the Timeless One' and when the sixth guru built this throne for God he built it deliberately a foot higher than the Mughal emperor's throne in Delhi to make it clear that God was mightier than the mightiest emperors. The Akal Takht is directly opposite the Golden Temple, divided from it by its white marble forecourt and the sacred pool that surrounds the temple.

The Akal Takht was so revered as a symbol of resistance that nobody, not even the sixth guru himself, ever used it as a residence. So when Bhindranwale decided to make it his new home there were mutterings among more traditional Sikhs about how very irregular this was. But everyone was too scared to say anything. Everyone except my brother-in-law's mother, Nirlep Kaur, and she chose to do this one sunny afternoon when I happened to be in the Golden Temple on a routine visit. I think it must have been just weeks before Operation Blue Star because I remember there was palpable tension in the air when I heard the sound of gunfire. When I asked one of the priests what had happened he said, 'Oh, it's just that Nirlep Kaur was here and she made a speech saying that people who hang their underwear in the Akal Takht are bound to meet a sticky end. Bhindranwale's men got angry and started firing in the air.' They would not have dared to attack Nirlep Kaur because one of her ancestors is part of Punjabi folklore for having freed the Golden Temple from the clutches of a Muslim governor named Massa Ranghar, who had at some turned it into a den of vice.

From my childhood I remembered Nirlep as a legendary beauty and a politician who, in the early seventies, had fought an election against her rich and powerful father-in-law, and won. She was estranged from her husband when she made this controversial entry into political life, and this made her victory the subject of much gossip among Delhi's prominent Sikh families. She was no longer a member of Parliament but continued to take a keen interest in Sikh politics and totally disapproved of Bhindranwale. My earliest memories of her are of someone who broke rules with impunity and who was completely fearless about consequences. That afternoon she arrived at the Golden Temple, made her little speech and strolled calmly back to her yellow Mercedes, undeterred by the gunshots. I met her as she was getting into her car. She chatted to me about this and that, and then drove off with a smile and a wave to the small crowd that had gathered. As a passionate Sikh, she saw through Bhindranwale's limited understanding of the religion and as a politician she could see the harm his violent politics was causing.

Some weeks later, in Delhi, I got home from a dinner party really late to find Sandeep Shankar, my trusty companion on Punjabi adventures, waiting in a white Ambassador outside my flat. The party had exhausted me because dinner had not been served till after midnight. The ambassador of Qatar, whose dinner party it was, had got it into his head to treat his guests to an Arabian night. There were tents everywhere, even inside the drawing room of his fine colonial bungalow near the Claridges Hotel. Deer and peacocks frolicked in the lawns and in one white garden tent mattresses had been laid out on the grass to create the atmosphere of an Indian concert. A qawwal from Hyderabad sang dolefully and not very well but the ambassador was pleased and cheered him tediously on with endless 'Wah, wahs', which inspired him to continue singing. So at 2 a.m. the last person I wanted to find at my doorstep was Sandeep.

'Not another rumour that they're going to attack the Golden Temple,' I groaned.

'Yes. This time they say it's based on definite information. The army is going in early tomorrow morning. We have to leave immediately.'

'I'll go up and change and get my toothbrush.'

'Just get your toothbrush. You're wearing a salwar-kameez and you have a dupatta so there's no need to change. You can buy something in Amritsar if you need to.'

We left for Amritsar with me dressed in a shiny black salwar-kurta, a dupatta that glittered with silver and gold embroidery and a pair of dangling earrings, which I instantly removed and put in my evening handbag. A hot breeze blew in through the open windows of our Ambassador and I was so exhausted that I fell asleep before we got to Haryana. When I woke it was nearly light and we were already in Punjab, somewhere beyond Patiala. Sandeep was still asleep but stirred when I asked the driver if he wanted to stop for tea. He said he would like to so we stopped at the next dhaba.

A long line of trucks stood outside it and Sikh drivers in grimy white vests and lungis lay asleep on the string beds that served as seating during meals and became beds at night. While we were drinking our tea two truck drivers woke and joined us. They were tall, heavily bearded Sikhs with big bellies. I asked if they had heard anything about an attack on the Golden Temple. They looked nervously at each other and the taller, fatter one, who had taken off his turban and had his thick, oily hair coiled on his head in a loose roll, asked who I was.

'We're reporters from Delhi.'

'So something is happening,' he said looking worried. 'We are trying to get to Amritsar, our families are there and we have also heard rumours of an attack.'

'When did the rumours start?'

'We heard yesterday as we drove through Delhi. Some taxi drivers told us they had seen trucks carrying soldiers moving towards Punjab.'

'It's possible that it was normal troop movement to the border.'

'They said they didn't think it was routine stuff. But who can say? There have been rumours for such a long time. Anyway we should all get going because if something is happening they will close Amritsar down. There will be curfew and nobody will be able to get in.'

'Is it a good idea for the army to go into the Durbar Sahib?' I asked, using the Sikh name for the Golden Temple. It was a question that they seemed to have thought about and the taller man answered without hesitation.

'No. They can kill the Sant and nobody would care, but if there's an attack on the temple most Sikhs will see it as an attack on the Sikh faith and there will be a bad reaction. But they say that Mrs Gandhi is being advised by people who don't know the mentality of the Sikhs.'

'What will happen if the army is sent into the temple?'

'There will be violence,' he said, sipping his tea noisily, 'terrible violence. They say she is surrounded by Madrasis who do not understand the way Sikhs think.'

The truck drivers finished their tea and drove off hurriedly, and we followed. There was no curfew in the towns we passed and no military movement on the highway. By the time we reached Amritsar, the sun was high in the sky and everything seemed peaceful. Nobody stopped us from entering the city and we soon realized that this was yet another false alarm.

We ate breakfast at the Amritsar International Hotel and saw no barricades and no soldiers, even though the hotel was in the same bazaar as the temple. After breakfast we set off on foot through the bazaar and stopped for tea at a teashop we always visited when we wanted to know what was going on inside the temple. The teashop was popular with Bhindranwale's followers. The owner was a Sikh so they spoke freely in front of him.

The teashop had a roof of corrugated iron sheets held up by narrow pillars of unpainted brick. There were five or six wooden tables and a few rickety chairs. There were no walls, so the owner could see everything that went on in the bazaar and everyone who went in or out of the temple. He was a source of information for journalists and the police. It was he who identified the killers of the first Sikh woman Bhindranwale's men killed because she was suspected of being a police informant. This was the only time they broke the fundamental Sikh tenet that women and children cannot be killed, no matter what.

'Sat sri akal,' I said.

'Sat sri akal,' the teashop owner replied, continuing to pour milk from one tin jug into another. We sat down at one of the rickety tables. There was nobody else in the teashop.

'Have you heard anything about an attack?' I did not look at him when I asked the question. He did not look at me when he answered.

'There have been some soldiers in civilian clothes hanging around.'

'Inside the temple?'

'No. In the bazaar asking questions?'

'What sort of questions?'

'They want to be sure they know how many men are inside and how well they are prepared,' he said softly, continuing to pour milk from one jug into another.

'Are they prepared?' I asked looking into my glass of steaming hot tea.

'Yes.'

'How do you know?'

'I know that there is that General inside helping the Sant set up barricades. And all night these trucks go into the temple. They are filled with guns and rockets.'

'How come nobody stops them?'

'Who will? The police don't dare go into the temple.'

Just then a group of young Sikh men walked in, laughing and talking loudly. The teashop owner rushed to serve them. They wore saffron turbans, long blue kurtas and short white pants, and they carried machine guns. They ordered glasses of banafsha, hot milk flavoured with an aromatic herb. Bhindranwale thought of tea as an intoxicant and all intoxicants were forbidden in his army. The men were in their early twenties, tall and well built. They looked suspiciously at Sandeep and me as they sat down, and I decided it would be prudent to identify ourselves.

'Sat sri akal.'

'Sat sri akal.'

'I am a reporter from Delhi. We are here because we heard there is going to be an attack on the Durbar Sahib.'

They laughed. 'Yes. We've heard that too, but by the grace of Guru Govind Singh we are fully prepared.' They held up their guns.

'Prepared to take on the Indian Army?' I asked the question, knowing that as Sikhs they would have grown up with deep respect for the army.

'Ready to take on any troops that the Hindu leaders in Delhi send,' said a tall, good-looking young man with a glint of laughter in his hazel eyes.

'Do you all come from the same village?'

'We come from the same army. We are all the children of Guru Govind Singh.' They laughed.

'Do you live in the Golden Temple?'

'You could say that.'

'Before you came here...to the temple...what work did you do?'

'We were in college,' one of them said, 'but why do you ask so many questions?'

'I'm a reporter.'

'You ask too many questions even for a reporter.' They laughed again, drank their milk and left without paying.

Inside the temple the crowds were larger than usual confirming that rumours of a possible attack that day were hugely exaggerated. Recitations from the Guru Granth Sahib drifted from a loudspeaker and the rich, rancid smell of ghee filled the air. We walked down the white marble steps that led to the white marble concourse around the temple's sacred pond. The light was blindingly white and I had to cover my eyes with my dupatta.

The temple floated like a gold box on the glistening water of the pond. The chanting from inside grew louder. We joined a queue of pilgrims as they muttered and genuflected their way to the temple. I looked for fortifications and Sandeep, a white handkerchief covering his head, took pictures as unobtrusively as possible.

When we got close to a set of rooms we knew to be the offices of Bhindranwale's spokesmen, we stopped to see if we could find someone to talk to. The offices were closed, which was unusual, but more unusual was the sight of several young men climbing down a flight of stairs that led to the temple's labyrinth of underground rooms where grain and other supplies were stored. They carried large jute sacks that could have contained food grain or guns.

The middle-aged man supervising the operation was small and wiry, with a long, sad face and a straggly white beard. I recognized him as Major General Shabeg Singh from a picture I had seen in a newspaper. I had been trying to interview him for weeks but had not managed because he avoided reporters. I knew he was bitter about the way he had been treated by the Indian Army and that he was helping Bhindranwale train his troops for a possible assault on the Golden Temple. He had said as much in the only known interview he had given till then. It appeared obscurely in a Delhi magazine or newspaper without being given the prominence it deserved. Not many people knew, then, that Bhindranwale's army was being led by a General who was the real hero of the Bangladesh war without ever having received sufficient credit for this.

'Sat sri akal.' I used the Sikh greeting in the hope that he would agree to an interview to a fellow Sikh.

'Sat sri akal,' he replied.

'What are you building?'

'Fortifications.' He used the Punjabi word. Morcha.

I switched to English. 'What for?'

'To face the army. We can easily take on the police and the paramilitary but we hear that Mrs Gandhi plans to use the army in which case we need to be better prepared than we were.' He said this in fluent English.

'Is an attack imminent?'

'I don't know...you tell me. You've just come from Delhi, haven't you? You should know more about when it's going to happen. Aren't you here because you're expecting an attack any moment?'

'Yes.' It seemed pointless to lie.

'So?'

'So, I'd like very much to talk to you.'

'Not just now,' he said, 'but I will be in my room in the Guru Ramdas Serai in an hour and we can talk then.'

'I'll be there.'

The General's room was on the first floor. Its single door opened on to a narrow veranda that overlooked the inner courtyard of the building and its small window had an angular view of the Golden Temple. Through it came the constant murmur of Sikh prayers. The tiny room's walls were painted green. Between two narrow beds stood a small wooden table on which there were several bottles of medicine. The General explained that both he and his wife had serious health problems.

'Do you live here all the time?'

'No. But I have been living here for a while to offer prayers after winning my cases against the Indian Army.'

'I've heard that you were treated unfairly by the army but I don't know much more than that.'

'"Unfairly" is the wrong word for what the army did to me,' he retorted angrily. 'I don't think any army in the world would do to a war hero what the Indian Army did to me. If it weren't for me there would have been no Mukti Bahini and if there were no Mukti Bahini there may not have been a Bangladesh.'

Mukti Bahini was the name given to the Bangladeshi resistance which, as the General confirmed, may not have won freedom for Bangladesh or offered much resistance without help from the Indian Army. The war for Bangladesh's liberation started as an indigenous movement after hundreds of thousands of Bengali muslims were massacred by the Pakistani army in what was then East Pakistan. In Bangladesh there are many who believe that more than a million people were killed. Students, university professors, writers, politicians, doctors, teachers, lawyers. More than ten million Bengalis fled across the Indian border after the massacres. They lived for nearly a year in squalid refugee camps forcing India to act. Before sending Indian troops to 'liberate' the Bengali half of Pakistan the Indian Army strengthened the Mukti Bahini by filling its ranks with regular Indian troops, in freedom fighter guise.

In the one conversation I had with the General in his room in the Guru Ramdas Serai that afternoon, he told me with considerable pride how he had transformed the Mukti Bahini from a ragtag bunch of volunteer fighters into a formidable military force. Before the Indian Army officially intervened to create Bangladesh it was the Mukti Bahini that took on Pakistani troops through sabotage and sneak attacks.

'I was decorated for what I did for the country and what does the country do for me? What does the army do? They trump up corruption charges, so flimsy they were thrown out of court, and the Army Chief dismisses me from the army dishonourably a day before I am due to retire. That means I get no pension.'

'Why? What were the charges?'

'I was building a house in Dehra Dun,' he said bitterly, 'and to save a little money I used army trucks to transport building materials. Is that such a crime? From this they tried to make out that I had been stealing supplies from the army and god only knows what else, and this man who is your Army Chief now – he was responsible.' The Army Chief he spoke of had retired by then.

'What happened after they threw you out?'

'I took the army to court and by the grace of god won all my cases, so I came here to give thanks. One night when I was asleep in the Guru Ramdas Serai someone came and woke me and said that the Sant would like to see me, so I went. He told me he wanted to create a separate country for the Sikhs, Khalistan, and asked if I would help. I told him I would help willingly and I have been here in the temple ever since.'

'But there's no way that you can take on the Indian Army and win,' I said hesitantly.

'If we cannot win, we can at least die giving them a good fight.'

'When are you expecting the attack?'

'Any time. Maybe even tonight.'

'But the temple is full of pilgrims.'

'So what? Do you think they care? Do you think Mrs Gandhi cares about anything other than ensuring that the throne of Delhi passes to her son and grandson? You're a Sikh, aren't you? You should be on our side. Why should you want to live in a country in which there is no justice and in which Sikhs are second-class citizens?'

'Why do you say that?'

'Look at what happened to me. Do you think this would have happened to a Hindu General? Never. They've caught senior officers for corruption, dereliction of duty, cowardice under fire, spying – all sorts of things. Nothing ever happens to them. They don't get thrown out without a pension.'

He fell silent and I asked if he would consider giving up his war against the Indian government if justice were done even at this late stage. He shook his head and said it was too late. The war had already started, he said, but I thought I detected a moment of uncertainty and resolved that if the temple did not come under attack that night I would go back to Delhi and tell Rajiv about my conversation. Rajiv was only a general secretary in the Congress Party at the time but I knew that his mother consulted him on most things and took what he had to say seriously. Maybe there was still the possibility of a solution that was political and not military.

That afternoon, I met Bhindranwale for the last time.

He was holding court on the roof of the *langar* or kitchen building. His audience consisted entirely of noisy young men who carried automatic weapons and shouted angry slogans. There were no pilgrims in this gathering. Its purpose seemed to be to rally the troops. Sandeep and I stumbled upon it because as was usual on all our visits to the Golden Temple we went looking for the Sant. He was already giving a speech when we arrived so we went and stood at the back behind the noisy young men. Since this was some distance from where the Sant sat with his lieutenants I did not think he had seen us. But perhaps my glittery evening clothes and the fact that I was the only woman there made me conspicuous because to my horror I heard him stop in the middle of his speech and summon me.

'Bibi, come here please,' he said as a hush descended over the gathering.

'Me?' I asked in the hope that I had heard wrong.

'Yes.' There was no choice but to do as he commanded. I noticed that Sandeep looked very nervous and had stopped taking pictures.

When I got to where Bhindranwale sat he stood up and raising his voice asked, 'Aren't you the woman who wrote an article called "Why I am ashamed to be a Sikh"?'

It was one of the few moments in my life when I have been really scared. Bhindranwale was in the habit of identifying people he wanted dead at meetings such as this one. If I admitted on this tense, hot afternoon in front of this bunch of hotheaded young Sikh 'soldiers' that I had written an article titled 'Why I am ashamed to be a Sikh' in *Sunday* magazine, there could be serious trouble. So I dithered.

Bhindranwale repeated his question in an even louder voice.

Finally, as softly as possible, I said, 'I wrote an article saying that I was ashamed to see so many guns inside the Golden Temple.'

Bhindranwale's reaction was to flounce off in a rage, after saying loudly, 'Our Guru has given Sikhs the right to bear arms.'

I was momentarily relieved to see him go but quickly realized that Sandeep and I had to negotiate our way down a narrow flight of stairs. Since I had been identified as someone who had displeased the Sant one of his more reckless followers may try to attack us on the way down. Sandeep seemed to have had the same thought and whispered, as Bhindranwale's troops began to disperse, that we should wait till everyone had gone.

So we waited till everyone left and walked uneasily down the stairs. I noticed that Harmindar Singh Sandhu, a former student leader and one of Bhindranwale's closest lieutenants, was standing at the bottom of the stairs. Deciding that aggression was my best defence I said that I thought it was disgraceful that the great Sikh community had come to such a pass that a defenceless woman should be targeted in this way.

He gave me a long, hard stare and said, 'Let's just say you are very lucky that you are a woman. I cannot say any more.'

The chance to tell Rajiv about my conversation with the General never came. Two weeks later troops were sent into the Golden Temple. And, despite Kewal Sahib's best efforts to ensure my presence in Amritsar I was not there when it happened.

Two days before Operation Blue Star began Punjab was put under twenty-four-hour curfew. Journalists who managed to get to Amritsar before the curfew were woken by soldiers in the early hours of the morning and ordered on to military buses that transported them across the Punjab border. Only two journalists managed to stay on in the city but saw very little. When they finally succeeded in sneaking out of their hotel rooms, the battle for the temple was over and the army was 'mopping up'. One of them managed to dodge soldiers and curfew to get within the outer perimeter of the Golden Temple and wrote the first article that revealed how badly the attack had been botched up. In the *New York Times* he wrote that he had seen Sikh men lined up in bazaars and shot in the back of their heads by soldiers of the Indian Army. I did not hear about this article till much later. Indian newspapers carried news from Amritsar that had been given to them by military officials, so in Delhi's newspaper offices there was not the slightest clue that Operation Blue Star had not been a resounding success.

Three days after the attack Kewal Sahib decided that it was time for me to try and go to Amritsar. The administration of the state had been handed over to the army in an undeclared imposition of martial law. So I went first to Chandigarh. My father knew the Army Commander, General Mehta (whose first name I no longer remember), from his army days, and gave me a letter of introduction. The plan was to try and persuade him to give us a curfew pass. I had heard from other journalists that without a curfew pass there was no possibility of getting to Amritsar. Those who had tried to enter the state without one had been arrested and sent home as soon as they crossed the Punjab border.

Sandeep and I arrived in Chandigarh as a hot, white dawn was breaking. It was too early to go to army headquarters, so we stopped for a shower and breakfast at the Mount View Hotel. The restaurant offered through its large glass windows a lovely view of the Himalayan foothills and everything seemed peaceful and serene, and very removed from what was happening in Amritsar. Sandeep and I ordered a 'traditional Punjabi breakfast'; enormous parathas stuffed with potatoes and cauliflower, which we ate with yoghurt. Sandeep had a theory that one paratha was so nourishing that it provided sustenance all day. He sensed we had a long day ahead of us and may not find food at all later.

After breakfast we drove to army headquarters. It was a place of unnerving orderliness. The red gravel in the long drive looked as if it had been clobbered into obedience. The bricks that lined the drive were placed at exactly the same angle and were painted white in exactly the same way. The trees stood as if at attention and their leaves looked as though they had been freshly polished. The colonial bungalow that served as the headquarters for the Army Commander had a wide veranda with doors that led to high-ceilinged offices with large desks and neatly placed furniture. In a large ante-room to the Army Commander's office we met his aides, two young officers in impeccably pressed uniforms, who sat drinking tea out of china cups.

Sandeep seemed so intimidated that he had the look of a frightened intruder.

'Stop looking so nervous,' I whispered. 'At the very most we'll be thrown out.' Then in my bossiest voice I asked to see General Mehta.

'Do you have an appointment, madam?' one of the officers asked politely.

'Of course not. I've just driven from Delhi and I want to discuss details of my visit to Punjab.'

'Are you a reporter?'

'Yes.'

'No reporters are allowed to go to Punjab.'

'I am. You can check with the General. I know him well and I have a letter for him from my father.'

The young officer was impressed enough by my demeanour to take my message to the General. Within minutes a tall, bald, middle-aged man with a big moustache and a blustery manner came noisily into the room and confronted me with a friendly but firm reprimand, 'What on earth are you doing here, young lady? And how is the Brigadier?'

'Very well. He sends you regards and this letter.'

'Well, well,' he said, taking the letter from me, 'come into my office and have a cup of tea.'

We followed him into a large, orderly room that smelled of furniture polish. The General settled himself behind an enormous desk that did not have a single piece of paper on it. He opened my father's letter, read it and chuckled. 'The Brigadier says we did a good job in Amritsar,' he said. 'That is a good endorsement from a fine soldier. He asks me to help you in any way I can. How can I help you?'

'We need a curfew pass to go into Punjab.'

'That is the one thing I cannot give you. No reporters are allowed just yet.'

'I know that but there is a press party coming from Delhi this morning. They are flying in with the President. We would like to join it. That's all. I'm sure that won't be a problem.'

'It will be a problem. The reason why they are flying straight from Delhi to Amritsar and then flying out again is because we don't want reporters wandering about the countryside making trouble in the villages.'

'What trouble could we possibly make?'

'You could start asking a lot of silly questions and that would be trouble, especially at the moment since mopping up operations in the villages are still going on.'

'Mopping up?'

'Yes. Now drink your tea and get on back to Delhi. There is not a chance that I can allow you into Punjab.'

'But what are these mopping up operations?'

'I can't talk about them,' he said impatiently.

'All right, General. Thank you for seeing us...we'll be off then.'

It must have been something about the cheery way I said this that made him suspicious, because he gave me a funny look and said, 'Now, listen here, young lady. I've known you since you were a baby and I will have no hesitation in taking you over my knee and spanking you if I hear that you've been trying to sneak into Punjab. Nobody is going to Punjab until we say so. Got it?'

'Got it,' I said with what I thought was a sweet smile.

'Right ho. Right ho,' said the General, 'but I warn you that I will not make any concessions. You will be arrested if you go into Punjab.'

We said goodbye and as we drove out of army headquarters I told Sandeep that I had a cunning plan. 'Our best bet is to take a circuitous route to Amritsar via Moga instead of going through Jalandhar, which is the usual route.'

'We can try,' he said uncertainly, 'but you do know that yesterday some journalists tried going into Punjab and were arrested?'

'They tried going through Jalandhar?'

'Yes. There were tanks blocking the highway.'

'I am willing to bet that they wouldn't have bothered to block the Moga route. Nobody goes to Amritsar that way because it takes twice as long.'

'All right. We can try. But please remember this is the army we're dealing with, not some inefficient civilian administration.'

We went back to the Mount View Hotel, drove around the city to make sure we were not being followed, and then took the road to Moga.

As soon as we crossed into Punjab we could see why the army was refusing to allow journalists in. Even in this relatively peaceful part of the state there were soldiers everywhere, and military vehicles with machine guns on the roofs. It was like entering a war zone. Soldiers stood at bus stops and checked passengers before they boarded and every time they saw a young Sikh man they pulled him out of the queue.

There were hardly any private vehicles on the road but surprisingly nobody stopped us. There was no curfew on the highway, and life seemed to be carrying on as normal until we drove off the main road into a village that we remembered from an earlier trip. We wanted to talk to ordinary rural Sikhs to get a sense of how they felt about the army being sent into the Golden Temple. We chose this particular village because its name was familiar. There had been a massacre here, or a police atrocity, neither of us could be sure which. On the surface things seemed normal. Green fields, houses built in disorderly fashion along narrow lanes, a bazaar that smelled of boiling milk, and a teashop in which a group of bearded old men sat on wooden benches drinking milky tea out of long steel glasses. It was only when I looked twice that I realized what was wrong with this idyllic Punjabi scene. There were no young men in sight; not one.

When I asked one of the elders about this he said, 'They've disappeared. They've all gone to Pakistan.' Then he went back to reading his newspaper.

'What is the news from Amritsar?' I asked.

'Oh, only that they've blown up the Durbar Sahib and thousands of Sikhs have been killed.'

'What about the Sant?'

'He is alive,' said one of the others. 'He escaped, and he is going to come back and lead the movement for Khalistan. Sikhs will not be able to live with Hindus after this. We will not tolerate this insult to our religion.'

'What do you plan to do?' I asked.

'We are planning to march to the Durbar Sahib and take it back from the army,' said an old man with watery eyes and shaking hands.

'Oh? How? There's curfew across the state.'

'We have our ways,' he said mysteriously, 'we have our leaders. You may not see them but they are here.'

In the next village we heard more stories about young men having left for Pakistan and old men planning a march to Amritsar to 'take back' the Golden Temple. Most Sikh men in Punjabi villages at that time were ex-soldiers. When merit was the only criteria for recruitment, Sikhs, Rajputs and Jats got in more easily because they tend to be tall and well-built. When the trouble started in Punjab it was these ex-soldiers, many in their late thirties and early forties, who trained young men in the use of weapons.

We stopped in other villages and it was the same story everywhere. The same tales of 'atrocities' in Amritsar and rumours that Bhindranwale was still alive. I remember being slightly frightened by it all because the Sant had in death become larger than he had ever been in life. I sensed that this would be the beginning of India's real Punjab problem.

Around dusk we got back on the highway because we needed to reach Moga before dark. We were stopped just before we entered the town. There was a tank blocking the road, with a group of jumpy young soldiers beside it. I noticed there were no officers with them and decided that the only way forward was to behave as officiously as possible. I ordered them to lift the barricade because I was in a hurry to get to Amritsar. When the questions began, I pulled out my father's letter, waved it in their faces and told them that I had an urgent message for General Brar. It was a serious name to drop because General K.S. 'Bulbul' Brar was directly in charge of Operation Blue Star. But it worked and they let us pass.

In Moga, which was then a small, overgrown village of a town, we got a room for the night in the best hotel. It reeked of oily food and dodgy sanitation, but the rooms were tolerably clean and we were too tired to complain. We planned to leave at 4 a.m. to get to Amritsar in the early hours of the morning when we knew curfew was being briefly lifted to allow people to stock up on food. By around 6 a.m. the next morning we got to the Harike Bridge over the Beas river. This was the last barricade before entering the city limits of Amritsar. It was a hot, hazy morning and the river looked like a depleted, muddy drain. Parked diagonally on the bridge, blocking all passage, was a tank and beside it a khaki tent in which a neatly dressed young lieutenant sat drinking tea out of a tin mug. A look of amazement spread over his face when Sandeep and I appeared.

'Good morning,' I said cheerfully.

'Good morning,' he replied with a frown.

'We need you to move your tank so we can get our car through. We're in a hurry to go to Amritsar,' I said with a confident smile.

'Nobody is allowed to go to Amritsar.'

'We are. We were supposed to be with the press party that is arriving at the Golden Temple at 11 today. We missed the plane so we drove instead and I have a letter for General Brar.'

'Who from?'

'My father.'

'May I see it?'

'Sure.'

He took the letter in his hands, examined it carefully and asked if it was a personal letter. I said it was and, incredibly, he handed it back to me and asked politely if we would like a cup of tea. We accepted joyfully and chatted to him about the 'success' of the army assault on the temple and the treachery of Sikh soldiers who had mutinied in regiments across the country. Then we shook hands and were on our way.

When we got into the car Sandeep said with a deep sigh, 'I tell you, Tavleen, I don't know what to say. Which fool was it who said women face disadvantages in journalism? If I had been alone I would have been arrested for sure.'

'Well, there have to be some advantages to being a woman,' I said, thoroughly pleased with myself, 'but I'm quite surprised that we pulled it off so easily.'

'What's the plan now?'

'I think we should actually try and find General Bulbul Brar because he is the only one who will be able to get us into the temple.'

'Right. How?'

'I suggest we ask for his headquarters at every barricade we pass. I'm sure they will tell us.'

The next barricade we were stopped at was inside the city. It was a police barricade and the mere mention of the General was enough for them to point us in the right direction. In an hour or so we arrived in an isolated suburb of Amritsar. The streets were empty and it was unnervingly quiet. We were about to stop to find someone to ask for further directions when we saw a truck filled with blindfolded Sikhs lying prostrate in the back. Their turbans had been taken off and used to blindfold them and their long hair fell in untidy coils. Their hands were tied behind their backs. They lay one on top of each other like dead bodies.

'Do you think they're dead?' I asked in a whisper. In years of covering political violence I had never seen anything like it. I have covered many communal riots and heard of people being taken away in trucks like animals, but this was the only time I saw it happen with my own eyes.

'No they're not dead,' Sandeep whispered back. 'Should I take a picture?'

'No, don't. There's a soldier coming towards us...'

'Jai Hind,' I said, using a greeting I remembered from growing up as an army child.

'Jai Hind,' he answered, looking suspiciously into the car.

'We have to see General Brar,' I said firmly, 'I have an urgent letter for him.'

'From whom?'

'From Delhi. It's an important letter.'

'Have you driven from Delhi?' he asked, a note of surprise in his voice.

'Yes.' This seemed to convince him that we were carrying an important letter for the General.

'Follow me,' he said getting into a jeep.

We followed him through a wooden gate guarded by soldiers, who waved us through when they saw our escort, and arrived at a low building with a wide veranda. On the door that led to a large hall was a sign that said 'Ops Room'. The hall was neon-lit and on its walls were large blue maps and diagrams in thick blue pencil. A group of army officers stood in front of a map of the Golden Temple listening to a tall, handsome man with thick greying hair who was pointing at something with a wooden stick. When he saw us he stopped and said, 'What the hell... Who the hell are you and how did you get in here?'

Everyone in the room turned and stared at us.

'General Brar?' I asked, trying to keep my voice calm.

'Yes. Who are you?'

'Brigadier Amarjit Singh's daughter. I have a letter for you from him.'

'How the hell did you get here?'

'We drove.'

'From Delhi?'

'Yes.'

'How in god's name did you manage that...' he said, taking the letter from me.

He read the letter and seemed not to know what to say when he finished. 'Well,' he finally said, 'now that you're here, what can I do for you?'

'We were hoping that you might help us get into the Golden Temple... and if you could tell us what happened...how things went. I understand that a group of journalists is arriving from Delhi today and is being allowed into the temple.'

'Yes. That's true. Well, I suppose it could do no harm to let you go in,' he said slowly. 'I still can't believe that you managed to drive all the way here without being stopped.'

'We were stopped,' I said, 'but I told them I had a letter for you and that worked.'

'Bloody fools. Shocking lapse, shocking lapse... Put that camera away, young man. No pictures. Not even in the temple. Understood?'

'Yes, sir,' Sandeep said putting his camera down on the table.

'Tea?' the General asked indicating that we should sit.

'Please, that would be lovely. Is the temple very badly damaged?'

'Yes. And what is sad is that it needn't have been if we had been allowed to spend a month using military intelligence to find out what was going on. We were forced to depend on those bastards in civilian intelligence and they couldn't even tell us how many entrances there were to the temple. If we had known we wouldn't have lost so many men.'

'Is the Sant dead?'

'Yes.'

'How did he die?'

'Crossfire. Early in the morning on the second day he walked out of the Akal Takht with General Shabeg and Amrik Singh, and they fell.'

'Did the fighting stop instantly after that?'

'It did. But we lost a lot of men...and the Akal Takht is badly damaged. We had to use tanks and heavy artillery. It was a mess.'

'In the villages they say the Sant is still alive. Where is this rumour coming from?'

General Brar frowned and looked wearily at his officers. 'This is a problem,' he said, 'we're not sure how to deal with it. He is dead. We had the body identified by his brother before it was cremated. But we know this rumour is going around the villages and it worries us. We fear that it is being spread to create an uprising, to get Sikhs to start marching on Amritsar.'

'But there's twenty-four-hour curfew, and tanks on all the highways.'

'Yes. But if they came out in really large numbers we wouldn't be sure what to do and firing into the crowd would only make things worse. It is a problem. Damn these politicians – they create these problems...'

'But the strategy for the attack would have been made by the army. Right?'

General Brar seemed not to hear my question and continued talking about how the army had been let down badly by civilian intelligence. 'I don't know really... What can I say except that we are really angry about the number of men we lost because civilian intelligence was so poor. Had we known how many entrances there were we would never have gone in through the main entrance which was so heavily fortified. We lost more than a hundred men in the first few minutes. The intelligence failure was so great we didn't even know how many men we were dealing with. And there are still snipers in the temple.'

'So, it's risky for us to go in?'

'Oh, you can go in. We will send you with an armed escort but whatever you write be careful not to incite any religious tension. Please, you will have to promise me that there will be nothing written that will cause alarm or communal tension.'

'Promise.'

In Amritsar the curfew was total. It was late afternoon and an oppressive, merciless heat hung over the empty city like a shroud. In the bulletproof interior of the armoured car, I felt like I was being boiled alive. Sweat poured so profusely out of every pore of my body that I stopped trying to dry it. I noticed that Sandeep was in the same state, but the soldier driving us and the young officer who sat beside him seemed unaffected. From the small, darkened windows I caught glimpses of armed soldiers lining the streets and dogs lying in every patch of shade they could find. There was not a civilian in sight and not even one policeman.

We drove up to the main entrance of the Golden Temple. The clock tower entrance, as pilgrims call it. There were two tanks parked in front of it. One had its gun pointing toward the temple's concourse, and the other towards the silent, empty square. The shops that sold religious artifacts were closed, as were the teashops and the little shops that sold Punjabi shoes and a bewildering variety of electrical goods. Sandeep tried taking a picture of the empty square but the young officer stopped him. He pointed to windows above the shops and said, 'Be careful, we're not sure if there are still snipers hiding up there.'

'How would they have got out of the temple?' I asked.

'There were several exits from the temple and once the battle for the Akal Takht was lost, many of the terrorists escaped through them and are still hiding in the city.'

'So in a sense it was a failed operation.'

'I don't know about these things,' he said with a frown. 'We are here to defend the country and we did our best.'

Sandeep and I took off our shoes before walking down the white marble steps that led to the temple's concourse. The soldiers did not bother to do so. The steps were burning hot because the red jute matting that usually covered them was no longer there, but I hardly noticed my burning soles because of the stench that filled the air. The soldiers covered their noses with handkerchiefs.

'Rotting bodies. There are hundreds still in the basement of the temple. We haven't been able to get them out because we don't know the entrances and we are afraid there could still be shooters down there. They were using the granaries as a base to attack us. You see those holes under the stairs? The first attack came from there as our men walked down. We lost a lot of men.'

Inside the temple grounds, we turned left automatically to make the usual clockwise perambulation of the sacred tank and it was then that I saw the first signs of what had happened. In one corner of the concourse lay an enormous pile of bloodstained clothes. Huge clouds of flies hovered over it and settled on the patches of blood. The clothes were brightly coloured and among them were sandals in pink and blue, some very small.

'There were women and children caught in the fighting?' I asked the lieutenant.

'What if there were?' he said calmly. 'These people were traitors. They were the enemy. Do you know how many men we lost?'

'No,' I said, unable to take my eyes off the pile of clothing. I found myself mesmerized by a tiny pair of sandals with Mickey Mouse's face on them.

'Officially we admit to only 700,' he said angrily, 'but at least twice that number died. We lost nearly 200 men in the first five minutes.'

'Didn't you know where the fortifications were? Didn't anyone give you a map of the temple?'

'A map of the temple,' he laughed derisively. 'A map? What a luxury that would have been. Forget about fortifications. Believe me when I tell you that we didn't even know how many entrances there were to the temple.'

'The temple looks completely undamaged,' said Sandeep shading his eyes.

'Yes,' said the Lieutenant, 'we lost a lot of men trying to save it. We had orders from the top not to return fire if it came from the temple.'

'Did it?'

'It was hard to tell from where I was,' he said, 'there was a lot of smoke and it was dark. During the day they would hold their fire. But the fighting was mostly around the Akal Takht. That's where the Sant and the General were hiding. We couldn't save the Akal Takht.'

When we had walked fully around the temple, the remains of the Akal Takht became visible. Where there had once been a fine building of white plaster and golden domes there now was a blackened shell. When we got closer I noticed traces of the frescoes on the ceiling. Despite not being a religious Sikh I was horrified by the damage and the young officer must have seen this.

'We had no choice,' the lieutenant said, seeing the expression on my face, 'we had to use tanks. There was no other way.'

'It was a political symbol,' I said for want of anything else to say. 'It will cause a lot of anger among the Sikhs.'

'Yes. There's no doubt about that. We've already had trouble with Sikh troops.'

'Were they used in the fight for the temple?'

'No. There have been mutinies in regiments elsewhere. But they're under control now.'

'What about ordinary Sikhs? There could be trouble across Punjab when they hear that the Akal Takht has been blown up.'

'Yes. But the temple is going to remain closed till the Akal Takht is rebuilt. Orders have already been given by Mrs Gandhi.'

Patches of dried blood stained the white marble of the concourse and the water in the sacred tank around the temple looked muddy.

'Why is the water this colour?' I asked, feeling a little foolish after asking the question.

'That's blood,' the lieutenant said, 'there are bodies in the tank. It will have to be drained. And look over there, right in front of the Akal Takht... That is where we found the bodies of General Shabeg and the Sant and you know that fellow who was the student leader.'

'Amrik Singh.'

'Right.'

'How did they die?'

'We're not sure... They walked right into the area where the firing was heaviest. It didn't make sense to us. The bodies were so mutilated it was hard to recognize them.'

It was later, on other trips to Amritsar, from talking to priests and those who remained of Bhindranwale's army, that I pieced together the final moments of Operation Blue Star. Those who stayed till the end said that on the last day of the fighting the Sant came out of the Akal Takht, saw the damage done to it because of him and it was then that he, General Shabeg Singh and Amrik Singh resolved to 'sacrifice themselves' because they knew that the Sikh community would never forgive them if they lived. So on the morning of 6 June they walked out of the Akal Takht and directly into the line of fire. Those of the Sant's companions who were still alive and in the Akal Takht disappeared quietly into the city from one of the many routes out of the temple that the army had no information about.

It soon became clear that the operation to save the Golden Temple had been a disaster. It was clear to the army, to journalists and to most political analysts. What never became clear was who was responsible for what happened. Was it Mrs Gandhi's powerful coterie of bureaucrats? Was it Rajiv and his friends? Was it a combination of both? Why had a woman so famous for her sense of political timing got the timing so badly wrong? Far from ending the Punjab problem Operation Blue Star served to dangerously exacerbate it and to deepen the divisions between Hindus and Sikhs. As far as I can remember none of these things were discussed in the Indian press because there was a sort of unspoken consensus that Mrs Gandhi had been right in doing what she did, that she had been forced to send the army into the Golden Temple because there were no options left.

When I got back to Delhi I was asked by an American friend, Mary Anne Weaver, who worked for the *Sunday Times*, London, if I would write a piece on what I had seen in Punjab. She would have written it but foreign journalists were not allowed into Punjab at the time. I wrote an article based on what I had seen in the villages on the way to Amritsar, saying that we were probably seeing the beginning of the real Punjab problem rather than the end of it. And, since it was for a British newspaper, I compared it with Britain's problem in Northern Ireland. It appeared under a headline that read something like 'The Seeds of India's Ulster'.

It was in my view an accurate description of what I had seen and since I had always opposed Bhindranwale's activities with brutal honesty, and at considerable personal risk, I did not think that anyone would read it and challenge my patriotism. I was wrong. The next time I met Suman Dubey, who was still a journalist and not yet one of Rajiv's personal aides, at a dinner party in Delhi, he made it a point to ask me how I could have 'written something like that piece in the *Sunday Times*'.

'What was wrong with it?' I asked with genuine surprise.

'You shouldn't have written an article criticizing the government in a foreign newspaper,' he said.

I never found out if he was speaking for himself or on Rajiv's behalf. What I did find out soon enough was that the general view in Rajiv's circle of friends was that Operation Blue Star had been a resounding success and any criticism of it amounted to treason. It took me a while to discover that the reason for this hyper-sensitivity was that Rajiv and his friends had been personally involved in advising a military assault on the Golden Temple. Mrs Gandhi's 'south Indian advisors' had gone along with the plan, but from all accounts were not the ones who initiated it. Was this Rajiv Gandhi's first serious political decision? Nobody will ever know, but by the middle of 1984, when Operation Blue Star happened, he had become the prime minister's closest advisor.

12 RAJIV

The rains came late in that long, hot summer of 1984 and those of us who could not leave Delhi suffered the intensity of long, still days that caused white vapour to rise from the road and make normal activity almost impossible. It was on such a day, when I was on my fifth lukewarm nimbu pani, staring dejectedly at the blank sheet of newsprint in my typewriter, that I heard that Mrs Gandhi was planning to topple Farooq Abdullah's government in Kashmir. It had been elected only the year before.

The news came from a reliable source in the Home Ministry and even he admitted that it was a mad idea. 'First Punjab…now this,' the official said. 'It doesn't make sense with Punjab still on the boil.'

It really made no sense at all that almost exactly a month to the date from Operation Blue Star Mrs Gandhi should go ahead and topple Farooq's government for reasons that were too flimsy to be valid. What was worse is that it was almost as if she acted out of pique rather than for political reasons. From the time Farooq became chief minister Mrs Gandhi and her circle of close advisors maligned him for being 'anti-national' for reasons so silly that they were laughable. On a visit to the Golden Temple he had spent some time chatting to Bhindranwale and this was portrayed as an act of treason. He organized a conclave of opposition chief ministers in Srinagar and this was seen as an attempt to thumb his nose at Delhi. But even if the reasons had been valid the timing of the move against his government was insane. Why would Mrs Gandhi, with her supposedly legendary sense of timing, destabilize two sensitive border states within a month of each other? It is something I have not understood to this day.

The plot to topple Farooq's government did not take into account that Kashmir had a long history of stolen elections and denied democratic rights nor did it take into account that Farooq was still very popular. He had brought levity to Kashmir's gloomy political history and ordinary Kashmiris loved him for it. His critics may have taken to calling him 'Disco chief minister' but ordinary Kashmiris loved his sense of fun and his irreverence. In his year as chief minister he had done little to improve anything, but people liked to see him riding his motorcycle around the streets of Srinagar and stopping to listen to the complaints of ordinary citizens. This was something important politicians did not usually do. He liked defying Delhi and this they especially loved because of Kashmir's peculiar history as a reluctant member of the Union of India.

While we in Delhi's newsrooms were still debating whether Mrs Gandhi would add to her political problems by destabilizing Kashmir within weeks of Operation Blue Star, Farooq was removed in an act of barefaced political chicanery that did little to enhance the image of Mrs Gandhi or Rajiv. In a midnight manouvre 13 members of his legislative party went to Raj Bhawan and told the Governor they were defecting from the National Conference in order to lend their support to Farooq's brother-in-law, Gul Mohammed Shah, whom Farooq had earlier expelled from his party and who had gone on to set up his own party, National Conference (Kashmir). Kashmir's governor was none other than Mrs Gandhi's old hatchet man, Jagmohan, the same man who had so faithfully obeyed Sanjay's instructions during the Emergency. Jagmohan had replaced Mrs Gandhi's cousin B.K. Nehru, who had refused to cooperate in this cynical exercise on the stated grounds that he would not help subvert a sensitive border state. Shah would not have succeeded in forming a government if the governor had not cooperated fully.

Gul Shah, married to Farooq's elder sister Khalida, had always thought of himself as the real political leader in Sheikh Abdullah's family and bitterly resented Farooq from the time Sheikh Abdullah anointed him as his heir two years earlier. I remember from Farooq's 'coronation' how unhappy Gul Shah had looked when Sheikh Abdullah announced at that rally in Iqbal Park that he was placing on Farooq's head a 'crown of thorns'. A little investigation was all it took to find out how much Shah resented being passed over. He had been Sheikh Abdullah's comrade and stayed in Kashmir while Farooq went to live in England in the years Sheikh Abdullah was in prison to come back only when his father became chief minister.

Farooq, oblivious to the plot against his government, happened on that day to be in Pahalgam, where my parents and sister were holidaying with her children and my son, Aatish. My sister told me later that Farooq had spent the day taking the children for rides on his motorcycle and returned to Srinagar late that evening.

As the resident Kashmir expert and since I had covered the Kashmir election the year before, Kewal Sahib decided that I should go up to Srinagar as soon as possible. I arrived two days after Farooq's government was dismissed on 2 July 1984. On my flight were Inder Gujral, Hemwati Nandan Bahuguna and other opposition politicians who were going there to lend moral support to the dismissed chief minister.

Sitting next to me on the flight was Bahuguna, former chief minister of Uttar Pradesh and a man who had been one of Mrs Gandhi's most trusted lieutenants. They fell out after Mrs Gandhi declared the Emergency. Bahuguna was a small man with a distinctive stoop and a face that looked like a withered raisin. He was highly intelligent and had a permanent twinkle in his eyes, as if he saw politics as a sort of absurd game. 'Now she has really gone and blown it,' he said to me with a smile. 'Kashmir is going to be the last nail in her coffin... Sadly it will also create problems for the nation.' He did not sound sad at all.

'What do you think will happen?' I asked, in search of a comment for the story I had to file that evening.

'Well, for a start this will prove to be a big boost for the secessionist organizations. They've been dormant for nearly ten years because they have no role to play in Kashmir if there is democracy. When the choice is between a military dictatorship in Pakistan and a democratic India, Kashmir will opt for India. It is when democracy is denied that people start remembering that they are Muslims.'

'Why do you think Mrs Gandhi did this?'

'They say it isn't her decision,' he said thoughtfully. 'I've heard at the highest levels in Delhi that she is almost in retirement and it is now her son and his friends who are calling the shots. And they obviously don't fully understand the consequences of their actions.'

'What do you think of Rajiv and his friends?'

'He is a sweet boy. Not very intelligent, but good. The problem is that he is not at all political and it's very difficult to rule India if you are not political.'

'What do you mean by not being political?' I persisted.

'Well, for a start, someone with even minimum political sense would never have toppled Farooq's government, especially not now with Punjab in flames. Someone political would never have attacked the Golden Temple because a political person would have found a political solution to Punjab instead of a military one.'

'Punjab is now irretrievable and they go and destabilize Kashmir,' said one of the other opposition leaders. He was a Punjabi Hindu and said he had driven through Punjab a week earlier and seen the beginning of a much more serious problem than had so far existed.

We flew over high mountains, half khaki, half covered in snow, and a little frightening in their cold beauty. As we began our descent, the countryside softened and below us lay fields filled with yellow mustard flowers and peridot rice paddies. From the first time I had come to Kashmir as a child I had marvelled at how Kashmiri rice fields were a lighter, more luminous green than anywhere else and on this sunny day they glistened as if someone had woven threads of gold into an embroidered landscape.

The scent of flowers greeted us as we stepped out of the aeroplane. It came from almond trees heavy with white blossoms, which we could see beyond the barbed wire that cordoned off the tarmac. Srinagar airport had changed since I was last here a year ago. Farooq believed that tourism should be the core of Kashmir's economy and in pursuit of this goal had transformed the arrivals lounge in the airport from the tin shed it had once been into a wood-panelled hall in which stalls advertised hotels, taxi services, trekking and fishing trips. A glass wall partitioned off the arrivals from the departures lounge and I noticed that the departures lounge was bursting with travellers who seemed slightly panicky. Women with small children formed the largest group. Was there already trouble in the city?

It was the first question I asked Shaukat, whose taxi was used so often by visiting journalists that it had a press sticker pasted permanently on the windscreen.

'Curfew,' he said. 'There's been twenty-four-hour curfew since midnight. I got here only because I rang your office in Delhi and asked them to ensure that I got a curfew pass.'

'Any violence?' I asked as we drove past the garden of almond trees.

'Not yet. But people are angry; they are saying Kashmir will never get democracy under India. Farooq has become a big hero now.'

'Where is he? Is he in Srinagar?'

'Yes. They say he is under house arrest because they won't allow anyone to drive down Gupkar Road. It's been closed even to journalists. They say he is going to come out this evening and drive through the city with the opposition leaders who are coming from Delhi.'

'What time?'

'Around five I've heard.'

'Great. We have time. Let's dump my luggage in the Broadway and try and get to his house.'

Police cars patrolled the deserted streets but there was a strange absence of tension, almost as if there was a holiday in the city. Kashmiri men in peaked caps and loose coats stood chatting and drinking tea, women shopped for groceries and in a field on the banks of the Jhelum children played cricket in the sun. When we got to the Broadway Hotel I noticed a bus leaving with a large group of tourists. The holiday atmosphere appeared to have fooled none of them into staying. Srinagar was known to explode suddenly and the first means of transport to stop functioning was usually India's one and only airline. Visitors could end up stranded in Kashmir for weeks.

My parents, sister and the children were among those who had decided to leave that afternoon on the earlier of the two Indian Airlines flights to Delhi. I was meant to take the one that left later in the afternoon but when I got to the Broadway Hotel I ran into Chaitanya Kalbag, who worked at the time for Reuters, and he pointed out that it would be madness to go back to Delhi on a day that Farooq could be arrested. Raghu Rai, who had made the mistake of leaving Amritsar two days before Operation Blue Star, agreed that it was better to stay and risk not being able to file my story than to go back to Delhi and find that Farooq had been arrested. So the first thing we did, on the way to Farooq's house, was to go to the Indian Airlines office and change our tickets, even though Raghu and I had sent our luggage ahead to the airport to be checked in by other journalists travelling on the same flight.

The entrance to Gupkar Road was blocked by a barricade. A group of Kashmiri policemen stood smoking and chatting. When I showed them my press card they smiled and waved me cheerily towards Farooq's house. They told Shaukat that the car would have to wait at the barricade, but he said something to them in Kashmiri and they laughed and moved the barricade and let us pass. The opposition leaders from Delhi had got there before me and were sitting in Farooq's garden amid beds of fat, overblown roses and chrysanthemums, drinking Kashmiri tea. When Farooq saw me he smiled and indicated with a wave that I should join them.

'Welcome. Welcome. You've come just in time. In half an hour we are planning to drive to the old city and cross the Jhelum to show people I am still their chief minister and will not be deterred by curfews and such things.'

'Don't you think they will arrest you?'

'I hope they do,' he said with a laugh.

'What happened?' I asked. 'When did you know that your MLAs had defected?'

'The next morning,' he said with a bitter little smile. 'And guess which ones went? The Jammu Hindus to whom I gave tickets because I thought it would make Mrs Gandhi happy to know that I was choosing what she calls mainstream politicians and not secessionists as she accuses us Muslims of being.'

After the opposition leaders finished their tea we drove in a convoy past police barricades to the Jhelum where we got into small boats to cross the river to the decrepit medieval buildings and crowded bazaars that make up the old city of Srinagar. As soon as Farooq was spotted, a huge crowd gathered and started shouting slogans of support. This inspired him to launch into one of his more passionate speeches, but within minutes a Kashmiri journalist, Yusuf Jameel, who worked for my newspaper as its Srinagar correspondent, took me aside to tell me that the Indian Airlines flight to Delhi had been hijacked to Lahore.

My first reaction was panic because I thought it was the flight that my family was on that had been hijacked. But it was the second flight, the one Raghu Rai and I would have been on, that had been forced to land in Lahore. On it was my bag in which there was a diary in which I recorded 'off-the-record' conversations that said things like 'RG said "I talked to

Mummy but she doesn't listen to me"'. Pakistani intelligence would have a lot of fun reading my diary, I thought.

'Kashmiris?' I asked Yusuf.

'Sikhs,' he whispered. 'I just got a call from a friend who works at the airport. The governor has rushed there. The flight has already landed in Lahore and the four hijackers have sought asylum in Pakistan.'

'Anyone killed? Injured?'

'Not that I know of.'

'We should tell Farooq.'

'He knows. His intelligence people have told him but he doesn't want to say anything before this meeting is over.'

'Should we go to the airport?'

'There is no point now that we know that the aeroplane is already in Lahore. Apparently the Pakistanis are making sure that it leaves for Delhi as soon as possible. But maybe it's a good idea to head for Raj Bhavan after this meeting and see what the governor has to say.'

Word about the hijacking spread quickly, and Chaitanya and Raghu said they would like to come to the governor's house with Yusuf and me. The sound of speeches followed us as we drove up the steep hill at the top of which was the governor's house. A lone sentry guarded the closed white gates of the Raj Bhavan.

'Do you have an appointment with the governor?'

'No. Press.'

'Let me check,' he said disappearing from his box. A few minutes later the gates were opened and we found ourselves in a long drive at the end of which was an old-fashioned Kashmiri house with sloping roofs, glazed verandas and a terraced garden beyond which we could see the lakes of Srinagar.

A butler in a white uniform led us down a long, sunless corridor whose walls were covered in portraits of governors past. At the end of the corridor, behind a thick door of polished teak, was the governor's office, an enormous room decorated with Kashmiri carpets and carved Kashmiri walnut wood furniture. Sunlight poured in through a picture window that opened on to a vista of Srinagar's lakes. The governor was almost submerged behind the huge desk at which he sat. He greeted us with an unsmiling namaste and indicated that we should sit on the stiff-backed carved chairs that stood beside a carved coffee table some distance from his desk.

He joined us after a few moments of appearing to be very busy and we went through stilted pleasantries. The governor was clearly not in the mood to see us and spent most of his time glowering into his teacup or gazing out at the view. We asked about the hijacking and who the hijackers were, and he said that initial information indicated they were Sikhs. We then turned to the local situation and asked if he expected instability in Kashmir as a result of the toppling of Farooq's government. The question annoyed him. Why should there be instability, he said curtly, when it was a political crisis that had been caused by the defection of 13 legislators, and as governor all he had done was facilitate a new government to avoid another election so soon after the last one.

We mentioned that there was unrest in the city because people believed that the government had been toppled at the behest of Delhi. Was he worried? Was he going to arrest Farooq? He did not like our questions or the tone in which we asked them and dismissed us after saying that he had no plans to have Farooq arrested unless he chose to break the law. Farooq was never arrested but Kashmir slid slowly into a mood of anger and defiance. Memories of secession flooded back from some long forgotten recess in the public mind and a slide began into chaos and violence that would a few years later turn into a full insurgency.

When I got back to Delhi almost the first thing that happened was that I got a call from someone in the Central Bureau of Investigation saying that they needed to ask me a few questions.

'What about?' I asked.

'About the recent hijacking of the Indian Airlines plane from Srinagar.'

'What? What can I know about it?'

'Well, madam, Mr Rajiv Gandhi has made a statement in the Lok Sabha referring to a woman journalist, close to the former chief minister of Kashmir, whose bag along with that of a well-known photographer were on the hijacked plane.'

'Has he?'

'Yes.'

I am not sure if I was seriously investigated as a hijacker but when I called Rajiv to find out whether he had mentioned me in his Lok Sabha speech he laughed and said, 'It's just politics. Don't worry about it.' It was Farooq Abdullah who was his target and not me. But it worried me that Rajiv could have drawn me into his political game so casually, knowing that it might cause problems for me. This was the first glimpse I got of Rajiv Gandhi the politician and I did not take it seriously at the time. But an incident that occurred some weeks later got me more worried.

My cousin Himmat Sandhu, an idle young man with nothing more serious on his mind than going to the next party, got arrested one night near Safdarjang's tomb. He was on a motorcycle and may have had a few drinks and talked rudely to the policemen who stopped him at a barricade. Nothing he could have said can justify what followed. He was taken to Tughlak Road police station and beaten brutally all night. The police wanted him to confess to being a terrorist involved in a plot to blow up the Bhakra Dam. Himmat identified himself before the torture began and told the policemen that they could verify his identity from our uncle who lived two minutes away in 17 Tughlak Road but they continued to beat him to within an inch of his life. And, in a gesture typical of Indian policemen when they are in torture mode, they forced him to drink their urine.

Luckily for Himmat a domestic servant from the house next to our uncle's on Tughlak Road happened to be in custody that night on some minor charge. When he was released the next morning he took the trouble to go and tell our uncle that someone from his family was being tortured in the police station. It is horrifying to think what could have happened to my cousin had this man not considered it his duty to inform my uncle. Nobody would have known where he was since there had been no official arrest. My uncle used his influence to have Himmat released and the first thing he did was to make up his mind to leave India for good. He migrated to the United States as soon as he could and has never come back to India again, not even for family weddings and funerals.

What happened to my cousin disturbed me enough for me to tell Nina and Sonia about it. I mentioned it in the hope that the information would reach Rajiv, or even Mrs Gandhi, to make the point that if something like this could happen to my cousin in the most exclusive part of Lutyens's Delhi it was terrifying to think of what could be happening to ordinary

Sikhs elsewhere. I thought Sonia would be shocked by the story and have to admit that it worried me that it did not bother her even slightly. She said that Himmat had been arrested because after Operation Blue Star security around the prime minister's house had been intensified and he had been rude to the policemen who stopped him outside Safdarjang's tomb. Perhaps torture in police stations was outside the realm of her comprehension, or perhaps she really was so deeply apolitical that she could not understand the significance of an instance of torture in a police station in Lutyens's Delhi.

It made me wonder about the kind of person she really was. She had an incredibly warm and friendly side to her that I had seen often. Having returned to Delhi with young Aatish to raise on a very meagre salary I found myself needing to depend on my parents for financial help. On what I earned I could not have afforded the rent of a small flat in Delhi so my mother agreed that she would pay the rent of a barsati in Golf Links that consisted of one large room, a toilet, a kitchen and a very nice terrace. It was here that Sonia would come, often with Nina, and always bearing gifts for Aatish. The smartest clothes he had as a small boy came from her. She would pretend that they had been bought for Feroze (Maneka's son) but had been too small.

Meanwhile, Aatish had learned to say his first full sentence and of all things it was, 'Indira Gandhi, hai, hai.' Death to Indira Gandhi. If he was happy he would say it cheerfully, if he was sad mournfully and if he was angry sulkily. When I told Sonia about this she laughed and said she could not believe that he said this spontaneously and that I must have tutored him to say it. I explained that his first word had been 'hi', his second word 'die' and the first full sentence came from a slogan he had heard from protesters in the street. She did not believe me, so when she came to lunch next I tried to get Aatish to perform. It should have been easy, since he said nothing else all day. But either because he has a sycophantic gene embedded in him or because his two-year-old brain understood the situation he decided not to perform. When I prompted him by saying, 'What does Indira Gandhi do?' he smiled sweetly up at Sonia and said, '*Kaam*.' Work.

It was hard for me to reconcile the Sonia of those lunches with the Sonia who could so casually accept police brutality. And I put it down to her inability to understand political things.

By the time the rainy season ended that year an ugliness was creeping into the political atmosphere, an ugliness that was almost tangible. I sensed a certain menace in the air. But even I could not have dreamt that the last few months of 1984 would bring unimaginable horror into our lives.

The season changed, as it always does at the end of September in north India, and cooler weather came. Before Diwali there were the usual card parties and long evenings of revelry. Naveen Patnaik won a lot of money from Akbar Ahmed one evening, and my sister, Udaya, had her usual luck. They played for small stakes and the card games were unserious but we heard that there were card parties at which the scions of rich business families lost hundreds of thousands of rupees. We did not know these people.

If there is one thing I have learned from my long years in journalism it is that history usually sneaks up on you when you are least expecting it. It gives journalists insufficient time to be good writers of that first draft of history that is supposed to be their job to write. This is what happened on 31 October 1984, the day after Diwali that year.

As usual, everyone had eaten and drunk too much on Diwali. The windows of my bedroom were open and I remember the air still smelled of fire crackers. I was dozing rather than asleep that morning when the telephone rang. It must have been ringing for a while because when I picked it up my bureau chief sounded annoyed.

'Mrs Gandhi has been shot,' Kewal Sahib said, 'they've taken her to the Medical Institute. Get there as soon as you can, before they close the gates.'

'What? When?'

'About fifteen minutes ago. We're not sure if she is dead and we're not sure who it was. Go immediately.'

'I can't believe it... God, I hope it wasn't Sikhs.'

'So do I...'

My first reaction was to open the window of my room wider and stare into the public park outside to see if the news had spread. It was a luminous, sunny early winter morning. Ayahs with their small charges gossiped on benches, toddlers tumbled around in bright sweaters and office-goers went by on bicycles and scooters. Nobody seemed to have heard yet. I threw on some clothes, raced downstairs and hopped into an auto-rickshaw. It would have taken less than ten minutes for me to get to the All India Institute of Medical Sciences but by the time I got there its black, wrought-iron gates were locked from the inside. A single armed policeman stood guard and I joined the small group of reporters gathered outside the closed gates. The enormity of what had happened sunk in and we stared at each other without speaking. More reporters came and like us they stared silently at the closed gates. When two foreign TV crews appeared they attracted enough attention for passersby to stop and ask questions. Television crews were a rare sight in those days. Someone said, 'The prime minister's been shot.' The news spread fast and before long a large crowd gathered behind us. They were mostly middle-class office-goers in badly stitched pants and terylene shirts. They parked their scooters by the hospital wall and stood with grim expressions on their faces. They murmured among themselves about 'consequences' and seemed more certain than us that Mrs Gandhi was dead.

Every reporter there that morning had heard something of what had happened. We tried piecing together the story as we waited. There were three men, we heard, of whom two were Sikhs. The Sikhs had been shot dead afterwards by Mrs Gandhi's security guards. The one who was not a Sikh disappeared before they could get him. There was a lot of shooting. She could not have survived.

We waited outside the closed gates of the hospital for hours without anyone officially confirming what had happened. Then, just as I was about to try and find another way into the hospital, I noticed an intelligence man I knew quietly coming up and joining the crowd.

'Is she dead?' I asked him softly.

'Yes,' he whispered back, 'but please don't say anything yet, they want to keep it quiet till the evening when Rajiv comes back from his tour.'

'Why?'

'The President isn't here and he will be needed to swear Rajiv in as prime minister.'

'Prime minister?'

'Yes.' Others noticed us talking and he disappeared into the crowd that was now muttering and getting restive.

'What did he say?' someone asked me.

'She is dead.'

The words were barely out of my mouth when the hospital's gates opened and a cavalcade of white Ambassadors drove out at high speed.

In one of them I saw Sonia, weeping. There was another woman with her. I thought it was Nina. The gates closed immediately but by now the crowd was sure that Mrs Gandhi was dead and that she had been killed by Sikhs. Their reaction was not grief, but rage. The air filled with talk of revenge but none of us knew what this meant. Not even Kewal Sahib, who was always so prescient about these things. When I called to give him the news that Mrs Gandhi was dead he said there would be trouble and he was worried about what could happen to ordinary Sikhs. But, the way he said it, I sensed that he expected just a bit of violence. On that day of pale gold sunlight, with a hint of winter in the air and the sound of children playing in a garden near the Medical Institute I was among those who would have said, if asked, that there may be just a 'bit of violence'. I would never have predicted that what we would see in Delhi in the next few days would be the worst violence since the Partition riots and that more than 3000 Sikhs would be killed in the carnage.

From the Medical Institute I went to Mrs Gandhi's house on Safdarjang Road. Naveen lived at the time in Safdarjang Lane, directly behind Mrs Gandhi's house, and I called him to ask if he had heard or seen anything.

'Not a thing,' he said, 'but the servants heard some shots and thought they were Diwali crackers.'

In the street outside the house the neem trees were shedding their plump, yellow pods. Uneven sticky patches of yellow stained the pavements and the bitter smell of neem filled the air. When I arrived the street was empty, but other reporters soon arrived and from 'sources' inside the house we continued to try and piece together the story. This is what we knew by that evening. Mrs Gandhi had stepped out of her house at about 9 a.m. and was walking through her garden towards her office, in a bungalow that adjoined her house, when her Sikh bodyguard, Beant Singh, greeted her with his hands joined together. Then he shot her with his pistol. Another bodyguard, Satwant Singh, opened fire with his automatic weapon. She had barely fallen to the ground when Sonia, the only member of the family at home that morning, rushed out. Sonia told me, many days later when I finally got a chance to talk to her, that she had heard the shots and come out to scold the gardeners' children for continuing to play with firecrackers when Diwali was over. That evening all we knew was that when she saw what had happened she looked for the ambulance that is always parked in the prime minister's house and found that the driver had gone for a cup of tea. So Sonia put her mother-in-law into a white Ambassador and took her to the Medical Institute.

I continued to wait with other reporters in the street outside the house for hours in the hope of gathering more details of the assassination and in the hope that we might be able to talk to Rajiv if he came home before being sworn in as prime minister. It got colder and darker and the smell of squashed neem pods mixed with cigarette smoke and the scent of hot tea. An enterprising chai-walla had set up shop on the pavement and offered us 'ready-made' tea in plastic cups and roasted chickpeas. Had there really been a third assassin who had disappeared? Why had Beant Singh and Satwant Singh been shot by the prime minister's security men immediately after they were arrested? As they were the only people who could have given information about a wider conspiracy if there was one should they not have been kept alive? We got no answers. All we learned was that Satwant Singh was seriously wounded but still alive and Beant Singh was dead.

Rajiv arrived late that evening and drove straight to Rashtrapati Bhavan, where he was sworn in as prime minister of India in a ceremony that was hurried and private. I was in my sister's house on Jantar Mantar Road when he made his first speech as prime minister. We watched him on television. In a calm, emotionless voice, he said India had lost a great leader. Someone who was not just his mother but the mother of the country, or words to that effect. Then he stopped and stared sadly at the camera while Doordarshan showed shots of H.K.L. Bhagat and his supporters beating their breasts and shouting, '*Khoon ka badla khoon se lenge.*' Blood will be avenged with blood.

'He should have said something about not resorting to violence,' my brother-in-law said with a worried frown. As a Sikh and the owner of the Imperial Hotel on Janpath he had reason to worry.

'Had Mrs Gandhi been in his place,' my sister said angrily, 'the first thing she would have said is if one Sikh is killed you will defile the memory of my mother or something like that. Why do you think he didn't say anything? Why are they showing shots of those people shouting "*Khoon ka badla khoon se lenge*"?'

'Because he wants revenge,' said my brother-in-law quietly, 'there are rumours that attacks on Sikhs have already started. A Sikh taxi driver in our hotel arrived this evening with his hair shorn off. He said he was surrounded by a mob in East Delhi and they tore off his turban and forcibly cut his hair.'

'There will be a bit of anger,' my sister said, 'that's only natural. But I'm sure it won't get out of hand because Rajiv is a decent man. He will definitely not allow innocent people to be killed. Right?'

'I don't know,' I said uncertainly, 'he is a good man but he will now be surrounded by Mrs Gandhi's advisors and they are the sort of people who will tell him that he needs to show the Sikhs that they cannot get away with killing a prime minister. It worried me to see his party MPs among the people shouting those slogans on television just now. Why would they show that on Doordarshan unless they were trying to send a message?'

The killings did not begin immediately.

The day after Mrs Gandhi's death was one of those especially beautiful days that you see in Delhi when summer ends and winter has not quite come. There was a light breeze that smelled of cold weather and dead leaves. The sky was the palest, most translucent blue flecked with gold. The menace I had sensed in the air the day before was so absent that when the *Sunday Times*, London, asked if I would go to Amritsar and write a piece on the mood there and how Sikhs were reacting to the assassination I readily agreed. Delhi seemed completely calm. But, as a precaution, I tried to get my mother to come and babysit Aatish, who would be alone with his ayah all day.

My mother refused to come and ticked me off for being paranoid. 'I know this country better than you,' she said, 'and there may be a bit of anger but there will be no killings or anything like that.'

By that evening there were mobs trying to burn down my parents' house in Panchsheel Park, where they now lived, and wandering about other exclusive residential enclaves of south Delhi looking for Sikhs to kill.

I took an early morning flight to Amritsar with the intention of returning late the same afternoon. Amritsar was so peaceful that I realized as soon as I got to the Golden Temple that nothing was going to happen here. Where there had been so much violence in the air four months ago there was now a tired sort of peace. I sought out a local politician who had once been in the Congress Party but had resigned when the army attacked the Golden Temple. He lived in a tall, narrow house in a bazaar in the old city, so close to the temple that it was filled constantly with the sound of Sikh scriptures from the temple's loudspeakers. His terrace had a view of the white marble concourse and the sacred tank that was now filled with clean, clear water. On this terrace we talked over a Punjabi breakfast of thick, milky tea and parathas lathered with butter.

He admitted that Sikhs were not unhappy about Mrs Gandhi being assassinated because they saw her death as retribution for desecrating the Golden Temple. He reminded me that anyone who had tried to desecrate this temple in the past had been punished. So were her assassins heroes, I asked. He hesitated for a moment, then admitted this but emphasized that the Sikhs he knew believed that justice had been done.

I met other Sikhs who confirmed this. From talking to Hindus in Amritsar that day I discovered that there were dangerous divisions between the two communities. Hindus were enraged by the assassination and wanted the Sikh community as a whole to be taught a lesson in some way. If this sentiment did not translate into violence in Punjab it was because in most Punjabi cities there are equal numbers of Sikhs and Hindus and in the villages it is Sikhs who are dominant.

It was dusk when my plane landed in Delhi. I remember that it was a typical early winter dusk with grit in the air and the scent of open fires. But there was something else as well and it took me a few moments to realize that what was different was the smoky haze that seemed to have found its way even into the airport's arrivals lounge. Passengers sniffed the air nervously. It could be a short circuit, I heard someone say. But when we came out it became clear that the smoke came from real fires. Big fires.

Outside the terminal was the longest taxi queue I had ever seen. Taxis came and went at such infrequent intervals that when one came I saw people begging each other to be allowed to share it. Some had given up and were standing on the highway flagging down private cars.

'Why are there no taxis?' I asked the pleasant-faced south Indian gentleman in the queue ahead of me.

'They say it's because most of the taxi drivers are Sikhs and they are not leaving their homes because there is violence in the city. They are burning Sikh properties is what my wife told me this morning when she called me in Bombay.'

'As they should, as they should,' said a small, weasel-faced man. 'They must be taught a lesson. Who do they think they are?'

After queuing for an hour I realized it was pointless waiting any longer. I walked to the main road and started walking towards the city. I was desperate to get home and see if Aatish and the rest of my family were safe. My patriotic mother had misunderstood not just the country but even the city she had grown up in. After several cars sped by an elderly gentleman in a black Fiat stopped and asked where I wanted to go.

'Anywhere in the city.'

'I am going to Rajouri Gardens,' he said.

'You can drop me anywhere on the way. Near Teen Murti House. Wherever.'

'Are you a Sikh?'

'No,' I lied.

'Even if you are don't say you are if we get stopped. I was stopped five times on the way to the airport. I came to drop my daughter.'

'Who stopped you?'

'The mobs. They're all over the city.'

The smoke got thicker as we got closer to the city. The streets were empty. The old gentleman drove slowly, hunched forward over the wheel and looking out of the window to see through the smoke. At the Ashoka Hotel, not far from the prime minister's residence, we were stopped by the first mob. There were young men and small boys. The youngest would have been no more than ten. They carried cans of kerosene in their hands and oily rags, and seemed to think they were playing a game. They swarmed all over the little black Fiat, thumping on the bonnet and banging at the windows.

'Any Sikhs here? Any Sikhs? Are there any Sikhs in here? Any Sikhs?'

My elderly companion smiled and pointed to his clean-shaven face saying it should be clear that he was not a Sikh and I was his daughter.

Disappointed, they waved us on. A few minutes later there was another mob and then another and another. On the streets were the remains of smouldering cars. Many of them were taxis with burned bodies slumped over the steering wheel.

'I better drop you home,' my benefactor said. 'I don't think you'll find a taxi anywhere in the city. Where do you live?'

'Golf Links...thank you.'

You can live in a city all your life and not know it at all. I was to discover this in the next three days. The people who lived in the Delhi in which I spent my childhood and growing years were old families of the city, mostly old Sikh families. I remembered the city from winter holidays because in the summer everyone went to Mussoorie or Simla. In winter Delhi was cold, but in a wonderful sort of way. Fires would be lit in the evenings and there would be hot water bottles in our beds and thick quilts made of silk and satin. The days were nearly always sunny and we would spend them in the garden soaking in the sun and eating pine nuts that came from Afghanistan and Kashmir. In this Delhi of big houses and sunny gardens there was not the smallest hint of violence.

So that evening when I got home and heard that the house of Amarjit and Amrita, friends of my sister, had been burned down and that their little girl had barely escaped with her life because her nursery was set on fire while she was asleep in it, I was not so much shocked as overcome by a sense of unreality. It did not seem possible. The story must be an exaggeration, I told my sister when she called. She said she had tried calling Amrita all day and had not been able to get through. One of Amrita's servants later turned up at her house to tell her what happened. Then someone else called to say that a retired general had died of a heart attack when a mob burned down his house in Greater Kailash. Then there were my own stories. My parents had been unable to leave their house because mobs had come hunting for Sikhs from both sides of the street in which they lived. If they had not been saved by a Hindu friend, who tore down the board on the gate with my father's name on it before the mobs arrived, who knows what may have happened.

The next day the violence got worse and it was no longer safe for my sister to continue living in her house on Jantar Mantar Road. She took the children and moved to the house of a Hindu friend. On the way there she had to disguise her two boys as Hindus by making them wear caps and heard her older son tell his six-year-old brother, 'Don't take off your cap on the way or they'll cut off your head.' They did not encounter any mobs, which was lucky for the mobs because my sister's instructions to her driver were to drive right through them instead of stopping. Other members of my family tried hiding in the home of a Hindu politician whom they thought they could trust, only to find that he had alerted the killers instead of protecting them.

Everyone I knew who had friends in political circles called them and told them what was happening in the city. They told them about the police refusing to register cases and the local administration doing absolutely nothing to protect citizens. But the new prime minister did nothing. Not even when senior political leaders like Chandrashekhar and Gandhiji's grandson, Rajmohan Gandhi, went to the home minister personally to urge him to call out the army for help was anything done in those first three days of November to stop the violence.

What we suffered in more genteel parts of the city was nothing. It was from across the Yamuna, where 'resettlement colonies' now formed an endless landscape of shanties that the worst stories came. By the evening of the second day it was clear that we were talking about thousands being killed in the colonies across the river so it was that I went with a group of reporters to East Delhi. Rajat Sharma, not then a famous TV anchor, was among them.

We saw the first bodies as soon as we crossed the river. They looked at first like logs, piled one on top of the other and burning in a large, circular fire that was still smouldering. Sunlight glinting off a gold ring made me look closer and I noticed that what I had thought was a piece of wood was a human arm. We stopped and got out of the car and Rajat started counting.

'Twenty at least,' he said quietly, 'and look over there. On that street are probably the killers.' We were in a small bazaar and behind the shops stood a group of young men and small boys. They grinned and waved at us and the boys pointed to the bodies and then flexed the muscles of their skinny arms like wrestlers.

'They are proud of what they did,' Rajat said with horror in his voice. 'They think they did a good thing.'

We drove through empty streets and bazaars that smelled of burned flesh. There were so many bodies and burned cars that the municipality had given up trying to move them. Rajat said there was no point in picking them up anyway because the morgues were full. He had seen bodies piled up to the ceiling in a morgue that day. Police vans patrolled main roads but in the narrow lanes that led to bazaars and apartment buildings the killers wandered freely, exultant and cheerful.

'It's sick,' I remember Rajat saying, 'it's like the day after Holi. You don't sense any remorse at all.'

One of the other reporters, a Brahmin, tried to analyse the violence by blaming it on the Dalits, who he said had been treated so brutally by high-caste Hindus for centuries that they had no qualms about killing anyone. It was a stupid theory because most of the victims in East Delhi were Dalit Sikhs from Rajasthan.

We had heard that of the resettlement colonies the one that was worst affected was Trilokpuri because the police helped the killers by forcing Sikhs into their homes and then allowing the mobs to burn down their houses. So it was to Trilokpuri that we headed that morning. Trilokpuri is one of the wretchedly poor suburbs that grew out of the wasteland in which Delhi's 'slum dwellers' were dumped when Sanjay Gandhi wanted to 'beautify' the city. There they built themselves one-room, windowless hovels. It was to resettlement colonies like Trilokpuri that new immigrants to the city came because an absence of low-cost housing made rents in more central parts of Delhi prohibitive.

As we got closer to Trilokpuri's narrow alleys, we fell silent. The windows of the car were open and the smell of burned human flesh was so strong we had to cover our mouths and noses. Packs of street dogs foraged in what seemed to be piles of burned garbage. It took us a while to realize that it was bits of human bodies that they were retrieving. I saw a dog chewing at a child's arm. In silence, we parked our car in a street in which every house had been burned and wandered through the roofless husks that remained. In every house there were communal pyres and half-burned bodies.

After the first few houses I decided I had seen enough, and I went back and sat in the car. A policeman walked by, smoking a cigarette, seemingly unperturbed by the carnage. When I asked why the police was not clearing the bodies he said, 'We cannot. The morgues are full and so we will have to cremate them here.'

'Where have the survivors been taken?'

'Women and children have been taken to camps and some are hiding in the gurudwaras.'

'Do you expect more violence?'

'Who knows,' he laughed, 'it depends on what the people at the top want.'

The day before Mrs Gandhi's funeral the violence stopped as suddenly as it had begun. Army trucks appeared in areas where the massacres had taken place and in minutes the mobs vanished. The killers went back to being tailors and carpenters, butchers and political workers. Nobody was punished, no questions asked. Most Indians believed that the Sikhs deserved to be punished as became evident from the massive mandate they gave Rajiv in the election that was to follow. Rajiv Gandhi reflected this mood when some weeks after his mother's funeral he justified the violence. 'When a big tree falls,' he said, 'the earth shakes.'

It took Atal Behari Vajpayee to refute this extraordinarily insensitive comment by responding that Rajiv was a child and did not understand that it is when the earth shakes that trees fall. But Vajpayee as the election was to soon prove was not as much in tune with the times as Rajiv was. And Rajiv was correct in describing his mother as a 'big tree'. She was more than that. Whatever her flaws she continues to be remembered by ordinary Indians as one of the country's greatest prime ministers. What appealed to middle class Indians was her strength and what appealed to illiterate, rural voters was her concern for their needs. She may not have succeeded in lifting them out of poverty but she more than succeeded in convincing India's poorest citizens that she was their leader. Their only leader.

PART 2

13 PRIME MINISTER RAJIV

Short of ordering the sun to rise Rajiv Gandhi could have done almost anything when he began his career as prime minister. It is hard to think of another leader who could have started with more goodwill, love and hope. There was so much that needed to be done. So much he could have done. He could have changed the economic policies that had kept India poor. He could have got rid of the corrupt courtiers who surrounded his mother and created within India's oldest and most important political party a culture of sycophancy and servility. He could have made up for the biggest failures of his mother and grandfather by investing in the areas they had neglected and for which India was already beginning to pay a heavy price. Education, health care, planned urbanization and modern services in rural India. Why he did not take even a tentative step towards a new direction remains a mystery.

For me there was personal disappointment almost from the start. He did nothing to stop the massacre of the Sikhs in those first terrible days of his rule and then went out of his way to justify the barbarism we saw unleashed on the streets of Delhi. I found myself wondering whether the goodness I had always seen as his finest quality had been a deception. The Rajiv I thought I knew would have stopped the bloodshed and would have risked his own life to do so. He would at least have been capable of the ordinary compassion that made my other Hindu friends form vigilante squads in Delhi's more genteel residential areas to defend Sikh families against the mobs. But Rajiv and his close aides showed neither concern nor horror at what happened.

When I personally approached a very important member of Rajiv's inner circle on the second day of the violence, I was dismissed as if I were wasting his time. I ran into this gentleman on the grounds of Teen Murti House where Mrs Gandhi's body had been laid in state for the period of public mourning. He was wandering about with an officious air and a walkie-talkie in his hand. When I stopped him and tried to tell him how terrible the violence was in the city he said, 'We know, we know. We're doing something about it.' Then he went back to talking on his walkie-talkie, dismissing me with a wave, as if he had more important things to do than worry about massacres in the streets of Delhi. The killings continued until the arrival of important foreign leaders for the funeral of Mrs Gandhi made it necessary for the violence to end.

The day after Mrs Gandhi's funeral I got a call from Aunty Sita, Arun and Mapu's mother, asking if I would come and see her in her daughter-in-law's family home in Nizamuddin. She was calling a few people, she said, to discuss the 'violence' and what could be done to stop it. Gita Mehta, the writer and Naveen's sister, was invited as well so we went together and Naveen came along out of curiosity. When we arrived we found that the other guests included the maharajas of Patiala and Kapurthala, a cousin of the Maharaja of Patiala, Randhir Singh, Romi Chopra, a Sikh businessman called Parvinder Singh who owned the pharmaceutical company Ranbaxy, and Sudhir Kakar, a psycho-analyst and cousin of Nina.

It was a curious gathering and it seemed obvious that Aunty Sita could not possibly have thought it up on her own. Aunty Sita remains for me one of the loveliest people I have met. She was married into the Kapurthala royal family when she was a girl of thirteen who spoke no English and had grown up somewhere in the wilds of rural India. The Kapurthala family were slavish Francophiles. Her father-in-law was so affected by Versailles that he ordered a palace just like it to be built in his Punjabi kingdom. Aunty Sita's husband took his child bride to Paris where she was taught French and English, dressed by Mainbocher and photographed by Cecil Beaton. She counted among her friends Barbara Hutton and the Duchess of Windsor, and was among the famous beauties of the thirties. After her husband died she behaved as a traditional Indian widow would, wearing only white, and filling her life with prayers and religious ceremonies. But I would always talk to her about her 'buried life and Paris in the spring' and then she would be full of stories and fun. In all the years I had known her I had only once heard her talk about anything vaguely political and this was when she told me about the violence in Kapurthala after Partition and how she and the other royal ladies did their best to help the refugees that were pouring in from across the border. What had persuaded her to call a meeting to discuss political violence?

Nina's mother lived in a small house in the shadow of the tombs of two of Delhi's most famous poets, Amir Khusrau and Mirza Ghalib, but the house was built without any acknowledgement of history or Delhi's architecture. It was modern and Punjabi. Aunty Sita and her guests had gathered in the drawing room where tea was being elegantly served. After some preliminary pleasantries she came quickly to the reason why she had summoned us. She said simply that she wanted to know how 'the violence could be stopped'. We thought she meant the massacres of the Sikhs but she explained that what she meant was the violence that had led to the assassination of Mrs Gandhi.

At this point Gita Mehta, who had been with me to the East Delhi colonies on one of my trips to the killing fields, said in shocked, angry tones that 'the killing of thousands of Sikhs in the past three days had trivialized the death of this one woman'.

It was enough to send Romi Chopra into a hysterical fit. In a voice shaking with rage he berated Gita for saying what she had and then said, 'The Sikhs are on trial. They have to prove their loyalty to this country.'

This outraged all the Sikhs in the room, including Parvinder Singh who was a close friend of Romi. It angered the usually mild-mannered Maharaja of Kapurthala enough for him to say, 'Look. I don't know who you are but I would like you to know that I have put my life on the line for this country in two wars.'

Romi lapsed into a smouldering silence but there was no stopping the other Sikhs present from telling Aunty Sita that they believed that the violence that had to stop was the violence being done against ordinary Sikhs. The Maharaja of Patiala, Amarinder Singh, said he had driven down from Simla the day after Mrs Gandhi was killed and throughout Punjab he saw villages that were lighted up as if it were Diwali. 'If I told you that there was grief over Mrs Gandhi's assassination I would be lying,' he said.

Aunty Sita's tea party deteriorated rapidly into a discussion of the possible consequences of the Sikh massacres and the frightening tensions that they had caused between Hindus and Sikhs. Nobody mentioned Mrs Gandhi any more. On the way out there was a small moment of levity.

Randhir Singh pointed to a painting of the god Krishna as a plump, naked child and told Naveen, 'And this I suppose is the great Hindu stud?'

Did Arun Singh call this meeting on Rajiv's behalf? Or was it just an initiative that Aunty Sita thought was necessary? This bizarre meeting was the first clue I had that Rajiv knew what was happening in Delhi.

Then came the Congress Party's election campaign and I began to wonder seriously whether I had completely misunderstood Rajiv. But, like the rest of India, I was still prepared to give him a chance. Why? Why did India so easily forgive Rajiv for violence that, as prime minister, he was directly responsible for? Why have other leaders, like Narendra Modi, never been forgiven for presiding over similar massacres? I have asked myself this question many times and the only answer I have been able to find is that it was perhaps because Rajiv, for a brief shining moment in Indian history, became for most Indians a living symbol of hope. It was the people who invested him with this hope because there was certainly nothing he said during the election campaign that indicated that he had moved away from the cynical, negative politics that his mother had come to represent in her last years.

The election came less than two months after Mrs Gandhi's assassination and no sooner did the campaign begin than it became clear that the Sikh massacres were going to play an important part. There is little doubt that he must have been told this by the advisors he inherited from Mrs Gandhi because in that first election campaign he ran as prime minister Sikhs, as a community, were maligned as enemies of the country. In newspapers across India the Congress campaign was launched with black-and-white photographs of Sikhs, under which a line of copy asked questions like, 'Can you trust your taxi driver?' Since the campaign material could not have been put together overnight it made many Sikhs ask whether the attack on the Golden Temple had been deliberately planned by Mrs Gandhi in the hope of consolidating the Hindu vote.

There was a menacing note even in Rajiv's campaign speeches, an attitude that implied that if you were not with the Congress Party then you were against India. He accused opposition leaders of being 'traitors' because of being electorally allied with the Akali Dal. But this campaign of hate and distrust was unnecessary. The reason why Indian voters were to give Rajiv the biggest mandate in Indian parliamentary history was because they saw him as a symbol of hope and change.

From the start of the campaign it was clear that Rajiv was undefeatable but one of the few people who either could not, or would not, see this was M.J. Akbar. He refused to accept that there was a 'wave' the likes of which I had personally never seen in any election. Not even in 1977 when there was that subterranean but massive wave against Mrs Gandhi and the Emergency.

When the election came Akbar was, for some reason, displeased with me and as punishment I was not allowed to cover any important constituencies or travel in states like Uttar Pradesh and Bihar. Those he was pleased with were sent to cover constituencies where big and glamorous battles were being fought, like Allahabad where Amitabh Bachchan had been enlisted to take on Hemwati Nandan Bahuguna. They duly reported what Akbar wanted to hear, that there was no Rajiv wave. I was restricted to Delhi and Haryana and reported that there was a wave in Rajiv's favour of quite phenomenal proportions. Since Akbar was predicting a victory for Charan Singh's Lok Dal, or some other equally bizarre result, this made him even more irritated with me.

I managed to persuade him to let me go to Madhya Pradesh, where Vasundhara Raje was contesting her first Lok Sabha election, against her better judgement, from the constituency of Bhind. She knew that there was a Rajiv wave and that as a Bharatiya Janata Party (BJP) candidate she had little chance of winning even from a constituency that had once been part of her father's kingdom, the former princely state of Gwalior. She would have liked very much not to contest at all that year, but had been unable to defy her mother.

Bhind was a wild, primitive place in those days, full of dacoits and lawlessness. I had last been there when Phoolan Devi surrendered. She was by then the most famous woman dacoit in Indian history for having massacred twenty-two upper-caste men in a village in which she had been confined for close to three weeks and gangraped. I remembered from her surrender, two years before this election, that there was almost no place in the entire constituency where a woman candidate could safely spend the night. So it did not surprise me that Vasundhara had set up her campaign headquarters in the Rani Mahal in Gwalior, a few hours' drive from Bhind.

The Rani Mahal was where the Rajmata had lived since her husband's death more than twenty years ago when Vasu was only eight. The palace was being used as the base camp for Rajmata Sahib's campaign as well. She was not contesting in this election but was there to campaign for Atal Behari Vajpayee who was contesting from Gwalior against her son. In what was celebrated in the press as an astute political move on Rajiv's part the Maharaja of Gwalior had been moved to this constituency, at the last minute, to defeat the BJP's president and most popular leader. Madhav Rao usually contested from Guna, another seat that was once part of the Gwalior princely state, and had never contested from Gwalior before. So this became one of the most interesting constituencies in the 1984 election. Madhav Rao Scindia had set up his campaign headquarters in the main Gwalior palace. The family and political drama that was being played out in the various wings of this sprawling royal residence would have made most Bollywood fantasies seem insipid.

The journey to Gwalior on a night train from Delhi in freezing weather in December is one of the more memorable of my life and for the wrong reasons. The only good thing about the journey was that I had a coupé to myself. But I left in such a hurry that I had forgotten to bring any bedding. The shawl I used as a blanket was too thin and by midnight it was impossible to sleep so I spent the remaining hours of the journey counting the cockroaches that raced about the floor and wondering if I could work up the courage to use the filthy lavatory or risk bursting my bladder.

When the first hint of dawn came through the dirt-encrusted shutters of my coupé I noticed that we were at the edge of a town. Through the misty darkness I spotted men wrapped in blankets defecating by the side of the track. They sat beside kerosene lanterns. The air smelled of shit and coal dust. Small bits of coal grit drifted in through the window and settled on the sill. I looked at my watch. It was 5 a.m. This must be Gwalior, I thought, and wondered why it looked so much worse than I remembered it.

Had it looked so bad when Vasu's ancestors ruled? I smiled to myself when I remembered asking her this once and her answer. 'Don't be stupid. Obviously not, because no maharaja would want a capital city that made him look bad. It's after Independence that cities deteriorated because they started to be built by nameless officials.' She had a point. The cities of my childhood were all beautiful and salubrious. And princely capital cities like Jaipur, Jodhpur, and Hyderabad particularly so. They had deteriorated under our 'socialist' rulers who thought of town planning as a luxury

India could not afford because we were always 'a poor country'. Beyond the narrow streets of the half-village half-town, on a hill veiled by mist and the smoke of open fires I saw the dark shadow of a massive fort. This was Gwalior.

The train halted for no obvious reason under a tangle of cables in the middle of nowhere and I was convinced that if it did not move soon I would freeze to death. I longed for some tea and as if in answer to my prayers a small boy, no more than twelve years old, materialized bearing a basket filled with terracotta cups and tea in a battered aluminum kettle. I bought three cups and drank them with the extra pleasure I always felt when I drank Indian railway tea. It was the terracotta cups that gave it that special flavour.

'Chai, garam chai,' the young boy yelled as he jumped from the steps of one carriage to the next deftly pouring tea into the terracotta cups from his battered kettle and collecting the bits of small change he was handed. He wore a tattered sweater and had wrapped a thin scarf around his head to keep out the cold. He had no shoes on his feet. Nearly forty years of socialism and this is what Indian children looked like, I found myself thinking. Children in rags always made me curse the economic policies that had reduced India, which had every reason to be rich, to a state of destitution and degradation. I was convinced that this was the result of the controlled, centralized economy created in the name of Nehruvian socialism.

Would Rajiv be able to change things? Maybe, I thought, as I sipped the hot milky liquid with its faint scent of mud. Maybe. If he got enough of a majority in Parliament he could do pretty much what he wanted because the country was desperate for change. Wherever I had been during the campaign I had noticed that instead of there being a sympathy wave for Indira Gandhi she had almost been forgotten and what people seemed to be voting for was change. Whatever my personal disappointment with Rajiv I understood well that to the average Indian voter he represented this change.

The country he had inherited from his mother was defeated, impoverished and dismal. A place in which more than 90 per cent of the people lived without such bare necessities as clean water, electricity and rudimentary public services. Government schools and hospitals, especially in rural India, were so bad that they provided neither education nor health care to those who were too poor to afford better private services. The economy was so tightly controlled by Mrs Gandhi's licence raj that it created neither jobs nor prosperity. The ultimate dream of young Indians in the eighties was to get a 'government job'. Rajiv had a real chance to sell India a bigger dream, I found myself thinking, as I watched the tea boy make his rounds.

After a mysteriously long halt the train finally began to move. When it pulled into Gwalior's dilapidated, smelly shed of a railway station I wondered if I would be able to find a taxi so early in the morning and was relieved to see that Vasu had sent someone to fetch me. He greeted me with a courtly bow, picked up my bag and led me to the white Ambassador that was waiting close enough for me not to need to walk too far in the cold.

We drove through narrow, smoky streets. Teashops were beginning to open for the day and the smell of boiling milk drifted through the closed windows of the car. At the end of an empty bazaar we turned left down a small road that led to one of the palace's ornate wrought-iron gates. The road tapered off as we drove past newly built houses that crowded together in rows on both sides. Vasu's mother had sold part of the palace grounds to a builder when they needed money to repair the Rani Mahal.

We drove into a courtyard with high, white walls and a big neem tree in its centre. The driver parked under it and the man who came to receive me guided me towards an enclosed veranda. It was used as a sort of reception area, beyond which lay two vast drawing rooms, a dining room and terraces that went down to a large, formal garden over which in the distance towered the fort. It was some distance away but so enormous that it seemed closer than it was. I walked up the wide marble staircase that led to the bedrooms and was happy to spot Vasu's maid standing outside her door as I was worried about stumbling into the wrong suite at so ungodly an hour. The Rani Mahal was small as palaces go but still large enough for visitors to get lost in.

Vasu's lovely, high-ceilinged sitting room was blissfully warm. Electric heaters were everywhere and she sat in front of one of them drinking tea and reading a newspaper. Campaign material lay in heaps all over the room and there was a general atmosphere of warmth and good cheer except on the face of the candidate. She gave me a gloomy look and said, almost before saying hello, that she wished she had not allowed her mother to persuade her to stand from Bhind.

'There is a Rajiv wave,' she said sadly, 'as a BJP candidate what chance do I have when they say that even Atalji might lose in Gwalior.'

'There is a Rajiv wave,' I agreed, 'a huge Rajiv wave everywhere. But do you think it's enough for your brother to be able to defeat Atalji?'

'Possibly,' she said, 'I can't see the Maharaja of Gwalior losing the first election he has ever fought from the constituency of Gwalior.'

'Well, we have to admit it was pretty clever of Rajiv to move your brother from Guna after Atalji had already announced that he was contesting from Gwalior. Another similar move was getting Amitabh Bachchan to stand against Bahuguna in Allahabad...they say Bahuguna is going to lose badly. Anyway, I am planning to go with your brother this morning on the campaign trail so by this evening I should have a pretty clear idea of how things look. The first story I have to file from here is on the Vajpayee–Scindia battle.'

'Right. You can come with me to Bhind tomorrow or the day after. But have some breakfast first.' Even as she spoke a maid walked in carrying mugs of hot tea and a plate full of hot buttered toast. Vasu left for her constituency shortly after breakfast and I prepared myself for the campaign trail with a hot *balti* bath that involved pouring masses of water over myself from a large, old-fashioned brass bucket. Suitably refreshed I then wandered off towards Jai Mahal, the main palace. When I came to its massive gates sunlight was just beginning to gild its roofs making it look more beautiful than it usually did. Once a magnificent palace, its orderly collection of white-washed Indo-European buildings had for long been in a state of decay.

It was still early in the morning and there was nobody guarding the gates so I walked unchecked through a vast garden filled with weeds and untended flowerbeds to the main porch in which stood a convoy of white Ambassadors. I identified Scindia's as the one covered in marigold garlands. It was my bad luck that the first person I met in the many-pillared veranda was one of Scindia's courtiers who knew that I was a friend of Vasu. I was worried that the family divisions would make Scindia give me a less than cordial welcome. The courtier's welcome was certainly less than friendly.

'What are you doing here?' he asked with a cold smile and a puff of his cigarette.

'Covering the election.'

'From the Rani Mahal? '

There was no point in lying. 'Yes. And I'm hoping to go with your candidate today to see his campaign,' I said with a cheerful smile.

He stared back coldly. 'Wait here. I'll speak to HH (His Highness) and see if we can accommodate you.'

'I can bring my own car.'

'Wait here,' he said again and disappeared into the courtyard.

It was too cold to sit and wait so I walked up and down the veranda, rubbing my hands together to keep them from freezing. On the walls were sepia pictures from another time. Princes in full regalia from an event in the thirties, princes at tiger hunts and princes with formally dressed white people. More recent pictures showed Scindia in school uniform, playing cricket, in formal attire for some ceremony and being invested as maharaja when his father died. On one of my perambulations I peeped into the courtyard into which the courtier had disappeared and saw the white crystal Lalique fountain that I remembered from an earlier visit. Lalique made many things for the Gwalior palace in the thirties, when it was built, and most of them could still be found in closed rooms and hidden courtyards around the palace. Vasu and I had once spent a week in Gwalior before the family trouble began and had wandered for hours through rooms filled with magnificent Lalique furniture. Beds, trolleys, dressing tables, chairs, all piled up in dusty rooms that smelled of old carpets. Most of the rooms in the Jai Vilas Palace remained unused after Vasu's father's death. Her mother believed in austerity and simple living.

I was beginning to wonder if the courtier had deliberately forgotten about me when a car drove up and an American journalist hopped out with a sunny smile and a cheerful wave. He demanded to know where the candidate was, and when I told him that I had not seen him yet he said with feigned horror that 'no candidate would dare keep a journalist waiting in the US'. He was about to barge into the palace demanding to see 'the candidate' when the courtier reappeared with a liveried waiter behind him bearing steaming cups of tea on a silver tray. He was more charming to the American journalist than he had been to me and said His Highness would be down shortly. He added that he had talked to HH and the plan was for me to travel with Scindia in his car for the first part of the day and to exchange places with the American journalist for the next part of the trip. This way we could get separate interviews.

No longer did we have to wait in the cold. The courtier led us through the courtyard with its white crystal fountain, past carriages from another time into a smaller courtyard and to a small, warm drawing room. The American journalist stared at the portraits of bejewelled princes on the walls, the Persian carpet and the Lalique drinks trolley and had begun a discussion about how well the maharajas lived despite the poverty of their subjects when Scindia appeared surrounded by party workers. He acknowledged our presence with a smile and a brief nod and headed straight for the cavalcade of white Ambassadors, with us racing after him. He indicated that I should sit in the back of his car with him. In front, beside the driver, sat an attendant with an old Louis Vuitton picnic box on his lap. The car smelled of marigold garlands and some sort of scent.

On our way to the first meeting, which was in the city, Scindia asked if I was staying next door. When I said I was he said with what seemed to me genuine feeling that he was sorry that his sister had been forced to contest her first election from a seat she had no chance of winning because there was a 'Rajiv wave'. I conceded that there was a wave and that if Vasu had a choice she would not have contested from Bhind but pointed out that she could not possibly have defied her mother. He nodded but seemed unconvinced. Before the conversation could proceed further we turned into a street of old-fashioned houses with wooden balconies on which women stood with baskets of rose petals that they showered on our convoy. In the street were party workers in white who shouted, '*Har vote pe naam likh diya*, Madhavrao Scindia!' On every vote we have written the name Madhavrao Scindia. In Hindi the slogan has a resonance that is lost in translation.

Scindia got out of the car and joined his hands in greeting. Masses of rose petals instantly showered down on his head from the balconies of the houses on both sides of the street. When I looked up I noticed that the women throwing them from the balconies smiled flirtatiously and half covered their faces. Party workers became increasingly frenzied as the narrow street filled up with passersby who stopped to see their maharaja. As I watched them I wondered if their enthusiasm was for Scindia, as their maharaja, or for Rajiv. He seemed to read my thoughts because when he got back into the car he said, 'See what I mean? It's like no other election I have ever seen. But I think it is more for Rajiv than for me, all this enthusiasm.'

I asked if he thought this was because of a 'sympathy wave' and he said without hesitation that his impression was that people wanted change. They wanted everything to change, he said. They wanted the officials who misused their power and failed to deliver public services to be curbed, a new kind of younger politician to take charge and for their lives to improve visibly. They believed all this would happen overnight after Rajiv became prime minister, he added, and admitted he was worried that Rajiv would not be able to live up to such expectations. As someone who had been a politician for more than a decade by then he knew how entrenched the old system was and how difficult it would be to get rid of those who had a vested interest in keeping it intact.

Gwalior in the eighties was a very small town. The old city, built in the days when it was still ruled by princes, consisted of an orderly collection of whitewashed, low-roofed houses and bazaars in the area that lay between the Jai Vilas Palace and the fort. At its edges were beginning to appear extensions of the town built in more recent times. These consisted mainly of rows of houses for officials of the government of Madhya Pradesh. They were identical, built with minimum imagination and at a deliberate distance from where the people lived. We drove down one of these newer roads and before we knew it were outside Gwalior's municipal limits, driving on a bumpy road past small splashes of rice fields in an otherwise cheerless countryside with signs of desperate poverty in the villages.

The road got bumpier the further we got from the city and every now and then Scindia's cavalcade would stop to greet villagers who waited by the roadside bearing garlands. After an hour or so we drove off the main road on to a dirt trail just wide enough for a car to travel on. Scindia said his first rural meeting that day was in a small village where he used to come with his father for hunts. 'Shikar' was just an excuse, he said, for his father to spend a few days camping in the rural wilds to hear and understand the problems faced by people in the villages.

As we got closer to this village the road became narrower, the countryside wilder. The neat patches of green disappeared and we were suddenly in a dun-coloured landscape of dunes and sandy valleys that undulated and rose in asymmetric disorder. After a few minutes the dirt road became too narrow for Scindia's convoy and we stopped. A group of villagers materialized out of nowhere, leading a small black horse that they offered Scindia. He gave us an embarrassed smile and said he had to get on it or they would think he did not know how to ride a horse. So he rode and the rest of us followed on foot. Our procession swelled as we went along, joined by swarms of young men and small boys. After walking for about half an hour we arrived at the village in which the meeting was due to be held. Small children in rags played in its constricted alleyways oblivious to mounds of fresh cow dung and rotting garbage. The American journalist looked horrified but for us Indians there was nothing unusual about half-starved children and rural squalor.

Scindia got off his horse in the village square and was instantly surrounded by villagers who fell at his feet, joining their palms in a gesture of both supplication and greeting. Some just stared in wonder. A very old man with deep wrinkles on his face and thick glasses stood up and addressed the maharaja, his hands joined as if in prayer.

'Your Highness, why did you take so long to come to us?' he said. 'Why did you not come earlier to see how we have suffered since the days when your respected and honourable grandfather, Madhav Maharaj, came to our village regularly just to make sure his officials were not cheating us? What days those were, days of plenty and prosperity. If the harvest failed or the crops were damaged by bad weather Madhav Maharaj would excuse us from paying taxes.'

When he finished Scindia stood up and raised his hands above his head in greeting. It was as if the whole village had come to hear what he had to say. Conscious that some of the adulation was for him personally, as the heir of the maharaja they revered, he spoke first of the old days.

His speech went something like this. 'This may be the first time I have come to this village but we know that my family has connections that go back more than half a century. As a child I came here with my father, and to this day I remember how delicious the food was that we would eat here at the end of a day's shikar.' His audience applauded. He smiled. 'But now I come to you not as a maharaja but as an ordinary man who wants your vote so we can bring about in India a generational change under the leadership of our young and dynamic new leader.' The applause was loud and long. I noticed that the emphasis of Scindia's speech was on the new rather than on what had passed. After his speech was over he got back on the horse and our procession wended its way back to the main road where the cars waited. Then we were off to the next village, and the next.

By late afternoon my American friend had seen as much as he needed to of local colour and we agreed we should go back to the city.

We drove back in his car and I asked to be dropped off in a bazaar that was not far from the Rani Mahal and wandered about trying to gauge the mood. I was already certain that Scindia would win but knowing that Vajpayee was very popular I wanted to see if urban shopkeepers, the traditional voters his party banked on, were still on his side. It did not take long to discover that although Vajpayee had supporters in this town, they were upset with him for having been an absentee MP. They resented his almost total absence since the previous election and said that even now with the campaign nearly over he had not held a single meeting in Gwalior. They said they had heard he was somewhere in southern India and that he had broken his leg but they hoped he would not use this to get their sympathy. They were willing to give Vajpayee a chance but it seemed to me that they had made up their minds to vote for Scindia.

That evening, when Vasu arrived defeated and drained from having spent yet another discouraging day travelling around Bhind, I told her this. She suggested that we tell Rajmata Sahib that Atalji should not begin his campaign in Gwalior by using his broken leg as an excuse for not having come earlier to his own constituency. This we did at dinner that evening and Rajmata Sahib said, without looking up from the simple vegetarian meal on her silver thali, 'I know that my son is going to win.' This sent her lieutenant and political mentor Sardar Angre into a fury and, as he always did at the mention of Scindia's name, he started to spit venom about his 'cowardice' and his unsuitability to be a maharaja. It was the sort of thing Angre said so often about Scindia that none of us reacted but after dinner was over Vasu decided that we had to find some other way to get a message through to Vajpayee.

By a fortuitous coincidence Jaswant Singh arrived in Gwalior later that evening. He was at the time a relatively unimportant member of the BJP but was known to be close to Atalji so Vasu and I tried to convince him that he should advise Vajpayee not to begin his campaign speeches by making excuses for his broken leg. Jaswant Singh, who went on to hold important portfolios like external affairs, finance and defence in Vajpayee's government, appeared not to have taken our advice seriously for when Atalji addressed his first public meeting in Gwalior he pointed to his plastered leg and said he would have been there earlier had it not been for his leg. He sounded defensive and apologetic and the speech he made was one of the most uninspired I had ever heard him make. He spent the rest of the election canvassing support from door to door, telling people how he was as much from Gwalior as the maharaja was, but came from an ordinary family and understood what it meant to be deprived because unlike his opponent he had not grown up in the privileged cocoon of a palace.

It made no difference. When Rajiv arrived for Scindia's grand finale, just before campaigning ended, the rally he addressed was so huge that people said they had never seen such a big election meeting in Gwalior. For me a new feature at this rally was the visibly heightened security. When Mrs Gandhi used to travel she usually had one escort car with a handful of sleepy policemen in it. Rajiv Gandhi and Arun Singh, who was now Rajiv's closest political aide, arrived in a convoy of white Ambassadors, most of which had their rear doors ripped out with commandos in black combat fatigues pointing automatic weapons in all directions.

What I remember most about Rajiv's speech was his attack on the opposition leaders whom he described as 'enemies of India'. He explained, as he had done in speeches throughout the campaign, that his reason for charging the opposition leaders with treason was because they had allied with the Akali Dal and other secessionist forces. Mixed with this unfair attack on legitimate opposition leaders and political parties were promises of change and a shining new future for India. He spoke in stilted, unsure Hindi but the vast crowd was not there to hear him so much as to see him. Compared to the aging, unattractive politicians that most Indians were used to he looked so young, so handsome, as he stood next to an equally young and handsome Maharaja of Gwalior that the aura of the young leaders was palpable even to us cynical hacks in the press enclosure.

The next time I saw Rajiv Gandhi was after he had won the largest mandate in Indian parliamentary history. Out of 543 seats in the Lok Sabha he ended up winning 416 with the second largest party being N.T. Rama Rao's regional Andhra party, the Telegu Desam, with 30 seats. The Marxist parties came third with 22 seats and the Bharatiya Janata Party was reduced to a humiliating 2 seats.

The election results came on a cold winter morning. I remember waking up to find a fog so thick and white outside the windows of my barsati that I could not see the plants on my terrace. Delhi has short winters, but there are days in December and January that can be so cold that anyone who has the option chooses to stay home glued to the nearest heater. This was one of them. If it were not for the election results I would have stayed at home.

There was another reason I did not look forward to going to the office that day. I was certain that Rajiv would win convincingly and knew that this would inevitably cause more tension between Akbar and me. Akbar had convinced himself, despite abundant evidence to the contrary, that there was no 'Rajiv wave'. I had discovered by then that his political analysis could often be based on emotions rather than on empirical evidence and for reasons that were not entirely clear he was at the time of the general election in 1984 a passionate supporter of the opposition parties and against the Congress Party.

Weeks before Mrs Gandhi was killed he had sent me off to the district of Ballia in eastern Uttar Pradesh for a long article on Chandrashekhar, the opposition leader he believed could defeat Mrs Gandhi in the coming election. Chandrashekhar was seen, by political analysts, as a possible candidate for prime minister. This was because he had between January and June 1983 walked from Kanyakumari, the southernmost tip of India, to Mahatma Gandhi's memorial, Rajghat, in Delhi with the stated aim of seeing first-hand the problems that ordinary Indians faced. The gesture was Gandhian, at a time when Gandhian idealism was totally absent from Indian politics, and so the 'padayatra' got a lot of support from ordinary people and the media. On Akbar's instructions I walked some distance with Chandrashekhar on this 'padayatra' and observed that he was more interested in getting to Delhi as fast as possible than in understanding the problems of the ordinary people he met on the long journey. But I wrote good things about the 'padayatra' because I knew this was what Akbar wanted and because at least Chandrashekhar was trying to infuse a new spirit into the cynical atmosphere of Indian politics.

Ballia was a dismal, primitive place but I noticed that the people loved Chandrashekhar. Not so much for what he had done for them but because they were proud that one of their own had become an important national leader. Chandrashekhar spent his growing years in Ibrahimpatti, a village near Ballia town, walked 10 kilometres to school every day and lived in a hut. His constituents liked him for having overcome these difficulties to become a national leader. They appeared not to mind that their hero had done so little for his constituency that it had remained a rough backwater in spite of his political success. To get to Chandrashekhar's village we had to get off at a railway station that did not have a platform. The photographer I was with happened to be from Ballia and was used to jumping out of trains when there was no platform. He showed me how to jump on to the filthy tracks and clamber up on to a decrepit platform that existed somewhere beyond the expanse of tracks.

When we got to Ibrahimpatti I saw that Chandrashekhar, an avowed socialist, had spent more money on building a temple for the people of Ballia than on a hospital. The temple was built in an elaborate south Indian style with many carved statues and arches and steps that led down to an attractive tank. Devotees flocked from far and near, but the hospital nearby, another of Chandrashekhar's projects, remained unfinished. Another thing that worried me was that the man who wanted to be our next prime minister had built himself a large farmhouse in nouveau-riche Delhi architectural style. And, in what seemed to me an act of disturbing vanity, he had left intact the hut in which he was born in a corner of the garden of his new estate. Unfortunately for Chandrashekhar his dreams of becoming prime minister died with Indira Gandhi's assassination. When he did eventually become prime minister, a decade later and only for a few brief months, it was ironically with Rajiv's support.

On the morning of the election results when I got to the office nearly everyone was already there drinking tea and warming themselves in front of electric heaters. Akbar's favourites looked a little sullen and I thought this must indicate that they had picked up more than a whiff of the Rajiv wave despite what they wrote in their reports. When early results confirmed a landslide for Rajiv we, the non-favourites, whispered gleefully about how Akbar had allowed his personal feelings to get in the way of his political judgement. The favourites treated us to filthy looks and pretended to be busy writing stories of great importance.

By late afternoon, when it was clear that Rajiv Gandhi was likely to win more seats in Parliament than any prime minister ever, Kewal Sahib suggested I go to his house and see what was happening there. I could not get away fast enough because I knew Akbar would not want to see me on a day when I was proved right and he so decisively wrong. The *Telegraph* office was in an old-fashioned colonial building called the IENS building on Rafi Marg in which many regional newspapers had their Delhi offices. The minute I stepped out into the corridor that led to the warren of small newspaper offices I noticed the celebratory mood. Journalists chatted to peons and everyone seemed to be revelling in Rajiv's victory as if it were their personal achievement. From Rafi Marg it was a short drive to Mrs Gandhi's house on Safdarjang Road, where Rajiv and Sonia had continued to live. By the time I got there all the results were in and it was clear that this was a victory on a scale that not even Rajiv could have dreamed of. The street that led to the house was filled with dancing party workers and the sound of drums. Boxes of soggy sweets were being passed around and marigold garlands tossed in the air as the slogans became more frenzied: 'Rajiv Gandhi *zindabad*.' Long Live Rajiv Gandhi. It was as if Mrs Gandhi had died a long, long time ago.

The gates to the house were locked but journalists were being allowed in along with more well-heeled supporters who came bearing flowers. Rajiv and Sonia stood at the entrance to the house receiving them. At some distance stood a group of senior political reporters. I went and stood with them. The drums and slogans got louder and more hysterical as the crowds outside the closed gates swelled, leaving little room for friends and well-wishers to pass. They came in looking dishevelled and bemused. Among them were businessmen bearing bouquets of orchids and senior bureaucrats with obsequious smiles on their faces. And there were socialites, friends and foreign diplomats.

Rajiv noticed our little group and signalled to someone to tell us to wait inside Mrs Gandhi's old office. We were led into a small, narrow room with a long conference table occupying most of it. On the yellow-washed walls were portraits of the late leader. I thought I recognized one as the painting by M.F. Hussain of Mrs Gandhi as the goddess Durga. It had been his tribute to the Emergency and was considered such an outrageous act of sycophancy on the part of India's most celebrated artist that the painting became a blot on Husain's reputation. Below the portraits, on a side table, lay wilting bouquets and garlands filling the warm room with the scent of dying roses. Before Rajiv arrived we whispered among ourselves that this room must have been Mrs Gandhi's private conference room.

It was here that she was headed on the ill-fated morning of 31 October to meet Peter Ustinov and his TV crew. It was hard to believe that it was just two months ago. So much had changed that it felt as if an aeon had gone by since then.

We did not have to wait long before Rajiv arrived. He came in smiling warmly and sat down at the head of the table and because I was seated closest to him, and the only woman in the room, I got to ask the first question.

'Congratulations, prime minister,' I said. He grinned when I called him prime minister. 'How do you read the election results? Do you think this was a sympathy vote or a vote for change?'

'Of course, there was the sympathy factor,' he said carefully, 'but wherever I went I noticed that people seemed to be hungry for change. They are tired of the old kind of politics and want something new.'

'What, sir, will be your first priority?' I am not sure who asked the question but I remember that Rajiv did not hesitate even slightly before answering that his first priority would be to bring peace in Punjab and in the north-eastern states. The problems in India's north-east were part of his political inheritance. Long before Punjab and Kashmir became India's most politically troubled states there had been secessionist movements in the north-eastern states which had been put down by Mrs Gandhi's government with a heavy hand. What complicated an already complex situation was that she had allowed an election to go ahead in Assam in 1983, despite knowing the extent of the seething rage over illegal Muslim immigrants from Bangladesh, and this resulted in a savage massacre of women and children in a village called Nellie. Assam had remained in ferment since then. That morning Rajiv said he was ready to talk to secessionist groups as long as they agreed to give up violence.

Everyone at this first press conference seemed bewitched by Rajiv. Veteran hacks who had long grown accustomed to treating the words of politicians with cynical disdain listened to India's new, young prime minister as if they were determined to believe everything he said. It was a short press conference and after Rajiv left the room we lingered and chatted among ourselves. The consensus was that he was 'prime ministerial material'. When I asked the person who said this why he thought this was so he said, 'I noticed first at Mrs Gandhi's funeral. He showed such grace and dignity and now look at the confidence with which he answered our questions.' Everyone agreed that the priority he was giving to healing the wounds in Punjab was another indication of his 'leadership qualities'. When we came out of the small, warm room we saw that Rajiv had been surrounded by dancing, slogan-shouting party workers who were now being allowed into the house in small groups. They showered him with rose petals and raced each other to garland him. Some fell at his feet, others gazed in wonder as if in the presence of a deity. In India gods are easily invented, and that day Rajiv became a god.

As I watched him standing there, surrounded by supporters, laughing as they covered him in garlands I found myself making a conscious effort to forget the massacres of 3000 innocent Sikhs just two months ago. I told myself that if Rajiv had justified the killing of helpless, ordinary people he had probably done it on someone else's advice. I remained concerned about his lack of compassion but believed that he needed to be given a fair chance. I remembered that he had spent most of his life with people whose compassion was confined to those they met in Delhi's drawing rooms.

Even in those heady first days after his magnificent election victory there were those who had their doubts about Rajiv, but they were very few and were mostly human rights activists and others of 'liberal' disposition who found his justification of the Sikh massacres impossible to forgive.

Among the doubters was the Rajmata of Gwalior and her concerns arose not from political considerations but from what she saw as evil omens. Within a month of Rajiv's becoming prime minister the gas leak happened in Bhopal on the night of 3 December 1984. It must have been a day or two later that Vasu and I had lunch with her mother. We did not know many details then, only that thousands of people had died from a gas leak in the Union Carbide factory in Bhopal, but since the tragedy came right after the Sikh massacres it troubled Rajmata Sahib. She said, 'So many people have died such terrible deaths since he became prime minister...it doesn't bode well.' It was the sort of remark that is hard to forget and it has lain buried in my memory since that winter afternoon.

Almost nobody else in India seemed to have any doubt that Rajiv would be a great prime minister. It would not be untrue to say that the whole of India fell instantly and completely in love with Rajiv Gandhi. He revived in the most pessimistic hearts a tentative, undefined hope. Despite my own doubts I could understand why. He was young, he was not a politician in the traditional sense, during the campaign he had said all the right things about ending corruption and building a new India, and he seemed to radiate a goodness that made people trust him instinctively. Everyone was ready to give him a real chance.

14 EUPHORIC EARLY DAYS AND A PLOT

My problems with M.J. Akbar increased immediately after the election results for reasons that had nothing to do with my abilities as a journalist. I think it was exactly the day after the results that he summoned me and said he would like me to arrange for him to get the first interview Rajiv gave as prime minister. I said I would do my best, of course, but pointed out that now that he was the prime minister I really had very little say in planning his interviews. But, perhaps because of that Sunday lunch I had taken him to so very long ago, he thought I had more influence than I did and insisted that I try. I did. I rang Sonia and told her that my job virtually depended on her being able to do something, and she was sympathetic and promised to help. She tried putting in a word on my behalf with the people who were handling the prime minister's media relations, but was told that Rajiv would have to give his first interview to a Hindi publication.

For reasons unknown and unclear a Hindi women's magazine was chosen for the first interview that Rajiv and Sonia gave together and an apolitical woman journalist was granted the honour. She was so overawed by this extraordinary privilege that she spent most of the article expounding on how she felt about being in the presence of 'our beloved prime minister'. In words of breathless excitement she wrote, 'I still can't believe that I am here in the house of our beloved prime minister and that any minute now he will appear. I wait in a long conference room with paintings of gods and goddesses and our deceased leaders on the walls... I am proud to be here as I have never interviewed a political leader before and that I have now been given the chance to interview a man who is the emperor of the hearts of not just crores of Indians but the hope of the whole of the Third World. A man whom the world is talking about today, a man who has taken time from his busy schedule to talk to me. This makes me excited and a little nervous. What will I ask him about...'

When the interview started she appeared to be at no loss for questions. She asked Rajiv about his childhood, his relationship with his mother, the toys he liked playing with as a child and every other apolitical question she could think of. When it came to Sonia she was totally enraptured and spent a whole page describing every detail of her clothes and make-up. 'A cream-coloured Oriya sari with a red border, red bangles on one wrist and a puja thread on the other. Her brown, dead-straight hair was parted in the middle and pinned back on both sides. She could have been your sister-in-law or mine. Her simplicity was breathtaking.'

In this interview, her first ever, Sonia talked about how she met Rajiv in a restaurant in Cambridge and how it was love at first sight for both of them. She spoke of how she had not been afraid to come to India because 'when you're in love you cannot be afraid'. When she was asked what she had learned from Mrs Gandhi in the twenty years she had lived in the house as a daughter-in-law she said, 'I learned to fast once a week.'

It was this that everyone in the office was laughing about the day the magazine appeared with Rajiv and Sonia, wreathed in happy smiles, on the cover. My colleagues found Sonia's innocent admission that all she had learned from 'one of the most powerful women in the world' was to fast once a week hugely entertaining. I defended her by pointing out that in most of those twenty years she and her husband had stayed as far away as possible from politics. But my colleagues were unconvinced and put me through a virtual inquisition. Did she read books? What were her interests? Did she speak Hindi? Did she like India? Why had she not become an Indian citizen until 1983? What were her connections with Maruti, Sanjay Gandhi's automobile company that never produced a single car? There was hostility in their questions and it was the first time I realized that Sonia, because she was a foreigner, could be a liability for our new prime minister.

After the interview to the Hindi magazine appeared the pressure on me to try and get Akbar the next interview became intense. I needed the job I had with the *Telegraph* because I was bringing up Aatish on what I earned from it. My mother paid the rent for my barsati but was not ready to pay for anything else. I made ends meet by borrowing from either Vasu or my sister towards the end of every month and when Aatish's clothes did not come from Sonia they usually came from his cousins, who were twins and, luckily, just two years older.

Akbar probably did not realize how much I depended on what I earned from the job he had so generously given me but Sonia did. She went out of her way to persuade whoever was in charge of the prime minister's media relations to allow Akbar to do the first political interview with Rajiv. When she finally succeeded she rang me late one evening to say that the interview had been fixed and she wanted me to give Akbar the news so that it would appear as if it was my efforts that had got him the interview. She said that Akbar should get to Raipur the next day so that he could fly back to Delhi with Rajiv and do the interview then. I remember thinking even as I passed on the news that Raipur was too far away for him to be able to get there by the following day but somehow Akbar managed, and when he returned to Delhi he had become Rajiv Gandhi's most ardent devotee.

I remember walking into the office soon after Akbar returned to find him in the middle of a dissertation on the virtues of Rajiv Gandhi. He looked at me, and had the grace to look embarrassed for a moment, but then he went on about why he believed that Rajiv was likely to be the best prime minister that India could possibly have. Behind his back there was much mirth and merriment in the office over the transformation that had come over him and someone with a 'reliable source' in high places reported that Mani Shankar Aiyar, who handled Rajiv's relations with the media, was wandering about rubbing his hands in glee, saying, 'One interview was all it took to have the great rebel editor in our pocket.'

Akbar treated assignments as if they were rewards to be handed out for what he considered 'good' behaviour. So when he told me that I should prepare to go to Pakistan to do a story on the aftermath of a referendum that Zia-ul-Haq had just held to legitimize his 'democratic' credentials I was not sure if he was sending me because he thought I would do a good job or as a reward for arranging the interview. The referendum was so obviously a fraudulent attempt by Zia to prove that he was not a hated military dictator that it could easily have been told from India. It was clear from reports in the Indian newspapers that the question people were asked was phrased in a way that would force them to say 'yes' to Zia's rule. If there were not enough 'yes' votes they would be managed. But I had not been to Pakistan in five years and wanted to discover the extent to which secessionist groups in Punjab were being backed by the Pakistani government.

So, within weeks of Rajiv becoming prime minister I found myself on a plane to Lahore on a winter afternoon. It was so cold in Delhi that I wore leather pants and a thick jacket which, I realized from the stares that my attire drew at Lahore airport, was wholly inappropriate attire in Zia's Islamized country. Not having been here since the process of Islamization began I had no idea how much Pakistan had changed but sensed the difference from the moment I landed in Lahore. It was not just from the way my Western clothes attracted attention but from a prayer room that I noticed for the first time at the airport and from the way women were more demurely dressed and men more bearded.

In Lahore I met old friends, spent long evenings talking about dictatorship and democracy, heard that Salmaan Taseer was in jail, and before heading off to Islamabad drove to Nankana Sahib, where one of the most revered gurudwaras in the Sikh religion commemorates the birthplace of the founder of the Sikh religion, Guru Nanak.

My visit to Nankana Sahib was technically illegal since my visa allowed me to go only to Karachi, Lahore and Islamabad, but I thought it was worth taking the risk because I had heard that this was where young Sikh boys had gone after the attack on the Golden Temple. Some were former members of Bhindranwale's army and others had crossed the border simply to escape the 'mopping up operations' that the Indian Army had conducted in Punjab's villages after Operation Blue Star. On this visit to Nankana Sahib I discovered two things. First, that the village in which the historic gurudwara exists was the ancestral village of my grandmother. She was a Mann from Mannanwala, and the grubby little village we drove through on the way to the gurudwara turned out to be the very same Mannanwala. I found this out by accident when my Pakistani driver stopped in the crowded bazaar to ask the name of the village. After Partition my grandmother had been so reluctant to talk about the country she was forced to leave that she had told me very little about what it was like, but she had proudly mentioned the name of her ancestral village. Since I was in the village illegally and did not want to draw attention to myself by seeking out my grandmother's family home, we drove straight through the village to the Nankana Sahib gurudwara. Later, when I told her I had driven through Mannanwala by accident on my way to Nankana Sahib, she asked me if I had gone to her childhood home and was very disappointed that I had not made the effort.

When we got to the temple I discovered, through discreet inquiries over tea with a very frightened Indian priest, that a large number of Sikh youths had indeed come here six months earlier and had all been taken to Faisalabad Jail. This puzzled me at the time but some months later in Amritsar, I found out from a senior police officer that they had caught a group of Sikh terrorists who claimed they had been trained to use automatic weapons and make bombs by Pakistani army officers in Faisalabad Jail.

When I got to Islamabad I managed to get a short interview with the military dictator himself. It was my first and last meeting with Zia-ul-Haq and I have to say that I found him utterly repellant. With his greased down, badly dyed black hair and his permanent smile under his caterpillar-like moustache he looked as if he were a clown playing a role. Except, he was no clown. He had been responsible for executing a legally elected prime minister and at the time I met him was in the process of building the religious schools and Islamist institutions that would turn Pakistan into the epicentre of jihadi terrorism it became twenty years later.

I came back to Delhi to find that while I was in Pakistan the inquiry into Mrs Gandhi's assassination had begun and had taken a most peculiar turn. The city was filled with rumours that R.K. Dhawan, Mrs Gandhi's former stenographer who had risen to become her most trusted political aide, was about to be arrested. This was because the judge inquiring into the prime minister's assassination had apparently concluded that 'the needle of suspicion' pointed towards the man who had been by her side all his life and was literally standing beside her when she was killed. It sounded like a completely bizarre plot since nobody could have had less motive to kill Mrs Gandhi than Dhawan. It was from her that he derived his enormous powers. But since all the newspapers I read on the morning after I returned from Pakistan hinted at Dhawan's imminent arrest I decided to pay him a visit.

He lived in Golf Links, five minutes from my barsati but I decided to walk to his house not because he was a neighbour but because I worked out that if he were under surveillance, which he would most certainly be,

I would draw less suspicion to myself if I walked than if I drove up at his gate. A mysterious woman arriving at his home on foot would be harder to identify than one arriving in a car with number plates that could be tracked.

It was a rainy morning and as I walked I glanced backward from under my umbrella to see if I was being followed. A tactic that would have been more useful if I had used it on my way home as I was to find out later that afternoon. R.K. Dhawan came from a Punjabi refugee family that fled to Delhi in 1947 to escape the violence in the newly created Islamic republic next door. I knew from people who had known him since those early days that the family was so poor that as a young boy he was put to work supplementing the family income by selling trinkets on the pavements of Connaught Place. He always denied this and liked to say, like most refugees from Pakistan, that he came from a rich, landed family in Punjab. He must have known that nobody believed his story but he was too powerful for anyone to challenge him even if his incredible rise from humble stenographer to huge riches and great power was always whispered about behind his back.

He was introduced to Mrs Gandhi by his uncle, Yashpal Kapoor, who like Dhawan had begun his career as a stenographer in the prime minister's office and rose to dizzying heights of political power under Mrs Gandhi's patronage. After Kapoor was implicated in the Allahabad High Court judgement that went against Mrs Gandhi in 1975 he faded away, but Dhawan went from strength to strength. He became Mrs Gandhi's gatekeeper, as I had already discovered from my visit to the Sheikha Fatima's palace in Abu Dhabi. Rumour had it that he was the kind of gatekeeper who did not let anybody pass without extracting a toll and that businessmen had given him so many Mont Blanc pens and Rolex watches that he could have opened a shop. With me he had always been helpful and friendly in a completely toll-free way.

That morning I was so worried about being followed that in a silly attempt to confuse hidden spies I stopped a couple of houses away from Dhawan's when I got to the square in which he lived. When I was sure there was nobody watching I went up to his door and rang the bell. Normally even on a rainy day like this his small garden would be crowded with petitioners, power brokers and politicians. That morning it was deserted. Dhawan answered the door himself. He had a cigarette in his hand and looked as if he had not slept all night. His dyed black hair was uncombed, and he looked frightened. When he saw me he tried to smile but gave up and ushered me in with an anxious look.

He led me into a drawing room that could have been a shrine to Mrs Gandhi. There were pictures of her everywhere. An enormous portrait of her covered the main wall and had a garland of fresh marigold flowers hanging on it and a small silver tray with incense below. On every table in the room there were pictures of her. Some in silver frames, and some laminated and standing stiffly on their own. Many had Dhawan in them, always deferential, always at her side, with an expression of utter devotion on his face. He saw me looking at the pictures and said, 'Can you believe that they think I did it?'

This is how I remember the conversation that followed.

'How have they come up with such a bizarre theory?' I asked.

'I wish I knew. All I know is that a few days ago I was called in by the inquiry commission to answer a few questions and now the papers are reporting that I was involved...'

'What sort of questions did they ask?'

'They wanted to know if I had asked for Beant Singh to be brought into the inner security circle and they asked me what I had seen...that day, the day she was killed.'

'Did you? Did you ask for Beant Singh to be brought back?'

'Yes. I mean, I could have. I had never seen him before. I didn't know that he was behaving strangely or anything like that because I have nothing to do with security. But it's possible that someone put his name up to me and I signed something.'

'On the day she was killed...that morning, the first reports said there had been three killers. Did you see a third man?'

'I didn't see anything,' he said wearily, 'it happened so quickly, one minute she was standing there next to me, alive and chatting away, and the next moment she was lying on the ground...bleeding. I can barely remember what happened after this. I must have been in shock because it wasn't till after other people rushed up that I realized what had happened.' His voice trailed off and he looked down sadly at the cigarette in his hand.

'Do you have any idea why they would be targeting you?'

'None.'

'There have been rumours from the start that the conspiracy is larger than it seems.'

'I know nothing about these rumours and I know nothing about a conspiracy if there is one.'

'Then why are they going for you? Do you have enemies in the new government who might be trying to get rid of you?'

'In politics there are always enemies. You know that... Sorry, I forgot to ask if you would like something to drink. Would you like some tea?'

'I would love some.' He signalled to a servant who had slipped into the room and was standing quietly by the door.

'What do you think could be the reason? Have you heard anything?'

'No, nothing more than the usual conspiracy theories.'

'What are these theories?' he asked with genuine interest.

'Oh, the usual kind. CIA, rumours that people high up in the party wanted Mrs Gandhi out of the way because they felt she was no longer capable of winning elections.'

'Who could win instead? She was the only leader, the others are pygmies compared to her.'

Tea arrived on a silver tray. I drank it while Dhawan smoked incessantly, his hands shaking as he put out one cigarette and lit another. After fifteen minutes or so I realized that there was little more that he could tell me, so I left. I got the impression that he barely noticed my departure. The rain had stopped but I unfolded my umbrella anyway and put on a pair of sunglasses. And, in what I thought was the manner of a skilled spy, I looked cautiously around as I stepped out of his house. There did not seem to be anyone around so I walked back to my apartment.

That afternoon, when I got to the office, a man who identified himself as Mr Sharma called and said he was part of the commission of inquiry into Mrs Gandhi's assassination and that he would like to meet me.

'Oh. Of course,' I said eagerly, thinking that I had found a source for inside information about the assassination inquiry.

'Can I come right away?'

'Right away? Is it urgent?'

'Not really but it would be good if we could meet soon.'

'Sure. Come to my office. It's in the IENS building on Rafi Marg.'

'I know. I will be there in ten minutes.'

He arrived so quickly that I had no time to discuss my meeting with R.K. Dhawan or Mr Sharma's telephone call with anyone in the office. Mr Sharma was middle-aged with gray, thinning hair and a sagging face and body. I noticed that his eyes darted about the office taking in everyone and everything. He wore a terylene bush shirt and badly cut trousers of indeterminate colour. But for that unusually alert look in his eyes he could have been any one of the thousands of government officials who work in Delhi. He did not waste time on niceties or small talk.

'You know R.K. Dhawan,' he said. It was a statement, not a question.

'Yes.'

'You also know the prime minister?'

'Yes.'

'When did you last meet him?'

'After he won the election, when he had his first press conference.'

'No, no what I mean is you know him personally, don't you?'

I answered in the affirmative but his line of questioning was beginning to puzzle me. His next question confirmed that there was more to Mr Sharma's visit than I had thought. 'You also know Farida Ataullah. Right?'

'Yes.' Farida was a Pakistani socialite whom I had not met in years but had once known well through Salmaan. When we lived briefly in Sharjah we stayed with her. Munir Ataullah, her husband, was a close friend of Salmaan. I knew that she had gone on to become a friend of Sonia. I had heard, from someone who was present, that the friendship began when Sonia admired a Cartier bag she was carrying and Farida instantly emptied her things out of it and presented it to Sonia as a gift. She was introduced to Sonia by Nimal Thadani, who was married to Rajiv's friend, Thud.

'Where did you meet her last?'

'With Mrs Oberoi at the Oberoi Hotel.'

'How long ago?'

'About five years. But why are you asking me all these questions?'

He dropped his inquisitional manner and replaced it with an obsequious smile. 'Oh, madam, it is nothing really. But I need to talk to you a little more so can we meet again somewhere quieter?'

'All right,' I said, not sure what else to say. 'Come to my sister's house on Jantar Mantar Road the day after tomorrow. I'm busy tomorrow with a story.'

'Certainly, madam, certainly. What time and what number is the house?'

I told him, and he was gone as suddenly as he had appeared. I noticed that my colleagues were giving me curious looks and partly to avoid answering any questions, partly because I needed to go to the Press Information Bureau for information on a story I was writing, I left the office. I walked up Rafi Marg towards Shastri Bhawan puzzling over the questions Mr Sharma had asked and wondered if I should warn Rajiv and Sonia that questions were being asked about one of their close friends by people investigating the assassination of Mrs Gandhi. Then, in one of those coincidences that make you believe there is more to life than we know, a white Ambassador pulled up beside me at the roundabout near Rail Bhawan. Inside it was Sonia.

'Can I drop you somewhere?' she asked, rolling down a shaded window.

'Sonia. My goodness...you're the very person I want to see. This man came to see me just now, asking funny questions...'

Before I got any further she put her finger on her lips indicating silence and pointed to the man sitting beside the driver in the front seat.

'When can we talk? It's important.' I mouthed the words without saying them.

'Come to the new house this evening,' she said. She was in the midst of decorating the prime minister's new house on Race Course Road, which has now become the prime minister's permanent residence.

It was not possible for me to go that evening because there was a dinner party for M.J. Akbar and like other members of the bureau I was expected to attend. I told her that I could not come that evening but would talk to Mapu and get him to pass on to her what I had to say. So I rang Mapu and told him what had happened and he passed on the story to either his brother or to Sonia, and he called me back to say that on no account should I see Mr Sharma again. But I had already made an assignation to meet him in my sister's house for the day after so Mapu told me to be sure not to 'say anything'. An unnecessary injunction since I had absolutely no idea about any larger plot involved in Mrs Gandhi's assassination.

What puzzled me more than anything was that Farida, a close friend of Sonia, was being considered a suspect. She was as empty-headed a socialite as I have ever met and to think she could be involved in an international conspiracy to assassinate a prime minister was beyond absurd. In any case as a friend of Sonia she should have been eliminated from the list of suspects. But knowing that intelligence agencies in Delhi often worked at cross-purposes I did not give it much thought until that night. I had barely fallen asleep when the phone rang. When I picked it up there was a long moment of silence, so I said 'Hello' many times over. I was about to put the receiver down and go back to sleep when a man's voice came on and said in fluent English, 'You bitch. You think you're very clever, don't you? Talking to higher-ups thinking you can protect yourself. We will fix you unless you keep your mouth shut. Understand?'

'Who is this? Who is speaking?' I asked, trying to sound confident. It was hard not to be frightened by the threatening tone in the man's voice.

'I could be anyone,' he said. 'Let's say I am Peter, will it make a difference? Whoever I am I warn you that it will not help you to talk to anyone.'

'About what?'

'You know exactly what. Please cooperate or there will be consequences.' He put the phone down.

The conversation with 'Peter', whoever he was, left me feeling very uneasy about the meeting I had fixed with Sharma. But I was not sure how to get out of it. I slept badly that night, troubled by the thought of another telephone call or perhaps even a midnight visitor. Like every other journalist in the city I knew that intelligence agencies were not to be trifled with.

When I met Mr Sharma again in my sister's garden I let him do all the talking. He spent the fifteen minutes we were together asking if I knew who had killed Mrs Gandhi. I told him that really it should be me asking him this question but if he was looking for conspiracy theories he should do some investigations in the Congress Party, which was bursting with conspiracy theories and rumours that Mrs Gandhi could not have been killed without the help of 'insiders'. We parted without learning anything important from each other but when I refused to agree to any more meetings with Mr Sharma I was sent a summons to appear before the Commission of Inquiry. The summons was worded in a manner that implied that I knew something about the assassination and was concealing vital information. I knew nothing but what worried me was how little the investigators seemed to know.

If there was a wider conspiracy in the assassination of Mrs Gandhi, it was never made public. What became clear to me from appearing before the commission was that someone seemed to be trying to put the blame on Rajiv and Sonia by implicating their friends. The questions I was asked when I showed up at the commission's shabby, makeshift courtroom in Vigyan Bhawan were all to do with my visit to Pakistan. The man who questioned me made it a point to do so in Punjabi, as if to inject a note of familiarity, and the inquiry went like this.

'You went to Lahore recently?'

'Yes.'

'Where did you stay?'

'At the Faletti's Hotel.'

'Where is the Faletti's Hotel?'

'I have no idea but I am sure that if you checked with someone who worked there they might be able to tell you?'

'You know Farida Ataullah?'

'Yes.'

'Does she stay with you in Delhi?'

'No.'

By the end of the inquisition I found myself seriously worried about the standard of our intelligence agencies. It did not surprise me when, some months later, the investigation into whether there had been a larger conspiracy to kill the prime minister of India was allowed to quietly die away.

In that first year of Rajiv's rule it was as if everyone wanted to forget the violence and bloodshed that had defined1984 as one of the most horrible years in India's democratic history. Rajiv's youth and his image of being Mr Clean brought to the jaded, cynical atmosphere of Indian politics such a sense of renewal and hope that nobody noticed that he was doing almost nothing to change the policies that had kept India mired in poverty for so many decades.

He did nothing to loosen the controls of the licence-quota-permit raj that his mother's socialism had imposed on the economy. That would happen under another prime minister a wasted decade later. He spoke of improving education, but instead of making the big changes that were necessary he tinkered around. Indian government schools were in bad shape. What was needed was a change in direction that would have made primary education compulsory and other radical changes in policy. Instead, Rajiv ended up building a handful of new schools that were called Navodaya or New Dawn schools. They were better than the average state school but too few to make a difference.

Early in 1985 when the euphoria of the election still infected the political atmosphere and Rajiv seemed to represent hope and change and magic he made a powerful speech at a party convention in Mumbai in which he attacked the 'power brokers' who had taken over the Congress. He seemed to indicate in this speech that the party would become more democratic in future and not rely on the courtiers and sycophants whom his mother had preferred to those who had real grassroots political support. But he did nothing to get rid of the 'power brokers'. When they realized that his speech was just a speech these men became more skilled at playing their power brokering games. The only thing that would have reduced their power in the Delhi durbar was if Rajiv had introduced a system of genuine elections within the Congress Party so that people who really deserved to be in public life rose to the top instead of courtiers. He did not.

Rajiv may have noticed the scum that had risen to the highest levels of political power because in those first heady months of being prime minister he attempted alternative methods of bringing change. He tried to reduce the power of politicians and bureaucrats by bringing in professionals and management types who worked directly under the prime minister's office and did not follow the usual, turgid rules of governance. They brought with them a semblance of urgency that for a short while fooled people into believing that the situation was really changing. It was not. This was mainly because Rajiv seemed unable to make the drastic administrative reforms that were necessary for India's unresponsive, colonial system of governance to improve.

New recruits, like the NRI businessman Sam Pitroda, who had built a thriving business in the United States, came back to India to try and help Rajiv improve telecommunications. In the eighties it sometimes took years to get a telephone connection. And, hard as it is to believe now that every other Indian has a cell phone, all of rural India was bereft of telephonic connections. In the cities the only people with easy access to telephones were politicians, senior government officials, rich Indians and those, like journalists, for whom special quotas were reserved on account of the nature of their professions. But even the Indians lucky enough to have a telephone depended on services that were so bad that lines went dead inexplicably and remained unrestored for days. It was a time of 'trunk calls' that could take a whole day to connect and if you were desperate you booked a lightning call that cost you twice as much. When I first went to England to train as a reporter on the Slough *Evening Mail* in the early seventies I was amazed that I was expected to 'phone copy' from the magistrate's court I was assigned to cover. This was unheard of in India. Filing a story meant finding a post office with a telex machine and then waiting, sometimes for hours, before your turn came to slowly key your report into the noisy, ancient machine.

When Pitroda suggested creating rural telephone services in India and setting up STD/ISD booths in villages and small towns to make services available to those who could not dream of getting a private telephone he brought about a telecommunications revolution. He was able to do what he did not just because he had a good idea but because he was able to cut through the red tape, in which most government work was trapped, and report directly to the prime minister's office. Rajiv was so impressed with Pitroda that he gave him charge of not just rural telephone exchanges, but drinking water, the greening of India and other intractable problems. Pitroda called them 'missions' and from his fancy office in the Akbar Hotel in New Delhi tried to implement them with missionary zeal. But these were serious problems that needed massive investment as well as institutional and administrative changes that Rajiv seemed unaware of so most of the missions fell by the wayside.

As prime minister Rajiv soon showed a weakness for the English-speaking, Doon School-educated Indians with whom he had grown up. Unfortunately, like him, they were apolitical and unfamiliar with the complexities of ruling a country as diverse and difficult as India so none of them could help bring the changes that the country so desperately needed. Even in his choice of bureaucrats Rajiv was inclined towards Doon School types like Mani Shankar Aiyar, who was given charge of his relations with the media. But he was a bumptious ex-Marxist with an offensive manner that did little to endear either him, or the new prime minister, to journalists and Rajiv paid a heavy price for this later when his troubles began.

In those exhilarating months it was as if nothing could go wrong with the world. It was a time when all the people I met, from Delhi's drawing rooms to the squalid alleys of the slum colonies his brother had created, seemed to have become devotees of Rajiv Gandhi. A handsome, young prime minister had a special allure where Delhi's socialite circles were concerned and I could go nowhere without running into some attractive woman or other who believed she was on the verge of having an affair with Rajiv. A woman, married into a political family, and who went on to become a well-known politician later but at the time was just an aspiring socialite, took every chance she got to tell everyone how charmed Rajiv was by her beauty. 'He notices everything about a woman,' she liked saying coyly. 'The other day he asked me why I had changed the colour of my nail polish.' Droves of attractive young women began to haunt the Congress Party office offering their services to the new government. Rajiv remained totally oblivious to their charms but the same could not always be said of his aides. As a result more aging bimbos entered the portals of Indian politics then than ever before or ever since.

The foreign press loved him almost as much as ordinary Indians did and endless articles were written about the 'Indian Camelot'. I started to write regularly for the *Sunday Times*, London, after Mary Anne Weaver went back to New York, and I found that although it was difficult to interest London in most Indian political stories I could always get in a story about Rajiv and Sonia. The fact that his wife was Italian and that they made a handsome couple added to their allure where the foreign press was concerned.

The only people who remained unimpressed were human rights activists. In Delhi, living in wretched conditions, were more than 3000 Sikh widows. Their stories were told by the activists in detailed reports on what happened in those terrible three days after Mrs Gandhi was killed. The reports were published as pamphlets and found their way into drawing rooms and government offices.

In the camps, the Sikh widows told their stories over and over again to anyone who cared to listen. They told of the involvement of policemen and politicians in the massacres and named the Congress Party politicians whom they had seen leading the mobs. The Sikh widows had powerful supporters. There were lawyers, journalists, college professors, leftist politicians and high-minded officials who brought them food and clothes and set up makeshift schools for their children. As a Sikh I did my bit by going to the camps as often as I could even if nobody in my newspaper was interested in more Sikh massacre stories.

Among the people who went regularly to the camps was Mala Singh, a friend of Sanjay Gandhi, a journalist who was less famous for her journalistic skills and more for her skills as an influential society hostess. Mala is married to Tejbir Singh, grandson of Sir Sobha Singh, who along with my grandfather was one of the five prominent contractors who worked with Lutyens to build New Delhi. She had inherited a robust social conscience from her parents, Ramesh and Raj Thapar, who had once been friends of Indira Gandhi but had fallen out with her when she suspended democracy. Mala was appalled that Rajiv's government had made no effort to order an inquiry into the Sikh massacres. So I think it was she who suggested one evening that I call Sonia and arrange a meeting to tell her about the importance of a judicial inquiry into the violence. But the suggestion that we talk to Sonia may just as well have come from Mapu in whose house the meeting was eventually arranged.

Sonia came with Nina. I think it was the first time that Mala had met her, because she looked a bit intimidated at first – unusual for Mala – but once she started talking there was no stopping her. She told Sonia about the conditions in the camps and that people were beginning to think of Rajiv's government as insensitive to so immense a tragedy. Sonia said nothing but listened very carefully. We realized how carefully she had listened when two weeks later an inquiry commission was set up under Justice Ranganath Misra. It served mostly to whitewash the Congress Party's role in the violence but that it was set up at all was significant for the prime minister had gone out of his way to justify the massacres.

It soon became clear that Rajiv's closest aide, his most trusted ally and his only true friend was his wife. She understood little of politics and made no effort to hide her contempt for Indian politicians, but she became a power centre because she controlled access to the prime minister's house and made sure that only those she approved of entered its portals.

In the first few months after Rajiv became prime minister Sonia spent most of her time decorating the new house in Race Course Road. Mrs Gandhi's old home opposite the Gymkhana Club was now hallowed ground. So many people came to see where she had been killed and where she had lived that it became necessary to turn her home into a memorial. A walkway of crystal was created where she took her last steps and her room was preserved as she left it on the last day of her life. Two large bungalows were found on the other side of the Gymkhana Club, on Race Course Road, for the new prime minister to live in. They were large government bungalows with gardens on all four sides, but because politicians liked living in Gandhian austerity the houses and gardens had fallen into a state of decay. Sonia spent the first few months of 1985 making improvements to her new home and after that amused herself in the long hours that Rajiv was away by learning to restore old paintings in the National Museum.

Sonia seemed to play no political role, but where social matters were concerned she played an increasingly important one. She began a process of weeding out from Rajiv's inner circle people whom she considered unsuitable or those she took a sudden dislike to. Among the first to go was Nina. As far as I knew Sonia had continued to see Nina for long lunches nearly every day so it came as a shock when I first heard that there was trouble between them. Arun and Nina were so close to Rajiv and Sonia that they were given a house on Race Course Road next door to the prime minister's new residence. A small gate in the dividing wall made it possible for them to go to each other's houses without needing to go out of the main gates. The first rumour I heard, not long after the meeting at Mapu's with Nina and Sonia, was that Sonia had locked the gate on her side of the wall.

Nobody knew why this had happened and none of their close friends talked about the closing of the gate. I did not know Nina well enough then to ask her straight out, and Mapu was too discreet to open his mouth about anything connected with his family. But in Delhi's drawing rooms gossip had it that Nina had been dropped because she was too outspoken and Arun too moralistic about anything to do with collecting money for political purposes. He had always made it clear, people said, that he would help Rajiv with his politics as long as he was never expected to handle party funds.

Arun continued to work for Rajiv's government till the Bofors scandal broke but he and Nina were no longer included in the intimate social circle that surrounded Rajiv and Sonia. In this circle were Amitabh Bachchan, now a member of Parliament from Allahabad, his wife Jaya, his brother

Ajitabh and Ajitabh's wife, Ramola, Satish Sharma and his wife, Sterre. The closest to Rajiv and Sonia were Ottavio and Maria Quattrocchi. When Mrs Gandhi was alive she discouraged her daughter-in-law from inviting foreigners to the house, so the Quatrocchis were kept at some distance from the prime minister's residence. But after Rajiv became prime minister the Quattrocchis had privileged access to the new house on Race Course Road. There were stories, spread by the prime minister's security guards, that when one of them had tried to use a metal detector on Mrs Quatrocchi, during a routine security check, she had kicked him and thrown a tantrum.

From the old inner circle, Romi, Vicky, Nimal and Thud, and sundry others remained. But the cosy lunches and dinners of yore came to a swift end once Rajiv became prime minister. If the Gandhis entertained at all it was mostly for official events. I heard of dinners for visiting celebrities that were carefully choreographed by Sonia to give them an elegance that social events by the Government of India usually lacked. Meals started to come course by course instead of all jumbled together and from those who attended these dinners came tales of a European touch to the food.

By Rajiv's second year in power stories about Sonia's shopping sprees began to circulate in Delhi's drawing rooms. The most dangerous gossips in Delhi are traditionally the sellers of shawls and carpets who wander from house to house with their wares. So it was from a Kashmiri shawl-seller that I first heard that the prime minister's wife was buying shahtoosh shawls in large quantities. It was not an environmental crime then to wear shahtoosh but to buy a shahtoosh shawl was the equivalent of buying expensive fur. Only very rich Indians could afford to. Then, from diplomatic sources in distant Moscow, where the prime minister and his wife made their first foreign visit, came the story of Sonia buying an expensive sable coat. In Mrs Gandhi's time this kind of personal expenditure would either not have happened, or would have happened so discreetly that nobody ever found out. Sonia's sable coat travelled back on the prime minister's flight, and people saw it and talked about it. According to the story I heard Sonia's taste in fur coats was so refined that she was not satisfied with Soviet tailoring and had the coat sent to Rome to be redesigned by the Italian fashion house, Fendi. These were the sort of stories that are never possible to confirm, but gossip rarely needs confirmation to be believed.

Other small sartorial signs of a gradual move away from 'socialism' soon became evident. Rajiv started to wear an expensive, gold Rolex watch and carry a Mont Blanc pen in the pocket of his humble khadi kurta. This elegant new touch was imitated instantly by other young members of the Congress Party. The style was not just imitated but embellished. Suddenly it became fashionable to add a pair of Gucci loafers to clothes made of Gandhian khadi. India had been through so many decades of enforced socialist behaviour that in the eighties there were not many Indians who would have recognized international designer labels. Certainly, there were no journalists in Delhi who had any acquaintance with them but what they did start to notice quite soon was that Rajiv's friends were all doing very well for themselves. Rumours of crony capitalism, an expression we only half understood then, started to spread. Contracts to export rice to the Soviet Union were said to have been handed to some of their friends and all sorts of other deals to others.

To those of us who still saw Rajiv and Sonia's friends in the drawing rooms of Delhi it was instantly obvious that they suddenly had a lot of money. No longer did they travel economy when they went abroad and no longer did they stay with friends in London and New York. They stayed in expensive hotels and this was so new and wondrous an experience for them that they liked slipping names like Claridges and the Meurice into accounts of their travels. I remember on a trip to Washington being astounded to discover that one of Rajiv's poorest friends spent a month occupying two suites in the Watergate hotel. Friends of Rajiv who had lived on salaries that barely enabled them to afford a small Indian car now drove around in foreign cars and in their drawing rooms suddenly appeared expensive works of art and antiques. Nobody asked too many questions because Rajiv was still very popular but rumours of 'deals' started to filter into newspaper offices.

By the middle of 1986, my relations with M.J. Akbar had become so fraught that I decided I was better off going freelance. I was writing regularly by then for the *Sunday Times*, London, which brought in more money than I earned at the *Telegraph*. I came to an arrangement with Aroon Purie, owner and chief editor of *India Today*, to do some freelance work for him as well and with a considerable degree of pleasure sent Akbar my resignation. His tantrums and sulks had now become so routine as to make constant difficulties for me professionally.

The final straw came when Sant Longowal, Bhindranwale's old adversary in the Golden Temple, was killed within weeks of signing an agreement with Rajiv in July 1985 to start a peace process in Punjab. Kewal Sahib's immediate reaction was to send me to Punjab and I would have left as soon as possible if Akbar had not been having one of his dinners. On this particular evening Akbar was in a bad mood. At some point someone mentioned that I was leaving later that night for Punjab to cover the Longowal story and he responded icily that this was out of the question. I was not to go, he said, because he had already decided to assign the story to someone else. He chose a reporter who spoke no Punjabi and had never been to Punjab before. He did this with such obvious spite that I made up my mind to leave the *Telegraph* as soon as I could find a way to. We were barely on speaking terms by the time I resigned and he did not bother to ask why I wanted to leave.

So it was that I happened to be in the *India Today* office on the afternoon the news came that someone had tried to shoot Rajiv Gandhi when he was visiting Mahatma Gandhi's memorial, Rajghat, on 2 October 1986. The failed assassin was a twenty-four-year-old Sikh called Karamjit Singh, who was such an amateur that he used a country-made pistol as his weapon. They found him within minutes, sitting barely concealed behind some bushes, and he readily admitted that he was trying to kill Rajiv to avenge the Sikh massacres. He told the police that he had been particularly disturbed by Rajiv's justification of the massacres in his 'when a big tree falls, the earth shakes' speech.

When I heard that Sonia had been with Rajiv at Rajghat, I called her to find out what had happened. She said that what had upset her most was that when they heard the shots the first people to duck were Rajiv's new and supposedly highly trained bodyguards from the Special Protection Group. I must have mentioned our conversation in the *India Today* office that afternoon because immediately afterwards Aroon Purie summoned me to his room to ask if I could do an interview with Sonia Gandhi. He said that people were blaming her for the negative stories that were beginning to pollute the atmosphere around Rajiv and everyone was curious about what kind of person she was and whether she really controlled the prime minister as people said she did. Although she went everywhere with the prime minister nobody knew anything about her at all. What did her voice sound like? How did she spend her days? What did she think of India?

I called Sonia and told her that *India Today* wanted to do an interview with her and emphasized that her image was really bad and that it might help her to give an interview and clarify some of the things that were being said about her. I told her that she was being blamed for interfering in government affairs and such things as throwing Arun Nehru out of the circle of Rajiv's closest advisors. Many people saw this as a mistake because Arun had acted as a buffer, taking the blame for many things including the Sikh massacres. She listened in silence and remained silent for a few moments before saying that she would check with the prime minister's media managers and see if they thought she should give an interview to *India Today*.

They did not think it was a good idea. So we agreed to do an interview disguised as a profile and that only Sonia and I, and of course *India Today*, would know that the profile was done with her cooperation. I asked her all the questions that Aroon wanted me to and produced a profile that was so anodyne that Aroon said, 'I don't mind being considered a *chamcha* of Rajiv Gandhi, but of Sonia...' I pointed out that I had said right from the start that I would not be able to say anything negative about her since we were doing the profile with her cooperation. Aroon was unconvinced and said that the very least we should do was put in the things that people were saying about her. He suggested that we put some bite into the piece by getting my colleague Dilip Bobb to work with me so that if I had problems with Sonia afterwards I could put the blame on Dilip.

So on the cover of the 15 December 1986 issue of *India Today* there appeared a profile titled 'The Enigmatic First Lady of India'. I am going to quote here the first two paragraphs and admit that the writing of them had more to do with Dilip than me. My contribution was to provide information about Sonia's likes and dislikes, her friends and her life as the prime minister's wife:

> Had fate – in the form of assassins' bullets – not intervened, she would have probably been quite content to linger in the shadow of her formidable mother-in-law, her assiduously protected privacy

> undisturbed by the fact that she belonged to the most famous family in the land. But destiny – and dynasty – willed otherwise. Unwarned, Sonia Gandhi was suddenly pitch-forked into the position she would have least wanted – India's First Lady.
>
> It is, as the last two years have painfully revealed, a role she is not comfortable in. Compared to the relaxed style of her debonair husband, she appears awkward and wooden. Though impeccably attired and carefully groomed, her face, framed by luxuriant chestnut hair, is an immobile mask. Perhaps deliberately, her public personality has given her the image of a mere ceremonial appendage to the Prime Minister. She is not a Lalita Shastri, but neither does she seem cut out to be Nancy Reagan or a Raisa Gorbachova. And the fate of someone who falls between two stools is not a happy one.

The article went on to charge Sonia with being the power behind the throne 'plotting the downfall of opponents, through cabinet reshuffles [she didn't trust Arun Nehru] and advising her husband on everything from the Kashmir coalition to Pepsi Cola's entry into India.'

The profile was not flattering but it was not as bad as it could have been. Considering how much vicious gossip there was about the Quattrocchis by then, the piece was not unfair. There was only an allusion to her friends using her name when they threw their weight around Delhi's drawing rooms and government offices. This was mentioned in passing. So, when I called Sonia to find out what she thought of the profile I did not expect the frosty response I got.

I asked her if she had seen the profile and what she thought about it, and I remember being surprised by the icy tone in which she replied that she did not think she was like the person I had described in the profile. In what way, I asked, and she mentioned the reference to her friends using her name.

I said, 'Look, Sonia, there are people using your name. I don't want to give you details over the phone. But let's have coffee and I will tell you exactly what is going on and who is doing what.'

We agreed to meet the next day or the next, but an hour before our scheduled meeting Madhavan, her personal assistant, called to say that Mrs Gandhi was unable to keep our appointment as she was accompanying the prime minister to Kashmir. He had been instructed to tell me that she would call when she returned to fix another time.

She never did. Some weeks later I wrote to her to offer condolences on her father's death and got a polite handwritten reply in her neat, carefully formed handwriting. My New Year's card in January 1987 was not written by hand and signed by both of them as it was the year before. It came from the prime minister's office and was formally signed by Rajiv Gandhi. I had been dropped.

15 INEXPERIENCE SHOWS

The trouble with serious political mistakes is often that they become obvious long after they were made. Or perhaps they were not as obvious to me then as they may have been had I been a wiser, more experienced observer of political issues. In 1986 my experience as a journalist was mostly as a reporter and I was so busy on most days of the week that I had little time to analyse the political events I was covering. This is my only excuse for not having understood sooner the gravity of the political mistakes Rajiv made even in his first two years as prime minister. But I was not alone in this. India's honeymoon with Rajiv was a long one, perhaps because compared to the other leaders in South Asia in 1986 he was so much younger and so full of promise.

And, perhaps because he talked so much about computers and taking India into the twenty-first century he created an illusion of change that seemed so much more important than his mistakes. It should have been clear even then that the illusion of change was only an illusion because even though he talked about computerization he did very little to computerize governance or make it easier to import computers into the country. It remained almost impossible to do this until the nineties after the economy was liberalized. Computers were unheard of even in journalism and I can remember using an electric typewriter in the early nineties and not knowing a single Indian journalist who owned a laptop.

The men who started what was to become one of India's most celebrated software companies, Infosys, remember well the trouble they had importing computers in the eighties. Why did Rajiv not notice that if he believed in computers he needed to make it possible for even students to import them easily and to do this he needed to change India's archaic rules about importing technology? I do not know. And I do not know why he never understood that there were many other outdated rules and regulations that needed urgent change and that it was by sheltering behind them that Indian bureaucrats had managed to make governance a labyrinth of red tape out of which only they knew the exit routes. Did he not change anything because he was too inexperienced a politician to challenge the bureaucrats? Did he fall into their clever little traps? I do not know.

What I do know is that politically in 1986 the most serious mistake he made was to throw away what was probably the last chance to find a democratic, domestic solution to India's Kashmir problem. His mother's reckless decision to get rid of Farooq Abdullah's government was now seen as a mistake by everyone who understood the Kashmir problem. It could easily have been rectified in 1986. As in the rest of India, people in Kashmir looked at Rajiv as someone who brought with him the chance of new political ideas and hope. The expectation in the Kashmir Valley was that instead of the cynical solutions that other Indian prime ministers had used to suppress Kashmir's legitimate democratic aspirations Rajiv would behave with sensitivity and understanding and show a real desire to find a solution to modern India's oldest political problem. All that he needed to do in 1986 was to order fresh elections and make sure they were free and fair and the Kashmir Valley may have gone back to being the favourite film set of Bollywood's film-makers and the favourite honeymoon destination of newly married couples across India.

Gul Mohammad Shah, who remained in power for twenty months with a lot of help from Governor Jagmohan, was seen as a usurper and was extremely unpopular. He was contemptuously called Gul-e-Curfew (curfew flower) in Srinagar because of the extraordinary number of days for which the city remained under curfew during his rule. To consolidate his fragile political power he tried to divide Hindus and Muslims and in the end his government was dismissed in early 1986 because of tensions caused by this. He left Kashmir a troubled place but the situation was far from irretrievable. A fair contest between Farooq Abdullah's National Conference and the Congress Party would have resulted in a victory for him and the Congress could have done what Mrs Gandhi refused to allow it to do in 1983, play the role of a worthy opposition. The average Kashmiri's faith in Indian democracy would have been restored.

Pakistan continued to be ruled by a military dictator who was nearly as hated in Kashmir as he was in his own country because memories of Zulfikar Ali Bhutto's grotesque execution were still fresh. Under Rajiv's youthful leadership India looked particularly good in comparison. I visited Kashmir regularly at the time and remember being surprised that despite the unjustifiable toppling of Farooq's government old wounds created by decades of rigged elections and the imprisonment of Sheikh Abdullah had almost been forgotten. All Rajiv needed to do was prove that he believed in democracy.

Unfortunately, yet again, his faith in his trusted advisors got in the way. One of them, Wajahat Habibullah, admitted to me many years later that they had been wrong in persuading Rajiv to coerce Farooq into an electoral alliance with the Congress Party. But by the time he admitted this at a lunch party in a sunny Delhi garden thousands of people had died in an insurgency that remains India's most intractable political problem. I remember the conversation with Wajahat as if it happened yesterday because I was stunned by how casually he said what he did. I remember thinking then that it was typical of the insensitivity that even the best Indian bureaucrats (Wajahat is among them) show towards the loss of human life. As if unaware of how many people had been killed because of the mistake made by him and Rajiv's other advisors in 1986 he said that he had read my book *Kashmir: A Tragedy of Errors*, which was published in 1995, and agreed with me that a crucial mistake had been made then. Once Farooq was forced to ally his National Conference with the Congress Party it automatically created a vacancy for less moderate Kashmiri parties.

By a funny twist of fate I happened to be in the remote city of Laayoune on the Atlantic coast of Morocco in March that year when I heard on the BBC that elections had been announced in Kashmir. It was a funny twist because what had brought me to Morocco was the decision by Rajiv's government to recognize the Sahrawi Arab Democratic Republic as a separate country. This was exactly as if Kashmir were to be recognized as an independent country. In the Sahara desert, in what used to be Spanish territory, a freedom movement led by the Polisario Front had existed since the seventies and its demands were almost identical to the demands of Kashmir's secessionist groups. They wanted a referendum and the right to self-determination under UN resolutions that recognized Western Sahara as disputed territory. The Polisario Front had the support of Algeria and other countries in the Soviet bloc but why Rajiv suddenly felt the need to recognize the Sahrawi Arab Democratic Republic as a separate country in the first year of his rule will remain a historical puzzle. The country he recognized was what Morocco considers its southern provinces so King Hassan of Morocco was forced to break diplomatic relations with India.

Weeks after this happened I accidentally met the roving envoy of the King of Morocco, Ambassador Abdeslam Jaidi, in circumstances that had nothing to do with politics or matters of high diplomacy. On a very cold January evening in 1986, just as I was settling down in front of a heater with a book and a glass of red wine, my friend and one of Delhi's most famous socialites, the late Raji Kumar, rang and virtually pleaded with me to come to dinner. He said he knew that this was a last-minute invitation but explained that it was a very last-minute dinner party. Someone had put Ambassador Jaidi in touch with Raji, who was an antiques dealer, to arrange for a shopping trip and to Raji's surprise the ambassador accepted his invitation to dinner afterwards. Raji told me that he did not know many people he could call at two hours' notice and the ambassador was interested in understanding why Rajiv's government had recognized an integral part of Morocco as a separate country. 'This man is very close to the king of Morocco,' he said by way of incentive, 'and I would really like you to come.'

I reluctantly abandoned my plans for a quiet evening at home and set off for Raji's house in Golf Links. When I arrived I found that not only was there no sign of Ambassador Jaidi but no sign even of my host. The only people in Raji's freezing drawing room was a Moroccan couple who spoke no English. They sat stiffly at one end of the room and for two hours all we did was smile politely at each other when we happened to look in each other's direction. Raji's staff seemed unaware that he had invited guests to dinner so there was not even food and drink on offer.

When Raji finally arrived with his important Moroccan guest it was after 9.30 p.m. and I was irritable and cold. So when Ambassador Jaidi greeted me by asking, as he shook my hennaed hand, why I was wearing henna, I said petulantly that I had been to an Indian wedding and this was an Indian tradition. 'Ah, we have the same tradition in Morocco,' he said, smiling graciously. And I being deliberately provocative replied, 'I know all about Morocco. I have friends in the Polisario.'

If the remark annoyed the ambassador he did not show it. Instead, with a very polite smile he said he would like me to visit Morocco at his invitation. When I told him that my friend Nooruddin from the Polisario Front had already invited me he said that I should not visit Morocco with the Polisario. They take people to Tindouf in Algeria and pretend that it is Morocco.

The rest of the evening was pleasant enough. I think we talked a little about the Indian government's decision and I explained that the government could have been persuaded to recognize the Sahrawi Arab Democratic Republic because of pressure from Algeria and the Soviet Union and we went on to talk of other things. I forgot about meeting Ambassador Jaidi till a few weeks later, when a business-class ticket arrived in my mail from the Moroccan government. Along with it came an invitation to attend the twenty-fifth anniversary celebrations of King Hassan's coronation. In my long years in journalism I have on principle stayed away from junkets of all kinds, but this was an offer I found hard to refuse.

So it was that in the first week of March I arrived in Marrakesh to find myself in a town that seemed to have come straight out of 1001 Arabian Nights. There were tents everywhere, Arab horsemen galloping about and lights and music in the medina. Ambassador Jaidi had arranged for me to stay at the Mamounia Hotel which was as romantic a hotel as I have ever stayed in. I entered the lobby to find myself instantly transported back to the thirties or at least to what I thought Morocco must have looked like in the thirties from what I had seen of it in Hollywood films. A black pianist played in the soft yellow light of chandeliers, there were men in dinner jackets, bejewelled ladies in long gowns and an elegant restaurant filled with laughter and the sound of clinking glasses. The next morning when I opened the windows of my room I saw an expanse of orange groves that, in the gauzy winter sunlight, seemed to stretch all the way to the Atlas Mountains in the distance.

I spent the next two days being entertained with the King's other guests in his magnificent palaces. There were journalists from all over the world but Pranay Gupte, who worked at the time in New York, and I were the only Indians. The festivities had a fairytale quality and it was easy to forget the real purpose of my being in Morocco. There were tournaments on horseback, feasts under tents, and evenings filled with music and magic. Pranay and I, and a gentleman from the Moroccan embassy in Delhi called Abdou, dined in charming little restaurants in the medina and had the sort of political discussions that can only happen over many glasses of wine and are afterwards forgotten. Abdou introduced me to Morocco's minister for culture, who was an Indophile, and in my collection of Moroccan photographs there is one of me chatting to the Hollywood star Michael York outside an Arab tent. He was among the celebrities who came to King Hassan's party.

When the festivities were over Abdou took me to some kind of military establishment where I was asked to point out on a map of the Sahara where exactly the Sahrawi Arab Democratic Republic was. When I named the towns that Nooruddin had told me about, I was flown to each one of them in an army helicopter with Abdou for company. The 'capital' of the Sahrawi Arab Democratic Republic consisted of no more than a tin shed in the desert and the other towns Nooruddin had told me about quite simply did not exist. As a result of this expedition, I flew all over the Moroccon Sahara for a day and saw the heavily guarded wall that the King had built to keep out the Polisario guerrillas, who operated from bases that were on the Algerian side of the desert. The day ended with a visit to Dakhla and Laayoune. These towns on the Atlantic were still very much part of Morocco.

When I came back to Delhi I wrote a story for *India Today* called 'A Sahara Mirage'. In it I described what I had seen of the Sahrawi Arab Democratic Republic and pointed out that it seemed more than slightly bizarre for Rajiv's government to have recognized a country that did not exist. I think I even asked in the article where the Indian ambassador would be presenting his credentials and where the embassy would be in a capital city that consisted of a tin shed in the desert. I came under immediate attack from colleagues of leftist disposition. They said that I had discredited myself by accepting hospitality from the Moroccan government. When I replied that this really was rich coming from people who had accepted Algerian hospitality on more than one occasion to cover the other side of the story, they said that Algeria was a socialist country and not a kingdom. My fiercest critics were revealed, decades later, to be in the pay of the Soviet Union when the KGB spymaster, Vasili Mitrokhin, published his memoirs after defecting to the West. They were highly respected journalists in an India that was then virtually a Soviet satellite.

The Soviet Union appeared to have a special allure for Rajiv just as it had for his mother but in the cloistered world that was political Delhi in the eighties nobody seemed to notice that a war being fought just beyond India's northern borders was slowly bringing the Cold War to an end and hastening the collapse of the Soviet Union. Rajiv did nothing to change his policy towards the Soviet Union. It remained the same as it had been during Mrs Gandhi's time, when she had supported the invasion of Afghanistan. The world was a very faraway place because private television channels did not exist in India and the three or four foreign magazines that came to Delhi were censored before being allowed into the country. It was also a time when foreign travel was beyond the reach of most Indians. India was so isolated from what was going on in the rest of the world that the immense changes taking place inside the Soviet Union in those last years of its existence were neither discussed in political circles nor written about in the newspapers.

When I returned to India from Morocco almost the first thing I did was call Farooq Abdullah to find out why he had agreed to an electoral alliance with the Congress Party. He happened to be in Delhi and invited me for a chat over coffee in his house on Safdarjang Lane. It was the house Naveen Patnaik had been living in when Mrs Gandhi was killed. When I arrived I found Farooq in his sparsely furnished drawing room chatting to M.J. Akbar. Akbar was about to make his first foray into television journalism and was there to interview Farooq. His crew was setting up chairs and cameras in the garden but he made no move to leave the drawing room. I asked Farooq if he was happy to talk in front of Akbar and he said he had no problem except that he was speaking to both of us 'off the record'.

As soon as we started talking I discovered that Farooq was dispirited and angry. When I asked him why he had agreed to such an obviously insane pre-poll alliance he said, 'Because I had no choice. They said that if I didn't agree there would be no elections in Kashmir for the next five years. By then I won't be able to control the situation.' He explained that the Jamaat-e-Islami, the most fundamentalist of Kashmir's Islamic parties, was building madrassas at an alarming rate across the Valley and that what was being taught in them was not just secessionist but poisonous. If I was not convinced of this, he added, I should go and see for myself.

When I did go, some weeks later, I was astounded to see how much the atmosphere in Kashmir had changed under Gul Shah's very unpopular rule. In the narrow bylanes of the old part of Srinagar, which they call 'downtown' and which I have always thought of as the political barometer of the Valley, I discovered that a carefully planned campaign was in progress to persuade Kashmiris that they could not live as part of India because they were Muslims. This message was taught to small children in the madrassas and to the general public through pamphlets that glorified the virtues of Islam and derided everything to do with India.

Nobody in Delhi appeared to have noticed what was happening. I may have been a novice when it came to political analysis but I could read the writing on the wall and see that there was big trouble ahead. It did not surprise me that when elections were held in Kashmir a few months later, a coalition of Muslim fundamentalist parties called the Muslim United Front emerged to pose a formidable challenge to the alliance into which Rajiv had forced Farooq. The Muslim United Front campaigned openly for Kashmir to secede from India and spread rumours that if they won enough seats in the legislature they would vote for secession.

It may have been this possibility that frightened Farooq or it could be that he panicked, but he appears to have done a few things that created a general impression that the election was rigged. Farooq has always denied that he rigged the 1987 election but in a state in which elections had been traditionally rigged for decades he was not believed. It did not help his credibility when the national press reported that there had been irregularities. In any case there were things that happened during the election campaign that toppled Farooq from the shining pedestal on which he had been placed after his dismissal three years earlier. He managed to form the government but could do nothing to stop the insurgency that began in the immediate aftermath of the election. Young secessionist politicians, who thought they had been cheated of victory, started slipping illegally across the border to Pakistan to learn about armed struggle from a military dictator who had already developed expertise in this area by training young Sikhs to spread subversion and terror in Punjab.

By Rajiv's second year as prime minister political commentators began to refer to Rajiv and his ministers as the '*baba log* government'. The term was coined by Indira Gandhi's former friend Ramesh Thapar and quickly became popular with journalists. *Baba log* is an expression that traces its roots to the British Raj when Indian ayahs used it for their English charges. It is a term of endearment except when used in the political context in which it was used for Rajiv and his government. It was cruelly apt when used to describe the manner in which Rajiv and his coterie of mostly Doon School-educated aides were running the country.

The kindest thing that can be said of Rajiv's other big political mistake in 1986 is that it was made out of naivety. In an attempt to become popular with Muslims he legislated to deny divorced Muslim women the right to alimony. He did this through a remarkably retrograde law called the Muslim Women (Protection of Rights on Divorce) Act, 1986. In doing this he succumbed to pressure from a fundamentalist Muslim pressure group that had been demanding a separate personal law for Muslims for more than ten years. It was led by a retired foreign service officer called Syed Shahabuddin. Rajiv's decision would lead to an upsurge of Hindu rage and a movement that would eventually end with the demolition of the Babri Masjid in Ayodhya the year after Rajiv was assassinated.

Why Rajiv decided to use his huge majority in Parliament to override a Supreme Court judgement remains as much of a bewildering mystery as his decision to first resist pressure to intervene in the Shah Bano case and then to change sides without explanation. He began by asking Arif Mohammad Khan, a Congress MP at the time and a personal friend of mine, to argue in Parliament against the demand that divorced Muslim women be denied their rights under Indian law. Arif, a former student leader and a man who believes that Islam and modernity can coexist, did this passionately. Then Rajiv changed his mind and Arif was so disillusioned by this that he resigned from the Congress Party.

But the Shah Bano story needs to be told from the beginning. A case came to the Supreme Court in 1985 in which a Muslim lawyer from Indore argued that he had the right to be exempted from paying maintenance to his divorced wife, Shah Bano, on the grounds that as a Muslim he came under the shariat and not Indian law. A Hindu judge ruled that this was nonsense and every Indian citizen came under Indian law. This caused conservative sections of the Muslim community to protest noisily, as they do so well every time they think Islam is in danger, and the Shah Bano case became the subject of a debate in Parliament. Rajiv ended up taking the wrong side after his initial vacillation and thereby sowed the seeds of a problem that nearly divided India once more in the name of Islam.

While the Shah Bano case was being debated in Parliament and creating tensions across the country nobody seemed to think it was worth interviewing the lady herself. These were times, please remember, when private television channels did not exist and when most editors thought reporters wanting to travel out of Delhi to do a story had a holiday on their mind. That is the only explanation I can find for why I happened to become the first person to get a photograph of Shah Bano. I was in Indore on some other assignment and decided to look her up. It did not take me long to discover the bazaar in the old part of the city, where she lived in a narrow alley lined with open drains. A tiny door led to a box-sized courtyard at the centre of a house made up of small rooms built one on top of the other.

I found Shah Bano seated on a string bed in the courtyard. She was a bird-like woman with a heavily lined face and beautiful green eyes. She seemed confused by the fuss her story had created. She told me that all she had asked for was an increase of Rs 100 in the Rs 180 monthly maintenance her husband paid her, and could not understand why this was too much to ask for. She said her husband made thousands a month as a lawyer and could well afford to give her more money. While she talked I took as many pictures as I could. I am widely regarded in my family as one of the world's worst photographers but discovered, to my delight, when I got back to the *India Today* office, that it was the first picture taken of her. Raghu Rai, who was picture editor of the magazine, sold it to a photo agency abroad and gave me $100. It was my finest moment as a photojournalist. There had been no other.

But apart from this small personal triumph there is little about Shah Bano's sad story that is worth celebrating. She accidentally became a pawn in an ugly game of religious politics that ended in a wave of hatred spreading across the country and violence that caused not just the demolition of the mosque in Ayodhya but the deaths of thousands of innocent people.

The cause of these terrible events was Rajiv Gandhi. When he realized that his decision to allow Muslims their own personal law had seriously antagonized Hindus his moronic advisors told him that the best way to make the Hindus happy was to open for Hindu worship a disused, disputed mosque in Ayodhya that Hindus claimed was built at the exact spot where the mythical god Ram was born. It did not win Rajiv much Hindu support because this was a game that the Hindu nationalist parties knew how to play better. But it did make him seem increasingly like a prime minister who did not know what he was doing.

16 THINGS GO WRONG

While it is possible to forgive Rajiv Gandhi the big political mistakes he made from inexperience and from not being a politician in the real sense it is harder to understand why he never made even those uncontroversial changes that needed to be made. Changes that should have come naturally to a man who professed to believe in taking India towards modernity and computerization. By the time he became prime minister Doordarshan was reviled even by semi-literate Indians as nothing more than a mouthpiece of the government and not a very effective one at that. Its news bulletins were so filled with items that were not real news that newspaper offices were awash with jokes about how they were only worth watching if you wanted to learn what should not be in the news. All India Radio, during the Emergency, was mocked as All Indira Radio and almost every journalist I knew relied on foreign radio stations to get the real story. Those of us who could afford to, bought expensive German shortwave transistor radios that we carried with us wherever we travelled. And the BBC's world service was possibly more listened to in India than any other country.

One of the things Rajiv could have done was give Doordarshan more autonomy and allow private television channels to compete with it even if only in the area of entertainment. Doordarshan's attempts at producing entertainment programmes were as amateur and ineffectual as its attempts to produce news bulletins, and on my travels in Punjab, where they caught the signal, I remember constantly running into people who said they preferred watching Pakistani television channels because of the high quality of their serials and plays. Rajiv could have changed things had he wanted to and I tried, one evening, to persuade him to see the wisdom of this change.

I think I may have rung Sonia to ask if I could talk to Rajiv and she suggested that I come over on an evening when he was home early from work. It was the first time I saw the house after she had redecorated it and it was full of light and pictures and beautiful things. She had completely and correctly abandoned the pseudo-socialist style of interior decoration that Mrs Gandhi preferred and created a home worthy of a prime minister and not some lowly socialist apparatchik.

It was one of those gentle Delhi evenings when you can sit in the garden without feeling too hot or too cold so we sat drinking iced drinks under a gazebo that was a new addition to the garden. Rajiv looked cheerful and happy and we talked of this and that and whether he was enjoying being prime minister, to which he said something like he was only doing his duty. I no longer remember how the subject of Doordarshan came up, but I asked why he did not relinquish state control over it. I said that it could never improve as long as it remained a tool of government propaganda and he sort of agreed with me. But he said that it would improve soon because he had found 'an intelligent, young bureaucrat' to take charge. The intelligent, young bureaucrat he referred to was Bhaskar Ghosh.

That was as far as he was prepared to go. I pointed out that as long as Doordarshan was controlled by officials sitting in the Ministry of Information and Broadcasting it was unlikely to improve because officials rarely came equipped with the creativity and imagination needed to transform a shoddy propaganda machine into a real television channel but my arguments fell on deaf ears. I think I even mentioned that when Doordarshan covered his own tours they did it badly but he said he was sure that Mr Ghosh would be able to make dramatic changes. The sort of changes that Doordarshan needed have not happened to this day and despite governments from other parties having come and gone no prime minister has seen the need to abolish the Ministry of Information and Broadcasting for being the anachronism it has been for decades. Television is today the most powerful tool of mass communication in India and an engine of change even in remote communities where literacy levels remain poor. There are more than 300 news channels in Indian languages that have become the main source of news for most of India and Doordarshan remains as dreary as it always was and as incapable of providing real news or entertainment programmes but it no longer matters because it has become irrelevant except in really isolated parts of the country where satellite dishes and private cable televisions have not yet reached.

It was, ironically, the year after Rajiv was killed that Rupert Murdoch's Star channels beamed their way into India via satellite. Suddenly, private channels in all of India's languages grew at such speed that keeping count became impossible and rural communities who had often not seen what the nearest town looked like were able to see big Indian cities like Delhi and Mumbai from the remoteness of their village huts. It changed the way they looked at the world and it has changed rural India in a way that ambitious government welfare programmes have failed to.

When Rajiv was prime minister we began to see the first hint of how powerful an engine of change television could become. It happened accidentally. Doordarshan allowed one of Bollywood's most famous directors to produce a television version of the Ramayana. This most popular of Indian epics is well loved and well known across most of the country because the story of Ram's extraordinary life is told every year in the weeks just before Diwali. But it is told by amateur actors who keep forgetting their lines as they stumble about on makeshift stages so the most serious moments of the epic are often reduced to farce. On celluloid with special effects and professional actors it became larger than life. And, so popular that in villages without electricity they used tractor batteries to run communal television sets around which the whole village gathered. What changed their lives were the commercial breaks advertising Sunsilk shampoo, Colgate toothpaste and Hamam soap. Most people in rural India were too poor in the eighties to spend Rs 20 on a bottle of shampoo but they could afford the Rs 2 sachets of Sunsilk shampoo that soon appeared in village shops. It was the beginning of a revolution in personal hygiene and lifestyle.

Had Rajiv allowed private channels to enter the television business change would have come to the villages of India much sooner than it did. Why did he, a young man who travelled every summer to Western countries and who in his years as a student in Cambridge University would have enjoyed watching British television channels, not see the need to allow private television channels in India? I do not know. My only explanation is that it could have been because, like his mother, he believed it was important for India to continue to follow the example set by the Soviet Union. It was already beginning to fall in the eighties but news from other countries travelled slowly to India and very little was known about Mikhail Gorbachev's attempts to start telling the truth about his country's brutal past.

I am ashamed to admit that I only learned about the immense changes taking place in the Soviet Union nearly a year after the Berlin Wall came down, when I travelled to Moscow in 1990 with the prime minister who took over from Rajiv. In my years as a political journalist I have been invited to be part of an Indian prime minister's delegation to a foreign country only twice and this was one of them. Vishwanath Pratap Singh, the man who became Rajiv's nemesis, was upholding the tradition of going to Moscow on his first trip as prime minister and I was invited to be part of the press delegation that went with him. We travelled on a special Air India flight and the crew who looked after us urged us to take along the free bottles of Scotch whisky, duty free cigarettes and packets of cheese and chocolates they gave us. 'They will come in very handy in Moscow,' they said, 'because there is a kind of barter system there.'

Little did we know how right they were till we ended up confined in the gulag-like Hotel Rossiya and discovered that a packet of cheese handed discreetly to the lady who guarded our floor could be exchanged for morning tea. She was a large woman with a grim expression and shabby, shapeless clothes and was meant to be a guest relations officer but looked like a warden. She helped us only if we bribed her with the foreign goods we had come armed with. The Rossiya was more penitentiary than hotel, but it had about it a hint of the atmosphere that existed in our own government hotels. Just as in our ITDC (India Tourism Development Corporation) hotels there was a peculiarly unpleasant smell in the rooms and in the bathrooms a small, hard cake of cheap Indian soap.

When we wandered about Moscow I remember being struck by other similarities with India. There were government-controlled shops filled with tawdry indigenous goods and the same black market for foreign goods. Male colleagues swore that they could hire prostitutes in Red Square for a packet of cigarettes. When I tried to file my copy from the hotels in Moscow and Tashkent I discovered the same ancient telex machines that were the bane of journalists in India and the same indifference among the officials to their work. But, I also discovered *glasnost* and *perestroika* and

Gorbachev's valiant attempts to reform the system. It saddened me that he seemed to be doing more to bring about change than Rajiv had done despite having history, democracy and a massive mandate on his side.

So trapped was Rajiv in the bad old ways of the past that when there was a drought in 1987 he reacted with the same disdain for the people that had defined Indian political leadership. The worst effects of the drought that year were in Orissa and the response of the state's Congress chief minister, J.B. Patnaik, was, as usual, to deny all reports of starvation deaths and famine. When newspapers reported that people in remote districts were eating red ants to survive the chief minister smiled and said that they were a 'delicacy' in Orissa. Reports of children dying of starvation, which he dismissed as propaganda by his political enemies, were followed by stories in the national press about women selling their babies for as little as Rs 40.

When the first stories reached Delhi in August, I suggested to the *Sunday Times* that I go to Koraput and Kalahandi to see what was really happening. The story interested my foreign editor in London because until then all the stories about Rajiv Gandhi in the Western press had raved about India's 'Camelot' and he was intrigued that the gloss was beginning to peel off. The Bofors scandal had broken by this time but it was not as big a story then as it was to become later in India. In the Western media it never did become a big story.

It was not till I got to Bhubaneshwar that I discovered that the villages from where the starvation deaths were being reported were more than 12 hours away by road. In Bhubaneshwar there was no sign of famine or drought and I quickly realized that the only way to find out what was really going on was to drive to the villages from which the reports of starving children were coming, no matter how long this took. I set off almost immediately and we drove till night fell. We were on a dark road at the edge of a forest, so the only choice I had was to spend the night in my hired car outside a teashop in what my driver told me was the district of Phulbani. It was as desolate a place as I have spent the night in but my driver, who seemed accustomed to this kind of night halt, told me cheerfully that I would discover the next day that it was one of the most beautiful parts of Orissa.

In northern India I could not have dreamt of spending the night alone in a car at the edge of a forest but my driver was so relaxed about it that

I sensed I had no reason to worry about unwanted nocturnal visitors. He seemed to know the owner of the teashop well and they sat drinking tea and listening to Hindi songs on the radio late into the night, which, in this unfamiliar jungle, had a most comforting effect on me.

The next morning I set off early for Kalahandi. I remember a long drive through beautiful countryside before I came to a town that was more an overgrown village than a town. In the dilapidated row of shacks that was the main bazaar I discovered the government of Orissa's token effort at famine relief. A free kitchen had been set up to serve a meal of lentils and rice to children under the age of five, but children older than five were prohibited from being fed. With a ruthlessness that I have never forgotten, the officials running this outrageous token kitchen turned away children they thought were over the age of five. All the children had pot bellies, discoloured hair and teeth, and a vacant look in their eyes. Classic signs of malnutrition. They stared in wonder at the huge cauldrons filled with rice and dal but when they were denied food they seemed too feeble to protest. They walked away quietly and waited for their younger siblings to bring their meagre meal to share with them. It was a horrible, sickening sight and so many years later I still find it hard to forget. Another memory from that morning is of a small baby, no more than a few weeks old, whose only living relatives were a six-year-old brother and an uncle. The brother and the uncle looked as if they had not eaten a proper meal in a while and the uncle, who lay listlessly on a string bed, told me that the children's parents had died a week earlier of hunger-related diseases. There had been no food in the house for weeks. I tried to summon up the courage to ask the uncle if I could buy the baby, who looked as if he would not survive another day if he was not hospitalized, but my courage failed me. It is something I am ashamed of to this day.

In the towns the situation did not appear to be as bad as I had expected. At least there was food available. There were shops selling potato chips and spicy snacks for those who could afford to buy them, and there were free kitchens, such as they were, for at least some of the children. It was when I came to the villages that I saw the real horror of the famine. To get to them I had to walk uphill along a dirt trail for more than two hours. On the way I saw stunted, scrawny, half-naked men walking down the trail carrying clay toys to sell in the towns. When the single crop failed, as it had that year, they made the clay toys in the hope of selling them to survive. They would have sold them for no more than a rupee or two if they managed to at all but this was the only form of commerce they seemed to know.

When I stopped to talk to them they explained, through my Oriya driver who acted as translator, that there was no food in their village and they had been surviving on birdseed and grass for months. While I was talking to them a government doctor came by after having visited some villages in the hills. He confirmed that most people he had met had not eaten a proper meal in months. The doctor was angry. He said, 'I have been sending report after report to Bhubaneshwar for months and they send me antibiotics and quinine tablets, and all these people need is food. The only food they have is birdseed and wild grass.'

When I got to the villages at the end of my long, dusty walk I found children dying slowly on the mud floors of mud huts. Their bellies were distended, their eyes glazed and the only sound they could make was a whimper. They had neither food nor clean water. Their parents had nothing to eat either, and were forced to just sit and watch their children starve slowly to death. To this day I think of it as one of the most horrible stories I have ever covered.

When I returned to Delhi the first thing I did was to try and get through to the prime minister to urge him to go to Orissa and see for himself the horror of what was happening. Rajiv was busy but I managed to meet the minister for human resource development, Arjun Singh, through someone who knew him well. He was the same man who had been chief minister of Madhya Pradesh on the night when poison gas leaked from the Union Carbide factory in Bhopal killing thousands of people as they slept. His reaction, from all accounts, had been to flee with his family to a safer place. His inability to provide even basic relief to the victims of the worst industrial disaster in history remains a monstrous example of inhuman governance. But nobody seemed to think this then, least of all the prime minister, and it did not surprise anyone except a handful of journalists that the delinquent chief minister was re-elected after the gas disaster. It was just the way India was. Most voters were illiterate and voted for reasons that were often hard to understand.

Arjun Singh looked at me with expressionless eyes as I gave him a list of the villages in which the starvation deaths were occurring. The list of villages, my detailed account of children starving slowly to death on the mud floors of huts seemed to make not the slightest impression on him. He promised to make sure that the prime minister went to Orissa, and he kept his promise. The prime minister and his wife went to Koraput and Kalahandi with Chief Minister J.B. Patnaik by their side. The chief minister made sure they only met people who were not starving. The prime minister then went on national television to pronounce that the reports of starvation deaths were nothing but 'opposition propaganda'.

It turned my stomach. It disgusted me to see Rajiv and Sonia smiling happily on Doordarshan, turning starvation deaths into a photo opportunity. The main purpose of the TV crew who followed the prime minister on this tour was to prove to the world that children were not starving in Orissa. When my story appeared on the front page of the *Sunday Times* I got angry reactions from Rajiv's friends. It bothered them that I had 'spoiled' India's image in a foreign newspaper, but it seemed not to bother them at all that children were starving to death under the rule of their friend. India's 'image' was more important because in their tawdry little lives it was only the death of children of their class that made a difference. My disenchantment with people I had grown up with and always thought of as decent multiplied after this.

In the years that have gone by since that terrible famine in Orissa I have found myself often trying to understand why Rajiv failed to respond with more compassion to the tragedies that happened on his watch. I have not been able to come up with a satisfactory answer except that the officials, who were by then his main political advisors, kept him insulated in the bureaucratic cocoon they built around him. It was a necessary cocoon from their viewpoint because had he broken through it he may have noticed their flaws and the colonial disdain with which they treated ordinary Indians. But this does not absolve him and nor is it my intention to absolve him. I continue to believe that had he responded more compassionately to the famine in Orissa he would have been forced to examine the hopeless, leaky anti-poverty programmes his government wasted so much money on. He would have been forced to acknowledge that the lives of all the children who starved to death in Orissa could have been saved just by ordering the chief minister to set up free kitchens in every village where starvation deaths were being reported.

If it is much harder today for children to die of starvation than it was in the eighties it is because of the vigilance of private television channels.

But malnutrition among children remains one of India's most shameful problems. Nearly half of India's children are considered malnourished by international standards, despite mountains of grain rotting in the open at the end of every harvest. There are solutions but Indian officials never come up with them because the political will to change things does not exist and because officials usually prefer massive, unwieldy social welfare programmes since the chances of money leaking into the wrong hands are limitless.

Could Rajiv have changed these things? I believe that no prime minister had a bigger mandate to do this than he did.

17 THE ARMS DEAL

By 1987 I was not alone in my disappointment in Rajiv. His honeymoon with India ended when in April that year the Bofors scandal broke. By the time news of bribes being paid to Indian officials by the Swedish arms company Bofors AB became public I already had an inkling about a 'big arms deal'. It came from my friend Akbar who had stayed in touch with some of the people he met when he was Sanjay Gandhi's lieutenant. Some of them had reinvented themselves as friends of Rajiv and it was because of a chance encounter with one of these people in London that Akbar discovered that Rajiv's government had just signed 'a huge arms deal with a Western country'. Most of India's defence purchases at the time were from the Soviet Union with whom we had a peculiar barter system that passed for trade. They would give us tanks and guns at throwaway prices and we would swap them for Indian consumer goods that few other countries wanted to buy. The ex-friend of Sanjay Gandhi who told Akbar about the arms deal gave him no details but hinted that a huge amount of money had been made by the prime minister and his friends. When Akbar told me this I paid no attention. There was no reason to, because one of the things Rajiv had done after becoming prime minister was to ban middlemen in arms deals. It had added to his image of being Mr Clean.

The story that a Swedish company called Bofors AB had paid Indian officials bribes to sell their 155mm Howitzer guns was not broken by the Indian media but by a Swedish radio station that revealed it in an obscure programme whose primary intention was to put Bofors in the dock for using dishonest methods to sell their guns. But it was in India that the revelation had its most devastating effect. No sooner did the news spread through Delhi's gossipy, murky corridors of power than the defence minister, Vishwanath Pratap Singh, declared that he had every intention of finding out who the bribe-takers were. When this happened Rajiv started behaving as if he had been caught in the act of personally accepting a bribe. It is possible that his personal image would not have suffered so much if he had not behaved from the first news of the deal as if he were guilty.

There is an expression in Hindi, '*chor ki daadhi mein tinka*', which translated literally is 'in the thief's beard is a sliver of wood'. Less literally translated it means that when you announce that the thief can be identified by the sliver of wood in his beard, the person who starts shaking his beard can easily be identified as the thief. Rajiv started to shake his metaphorical beard from the moment the scandal broke. He ordered Arun Singh, who was still in the government as a junior minister in the Defence Ministry despite the severed relations between Nina and Sonia, to make a statement in Parliament denying that bribes had been taken. He himself made a statement in the Lok Sabha in which he said that neither he nor any member of his family had been bribed by Bofors. At this point it was unnecessary.

V.P. Singh, meanwhile, continued to investigate the story with gleeful enthusiasm. His image was that of a man of impeccable integrity. When he was chief minister of Uttar Pradesh he had allowed bandits to kill his brother rather than pay a ransom. He had a reputation for being incorruptible. As finance minister in Rajiv's government, a job he had before being moved to defence, he had become famous for income tax raids on rich and powerful businessmen and for treating them like common criminals. Among those raided were friends of Rajiv and financiers of the Congress Party so V.P. Singh was shifted to the Defence Ministry, where he started digging into shady defence deals even before the Bofors scandal broke.

V.P. Singh's eagerness to find the officials who had taken bribes from Bofors was matched by Rajiv's public reluctance to do so. When Bofors officials came to Delhi and offered to reveal the names of those they had bribed, V.P. Singh had no hesitation in saying that this would be in the best interests of India. Rajiv, for his part, seemed to become very nervous about the possibility of revelations and refused to let the Swedish officials name any names on the tenuous grounds that this would be a threat to national security. It put him in direct confrontation not just with V.P. Singh but with his friend Arun Singh, who found himself in the very difficult position of having lied in Parliament. He agreed with V.P. Singh and Chief of Army Staff General K. Sundarji that it was in India's interest to find out the names of the bribe-takers and if this meant cancelling the deal with Bofors then so be it.

In Delhi's drawing rooms whenever I heard someone mention Bofors it would be in the context of Arun Singh's unhappiness over the way it had been handled. This was usually said in a manner that implied that as a man who valued his integrity above everything else if Arun was unhappy with the Bofors deal it had to mean he was sure he knew who may have taken the bribes and that this somehow implicated his former friend.

Arun and Nina continued to live in the house next door to the prime minister's on Race Course Road but a permanent frost had settled over their friendship. Rajiv and Arun continued to meet in a professional capacity but there seemed to be no friendship left between them. The Bofors scandal seemed to physically change the lives of Arun and Nina Singh. Even the atmosphere in their elegant home changed. Like Sonia next door Nina had transformed her government house by filling it with beautiful things and restored the old colonial character it must have had before the PWD imposed upon it a socialist aesthetic. From being a happy home filled with the sound of children, laughter and dogs and a place of garden parties and cosy dinners, it became an unwelcoming, tense sort of home. Nina looked unhappy and worried all the time because she was aware that Arun was planning to resign from government and was not sure what would happen to their lives after this. I did not see much of Arun, but whenever I did he looked as if the burdens of the world rested on his shoulders.

After returning from one of my trips to Amritsar, around the time that the strain over Bofors was building, I tried to warn Arun that Sikh militants, who had regrouped in the Golden Temple, were spreading rumours that he was personally responsible for planning Operation Blue Star. He listened to what I said with a half-smile and shrugged his shoulders afterwards as if he did not care one bit that there could be a threat to his life. He never talked to me about Rajiv or Bofors but from speaking to Nina and Mapu I managed to glean that he was deeply upset that Rajiv had put him in the position of making a false statement in Parliament. Meanwhile, V.P. Singh continued to investigate the Bofors case with unconcealed determination and was so passionate in his pursuit that

Rajiv found it necessary to sack him from his government. This added to the impression that Rajiv knew who had taken bribes and was terrified that this knowledge could become public.

Bofors was India's first major corruption scandal and inevitably became the biggest story where the media was concerned. The *Indian Express* and *The Hindu* were the two newspapers that went out of their way to find out who had taken the Rs 64 crore that had been paid through a series of shell companies. It would be ten years before Swiss banks revealed that a large share of the bribe money was paid into accounts that belonged to Ottavio Quattrocchi and his wife, Maria.

Years later, when Sonia Gandhi became the most powerful political leader in India, she tried to distance herself from the Quatrocchis by pretending that she barely knew them. But in the year that the Bofors scandal shattered Rajiv's image of being Mr Clean everyone from Delhi's drawing rooms to its corridors of power knew that the Quattrocchis were as close to the Gandhis as it was possible to be. They went on holidays together and Quattrocchi liked to flaunt his closeness to the prime minister. At dinner parties he was often heard boasting about his influence with Rajiv's government and those to whom he boasted did not hesitate to spread the word around because the Quattrocchis were not popular in Delhi's social circles. They were not a pleasant couple. Ottavio was loud and full of bluster, and Maria had a coarse, bossy manner. If they were invited everywhere it was only because of their obvious closeness to Rajiv and Sonia.

I remember a dinner party in the house of an American diplomat at which an uncle of mine, who lived in the United States, took me aside and asked me if I knew someone called Ottavio Quattrocchi. When I asked why, he said, 'He just came up to me and said he was so close to the Gandhi family that he could arrange for me to get government contracts.' My uncle was with a big American construction company. Was I surprised by what he told me? Not at all, because I had heard such stories many times before. Was I surprised that the Quattrocchis were using their proximity to the Gandhis to peddle influence? Not at all. What did surprise me was the manner in which Rajiv handled the Bofors scandal. Since there was no evidence then, or even at the end of endless inquiry commissions, that linked the bribes to him or his family why did he behave like a thief caught in the act?

When Rajiv refused to allow Bofors to reveal the names of the bribe-takers in his government rumours inevitably began to spread far and wide. Anonymous officials leaked stories about Sonia's two brothers-in-law having been present when Sweden's Prime Minister Olof Palme and Rajiv signed the deal in Stockholm. These stories remained unconfirmed despite meticulous investigative journalism by the *Indian Express* and *The Hindu*, but what did get confirmed was that people close to Rajiv and Sonia had been recipients of the Bofors kickbacks. *The Hindu* got hold of a diary that allegedly belonged to the chief executive officer of Bofors AB, Martin Ardbo, in which 'R' for Rajiv and 'Q' for Quattrocchi featured in entries that said special attention needed to be paid to them. The story was reprinted in newspapers across the country.

Rajiv and his media managers did their best to erase the Bofors stain but it refused to go away. High-level corruption was fairly rare in India in the eighties. Kickbacks in government deals were not routine, as they have now become, so for the biggest scandal to break with Mr Clean Prime Minister at its centre made the Bofors story very compelling and something everyone started to talk about when Rajiv's name was mentioned, anywhere. I remember hearing about Bofors in remote villages where access to newspapers was limited to the mofussil kind. In village teashops people joked about the biggest thief in India sitting in the prime minister's house and mocked Rajiv for being 'Italy's son-in-law'.

Rajiv reacted to his sudden unpopularity with a mixture of disdain and defiance that did not help at all. In a column I wrote in the *Indian Express* in December 1987 I described his reaction to a no-confidence motion in Parliament in these words:

> Then the prime minister arrived and proceedings began with Madhav Reddy of the Telugu Desam moving the motion. He barely started and the heckling began when he said that the prime minister was hardly ever in the House and this reflected his disdain for Parliament. Congress(I) MPs hissed, booed and hooted, ministers joining in, while the prime minister sat smiling happily until things seemed to be getting totally out of hand, when with a wave of his hand he silenced his supporters. Fortunately, he did not stay throughout and when he was not in the House most of his party went with him, so the Opposition got the chance to raise important issues. The drought, the problems with

> defence deals, the rise in prices, the non-punishment of those involved in the Sikh massacres of 1984 and the worsening communal situation.
>
> When the prime minister returned to make his two-hour reply what did he say? That the Opposition parties were talking rubbish because they were filled with men who had a 'total bankruptcy of thinking, ideas and vision' and were capable only of making 'petty, personal remarks'.

By the end of 1987 everything that could go wrong had started to go wrong.

On the domestic front Rajiv confirmed that he deserved the '*baba log*' label when he sacked the foreign secretary at a press conference. He did not meet the press often so this press conference was attended by every journalist I knew in Delhi and many more. There was so much interest in the press conference that it was held in the largest hall in Vigyan Bhawan, where international conferences were usually held. The prime minister addressed us from the stage and the foreign secretary, A.P. Venkateswaran, was sitting in the front row along with other officials, when in answer to a question Rajiv announced that we would soon be getting a new foreign secretary. Venkat, as he was popularly known, had no choice but to leave the hall in embarrasment.

I was not yet writing a regular column for the *Indian Express* when Venkat was sacked but it was such an extraordinary event that I brought it up in a column I wrote in December and the tone of what I wrote reflects how Rajiv was beginning to be increasingly seen as a joke. Here is what I wrote in a column dated 13 December 1987:

> Shortly after the public sacking of Foreign Secretary A.P. Venkateshwaran earlier this year, I was summoned for a private chat by a former high official of the Ministry of External Affairs. Like many other once-exalted mandarins he now works in some obscure political capacity and one of his tasks is to keep a beady eye on adverse changes in the prime minister's image. It was in an attempt to rectify the damage brought about by the public sacking that I was summoned. We talked for a while of this and that and took many sips of hot sweet instant coffee before he said, 'Well what are people saying? Do they say the prime minister was wrong to have done what he did?' I confirmed that this was basically

what people were saying and more... A look of impatience crossed the face of the former high official and he interrupted me to say, 'It's only people who do not understand the prime minister who talk like this. Anyone who knows him would know that there are many things that would have irritated the prime minister about someone like Venkat. After all the prime minister is a man of some style and sophistication and Venkat had this habit of sitting with his leg crossed over his knee. This used to upset the prime minister.'

This crumbling of Rajiv's shining image was happening at a time when the country's political problems seemed to get more difficult by the day. In Kashmir the election that brought Farooq Abdullah back as chief minister resulted in disharmony and not peace. The Islamist secessionists who had contested under the banner of the Muslim United Front were beginning to return to the Kashmir Valley as armed insurgents. In Punjab, Khalistani terrorist groups had not only regrouped but had gone back to using the Golden Temple as their shelter and political headquarters. Rajiv's peace initiatives in the north-eastern states floundered and he made a disastrous intervention in Sri Lanka that would one day become the reason for his assassination.

For many years the leaders of Tamil secessionist groups had been such honoured guests of the Government of India that when they came to Delhi they lived in luxurious suites in the Ashoka Hotel. It was in one of these suites, in either 1986 or early 1987, that I first met Velupillai Prabhakaran, whose Liberation Tigers of Tamil Eelam (LTTE) would one day be responsible for assassinating Rajiv. What struck me most at that first meeting with Prabhakaran was that he had the eyes of a dead man. Or, perhaps, the eyes of a cold-blooded killer. When I met him in his suite in the Ashoka Hotel he was being fawned over by south Indian politicians.

In July 1987, as a result of an accord with the Sri Lankan government, Rajiv sent an Indian Peace Keeping Force (IPKF) to Sri Lanka to disarm the LTTE, virtually the only Tamil militant group left after Prabhakaran had finished killing off the others. I was among a group of Indian and foreign journalists taken to Jaffna to witness the 'LTTE surrender'. We travelled in an unnervingly narrow army transport plane and were then transferred to helicopters that flew extra high to avoid potshots from the LTTE. The army officers travelling with us tried to reassure us by saying they were just communication flares, but their worried expressions indicated that they were not completely sure that the Tamil militants were not trying to shoot us down.

After we landed safely we were bundled into army trucks and driven to a military airport where the surrender was to take place. On the way we stopped because the photographers with us wanted to take pictures. When a couple of them stepped off the road and started wandering about, as photographers are wont to, the officers with us became hysterical with panic and ordered them to come back on to the road immediately. Afterwards they explained that they had cleared only the road itself of mines laid by the LTTE, not the surrounding area.

The so-called surrender was a farce. One LTTE man, a close lieutenant of Prabhakaran, handed over a pistol to the Indian General in charge of peace-keeping. That was it. When we asked why this was the only weapon being surrendered, the General explained that it was only a symbolic surrender but he looked unconvinced. Having driven through the empty streets and bazaars of Jaffna we understood why. It was as if the town had been evacuated of its residents and all normal activity suspended by a curfew to fool us who came from Delhi into believing that peace had been won. Nobody was fooled and foreign correspondents in the party insisted that we see more than empty streets. They pointed out that they had not come all this way to be denied the right to meet ordinary people and so we were driven to Jaffna's main hospital where we talked to Tamil civilians with severe injuries. When we asked if they were victims of LTTE attacks they looked shocked and said that their injuries were the result of bombing by the Indian Army. It was a disastrous visit as an exercise in public relations for the Indian Army, but it revealed that Rajiv's Sri Lanka policy was dangerously confused.

Indian troops in Sri Lanka went up to more than 80,000 at the height of their operations to defeat the LTTE but the army officers I spoke to, at various times during the two years that the IPKF was in northern Sri Lanka, told me that they were ordered to fight with 'one hand tied behind our backs'. Since the LTTE had at one point been trained by India and the headquarters of the Tamil secessionist groups had been in Tamil Nadu it was almost a phony war that the Indian Army was ordered to fight. But there was nothing phony about the LTTE's war against India. Prabhakaran was not a man with a great political vision for his people but he was an excellent leader of his guerrilla army and nearly 1500 Indian soldiers lost their lives trying to keep the peace in Sri Lanka.

For this I blame Rajiv less than the bureaucrats, mostly Tamil, who advised him on his doomed policy in Sri Lanka. They must have realized that they were dealing with a prime minister who was a novice when it came to matters of foreign policy and through a mixture of flattery and chicanery they persuaded him to go down a road at the end of which there could never have been victory. Every time I travelled to Sri Lanka I came away a little ashamed of being Indian because of the arrogance with which our diplomats treated both the Sri Lankan government and the leaders of the Tamil insurgency. A wiser prime minister, someone more acquainted with the manner in which a big country like India should behave with its small neighbours, may have controlled his officials better. But Rajiv was not that prime minister and for this he would one day pay with his life.

The summer of 1988 was hot, relentless and long. So when someone invited me to a conference on the 'Kashmir problem' in Srinagar I seized the chance to spend a few days in a cooler city than Delhi. The conference was boring and pointless. Pompous people talked pompously and at excruciating length about 'solving' the Kashmir problem but offered no solutions.

It did not bother me much because Srinagar was at its most beautiful. One tourist season had ended and a new one had not yet begun, and the city was nearly empty. I stayed in a houseboat on the Dal Lake and spent long evenings watching the sunset from the carved veranda of my house boat. I have memories of the setting sun gilding the mountains and bathing the lake in magical hues. From hidden mosques would come the call to prayer and, as if to remind solvers of the Kashmir problem that Hindus lived here as well, temple bells would start up. When the evening chill set in I would eat a meal of spicy kebabs and haaq (a special spinach that grows only on the edges of the Dal Lake) with fat Kashmiri rice. Then I would curl up on the drawing room's big sofa and read to the sounds of shikaras in the water, children laughing and women singing Kashmiri songs.

My little holiday did not last. On the third day of the conference I got a call from my foreign editor in London, and he was cross. He wanted to know what I was doing in Srinagar when I should be in Amritsar. A police officer, someone I knew quite well, had been shot outside the Golden Temple and I needed to file a story by Friday. This was Wednesday. I got to Amritsar as fast as I could and found the city under curfew. A small army of journalists was ensconced at the Mohan International Hotel where I was staying. They sat in the lobby drinking coffee, pacing up and down, and looked busy doing nothing. There appeared to be nothing to do other than wait for the police commissioner to hold a press conference later that day. There was no point in trying to go into the temple, they said, because nobody was being allowed in.

I decided to take a chance. Armed with curfew passes for myself and my taxi driver I drove through silent streets ominously reminiscent of the aftermath of Operation Blue Star. The temple had police barricades outside every entrance but there seemed to be a ceasefire of sorts and I was curious to know if this would give me a chance to go into the temple.

'What has happened?' I asked the young policeman who stood at a barricade close to the temple. 'Why is everything so quiet?'

'They could be trying to remove the bodies before they start to rot,' he said unconvincingly.

'How many people are dead?'

'The truth is we don't know,' he said, looking around to see if anyone was listening. 'We only know that there are bodies inside because we can see them from one of our lookout posts.'

'Can I see?'

'Sure,' he said, 'come with me.'

He took me into a building with a narrow staircase that led to a small room at the top. From its barred window there was a view of the courtyard of the temple's kitchens. It was empty but for the body of an elderly man who lay on his back with his arms held up. He was in rigor mortis and in his hands there were two rotis. He appeared to have been trying to get to the kitchen building when he was shot.

'Crossfire,' the policeman explained. 'They were firing from that building that you see on the other side of the courtyard and we were returning fire from here. The old man was one of the first to be hit.'

'Are there other pilgrims inside? He looks too old to be a militant.'

'There may be. We don't know much. We only know that there are several shooters inside and since yesterday morning they have shot at us every time we have tried to go in.'

'What would happen if I tried to go in?' I asked without any real plan to go into the temple, and it surprised me when he seemed eager that I should.

'Well, if they let you in because you're press you might be able to bring us some information. But we can't take responsibility for your safety. You go at your own risk.'

'All right,' I said, not feeling very brave but certain that unless I went into the temple I would have no story to file. A press conference by the police commissioner was no story at all for a Sunday newspaper in London. So I decided to take my chances and go into the Golden Temple. I entered from an entrance that led to the temple's kitchen and saw two more bodies. This scared me and I was about to turn back when I heard shouts from the veranda of the kitchen. A group of elderly pilgrims sat huddled together looking terrified.

'Help, please help us. We have had no food or water for twenty-four hours,' an old man with a long white beard said in a quavering voice. With him were three old women and another old man. I ran across the forecourt towards them, trying to ignore the possibility of being killed in crossfire.

When I got to the veranda I tried to reassure the terrified pilgrims. They could come back with me, I promised, as soon as I found out what was going on inside the Golden Temple. There was no shooting going on so I decided to push my luck and try to get to a room outside which the militants had optimistically hung a board that said 'Khalistan Headquarters'. The 'headquarters' had come up after Operation Blue Star and it was here that I always came when I wanted information on militant activity. To get to 'Khalistan Headquarters' I needed to go all the way around the temple and had got only halfway, as far as what is called the Manji Sahib entrance, when I heard the sound of a gong and saw a group of young men running towards the steps I had just come down. They were carrying a white sheet with something heavy inside it.

Realizing that I could get as much information from them as from the Khalistan office I shouted to attract their attention. I think I yelled 'Press, press!' or something equally inane but loud enough for them to hear. I admit that the gong had frightened me into wanting to get out of the temple as quickly as possible so I was more than a little relieved to see this small gang of Khalistani fighters. There were four of them and one of them waved to me cheerfully, indicating that I should join them. Just as I reached them I heard the gong sound again.

'Is that the end of the ceasefire?' I asked the stocky young man who had waved.

'Could be. Who knows?' he said with a grin.

'Does this mean I am in some kind of danger?'

'Not as long as you're with us. Come.'

They laughed and led me to a narrow red-brick tower that was as old as the temple. These towers are called *bunga* in Punjabi and were once used for military purposes, as lookouts and for storing weapons. The entrance to the tower was a dark, windowless square space that smelled musty and damp. The steps leading up to the top of the tower looked disused. The young men I was with had about them a sort of mad exhilaration, like children playing a game. Their eyes shone and they talked excitedly about how they were winning the battle. 'We will take the temple back and hoist the Khalistan flag in a few days.'

'How many of you are there?'

'Countless. It's the army of the Guru and that army has countless warriors.'

'You know that you can't take on the Indian state...the army. You know what happened last time.'

'They won't be stupid enough to send the army in again,' said the stocky young man confidently, 'and if they do then the army of the Guru will only grow and grow.'

'Can you tell me your names? Which group do you belong to?' I asked, remembering that I was here to try and get some information.

'We belong to the army of Guru Govind Singh and we have no names,' the man said. They laughed.

'Right. Well, listen, there are some elderly pilgrims trapped in the kitchen. Can you assure me that if I come back with the Red Cross you will let them come out with me?'

'Yes. No problem.'

'And can we take the bodies out?'

'No problem.'

'Are there any inside the temple?'

'Not that we know of.'

The stocky young man said that if I wanted to see some action I should stay with them and watch the 'fireworks' at night. I decided I had seen enough action for the moment and went back into the courtyard and tried to persuade the elderly pilgrims to leave with me but they said they were too scared to – unless I could guarantee that the ceasefire really was a ceasefire. I told them truthfully that I could not guarantee anything as I was not sure and promised to return for them. Then I ran back across the open courtyard, keeping my fingers crossed and hoping for the best.

The policeman who had encouraged me to go into the temple was waiting for me at the barricade and with him was someone else who could have been his superior. I told them I had not been able to get any information yet but needed to go back in with the Red Cross to rescue some pilgrims. They were interested only in the militants.

'Didn't you see anything inside? Didn't you meet anyone?'

'Well, I met this group of militants carrying a sheet full of guns...they're in that tower over there. The red brick one.'

'Did you get any names?'

'No. They said they were soldiers in Guru Govind Singh's army and had no names.'

'Can you describe any of them?'

'The one who did most of the talking was a small, stocky man with a happy face. He was confident that they were winning.'

'Did he have a scar under his right eye?' I thought for a minute and remembered that he did, a scar that looked like a knife wound.

'Yes. He did.'

'Then that's Penta. Madam, you will have to come with us and speak to the DG Sahib. This is important.'

The director general of police was K.P.S. Gill, who was then nowhere near as famous as he was to become some years later when he ended the insurgency in Punjab by using against the insurgents the same brutal methods they used against his policemen. I told Gill about the pilgrims trapped in the temple and asked if it was safe for me to go back with the Red Cross and rescue them. He said that he would ensure there was no firing from his side. So I went back into the Golden Temple with a handful of other journalists. Among them was Satish Jacob from the BBC. I told them that I may have met Penta but like me they seemed not to know who he was. It was only when I got back to Delhi that I found out that he was one of the new generation of terrorists who had been inspired to join the Khalistan movement after the pogroms that followed Mrs Gandhi's assassination.

Since there was now an official ceasefire it seemed stupid not to go as far as the Khalistan Headquarters to get detailed information on this new insurgency. So back we went using the route I had taken earlier along the concourse of scalding white marble. Even with the assurance of a ceasefire we were scared and kept glancing up at the many windows behind which snipers could have been hiding. After what seemed like a very long walk we arrived at the little brown door under the sign that said Khalistan Headquarters.

Stooping, we entered the small, bare room with its green-washed walls. There was a mattress on the floor and pictures of Sikh gurus on the walls. On the mattresses sat a group of armed men wearing the short knickers and long kurtas favoured by Sikh priests, the symbolic kirpan hanging by their sides. Their beards were untrimmed and greasy and they wore black turbans. I recognized one of them as the spokesman of the Khalistan 'government'. Unlike the men I had met earlier in the tower this group looked nervous and scared. They denied that the new battle had been started by them and indicated, without actually saying so, that they would be happy to surrender if that could be arranged without them losing face. It was clear from the way they talked that they did not want another long and bloody battle for the temple. They were just not sure how to avoid it.

As it turned out, it would be another ten days before they would be able to come out of the temple because some of the other groups wanted to fight till the end. This new phase of the struggle for Khalistan did not have a Bhindranwale type of leader leading it. There were several groups of militants led by smaller leaders who usually made it into the national newspapers only when one of them was shot dead. The second generation of militants who made up the new army of Khalistan were in many ways more dangerous because after the Sikh massacres in Delhi and Rajiv's justification of them there were real reasons for anger in the Sikh community.

The second battle for the temple was called Operation Black Thunder and it was fought by the government with a strategy very different from the first. Specially trained commandos arrived from Delhi and surrounded the temple complex but only opened fire if there was firing from inside the temple. They wore black combat fatigues, carried sub-machine guns and had about them an air of such menace that even journalists were afraid to engage them in conversation. When someone tried, they responded with silence, continuing to keep their eyes fixed on targets inside the temple. If anyone was seen moving inside the temple grounds they opened fire. If there was any shooting from inside they responded so aggressively that by the fifth day there was no more shooting.

By the tenth day white flags were raised above the golden dome and a small group of defeated, dirty men filed out and gathered in a courtyard beyond the temple's kitchen. There were no more than sixty of them. Among them I spotted Penta. A photographer from *India Today*, Pramod Pushkarna, saw me looking at him and gave me a questioning look. I signalled with the slightest nod that it was the man I had met earlier. We left immediately afterwards but no sooner did we step into the street outside than a huge commotion erupted. We rushed back to find that Penta had killed himself by swallowing a cyanide capsule. Khalistani militants had started carrying these capsules on strings around their neck in imitation of the LTTE. Within days Pramod received the first death threat. A man who did not reveal his identity said 'they' had seen him and me identify Penta and that this had caused him to commit suicide so we had better watch it.

I did not know whether to take the threat seriously, so I went to the home minister, Buta Singh, to ask if I needed police protection. He listened carefully to my story and at the end of it said that I might draw more attention to myself if I had police bodyguards. So what should I do, I asked, and he suggested that if I was worried about my small son becoming a target then I should make sure that he changed the route he took to school every morning. That was the only succour he could offer.

It seemed like surreal advice but everything about Delhi was beginning to seem surreal to me. I would come back from covering a war or a communal riot in which hundreds of innocent people had been killed only to end up at the same dinner parties, listening to the same sort of inane 'political conversations' that the denizens of Delhi's drawing rooms specialized in. These conversations would usually be about the issue that had made headlines in that morning's newspapers. Everyone would have some banal view and this would pass as political analysis. Or I would end up in some government office meeting officials to try and explain to them how serious the situation was in wherever I had been and they would indulge me as if I were a precocious child telling them things that they knew long ago. I found myself getting increasingly disenchanted with the sort of people who were in charge of ruling India and at the same time I began to understand better how the simplest political problems had been allowed to grow to enormous proportions just by being handled wrongly.

18 MISTAKES

By the middle of Rajiv's term as prime minister I started asking myself why things had gone so wrong for him. How had he squandered the largest mandate in Indian democratic history so quickly? It was in trying to answer this question that I began to wonder whether the problem was that he had entered politics not as someone who had a real interest in public life but as a prince. Had Sanjay Gandhi not been killed would Rajiv have been in politics at all? And had Sanjay not been Mrs Gandhi's son would Sanjay have been in politics? Would they not have spent their lives oblivious to India's gargantuan economic and political problems? And in asking these questions I became aware for the first time, at least consciously, of the dangers of dynastic democracy. If Rajiv had not understood how much hope Indian voters had invested in him was it not so much his fault as the result of his desire to 'help Mummy' rather than the people of India?

The more I thought about this the more aware I became of the kind of people Rajiv had chosen to surround himself with. Sycophants, servile officials and only those friends who were prepared to defer to him. He had chosen his team as an unwise maharaja may have done in another time. Anyone who could have advised him truthfully about what he should be doing, anyone who could have told him frankly that he was becoming unpopular because the changes that ordinary people hoped he would bring had not come about, was no longer in his court. There was nobody in his inner circle who could have told him that Bofors may not have caused so much damage to him personally if he had brought about even a measure of the changes that ordinary Indians so badly needed.

Changes in the corruption that they faced every time they dealt with a government official. Changes that would have reduced the discretionary powers that allowed officials to institutionalize corruption. Changes in the standard of living that would have brought better schools and health care. Changes in economic policy that would have brought higher growth rates and created better job opportunies. Nothing at all had changed and by 1988 it started to become clear that nothing was likely to change. Would he have done better if the shadow of Bofors had not fallen? Who knows.

The Bofors scandal cast a long shadow. The average Indian villager did not understand the full implications of what was involved nor was he certain that Rajiv had personally taken the bribes but what most people seemed to believe, with certainty, was that Indian money had been stolen and hidden away in foreign banks. They linked this with rural logic to their prime minister being married to a foreigner. On my travels I found myself running into more and more people who brought up the 'foreign woman' factor. It became the stuff of poems and jokes. I remember a catchy line from a song by a village poet: 'Italy *ke damad, tere bas ka Hindustan nahin.*' Italy's son-in-law, how will you ever understand India?

Did this mean it was Rajiv's wife's foreignness that alienated him from ordinary Indians? In view of Sonia Gandhi's spectacular success as a politician after Rajiv was killed it might sound absurd to suggest this, but I think it did. It certainly alienated him from Congress Party workers in more rural parts of the country. They said that because 'Memsahib' was always with the prime minister on his tours he never spent enough time in the villages. When Indira Gandhi was prime minister she would come to rural areas and spend the night there, they said, but Rajiv always had to fly off to the nearest town so that 'Memsahib' could sleep in a proper bed. Whether this was true or not it was perceived to be true.

As Rajiv's unpopularity grew so did jokes about his token tours in the 'real India'. A well-known Hindi satirist called Sharad Joshi wrote a hilarious skit called *Pani ki Samasya* (The Water Problem). In the satire he had Rajiv arriving in a village and asking where the villagers got their water from. They explain that it comes from the river and he asks if they walk to the river or take public transport, unaware that in the eighties there were no taxis in rural India. When they tell him that they have to walk to the river he points out that the water they bring back must be quite hot then. When they admit it is he orders an official to check if the World Bank can be persuaded to build a shed over the river.

An audio rendering of the skit was available on cassettes in shops across north India. An apolitical friend gave it to me in Delhi and when I listened to it I could not help thinking that had Rajiv listened to my advice and seen to it that Doordarshan's production standards were made more professional this skit may never have been possible. Doordarshan's cameras captured every word he said on his rural tours and not everything he said was clever so he would sometimes be shown asking silly questions like whether some villager's house was rented or owned by the man who lived in it.

Rajiv was mocked for not understanding Indian realities in jokes, satirical skits and conversations. What he most certainly appears not to have understood were the changes that were taking place in India's villages. They happened mostly because of the increasing popularity of television. India's villages in the eighties were so steeped in superstition and backwardness that celluloid images were seen by illiterate people as manifestations of the divine. A film called *Jai Santoshi Ma* about a goddess nobody had heard of till the film came out created a new cult. The film told the story of an unhappy woman who was tortured and starved by her husband's family while he was away working in some distant city. What keeps her alive in the film is her enduring faith in the goddess Santoshi, for whom she fasts every Friday and practises other austerities. The film became a runaway hit but nobody noticed that this was a new goddess invented in Bollywood. Not even my well-educated, Westernized friends who started to keep the Santoshi Mata fast after seeing the film. When the film was shown in rural cinema halls people placed offerings of incense, flowers and money in front of the screen as if they were participating in a religious ritual.

But with television the most illiterate viewers seem to have worked out that what they were seeing was real. Television made it possible for them to see, often for the first time, cities like Delhi and Mumbai and observe that these were places in which other Indians lived in nice houses with plump, glowing children. It made them aspire to the same things in their own lives possibly for the first time. For this to happen the economy needed to grow faster than the annual average of 3 per cent that it had grown at since 1947 under the socialist policies of Rajiv's mother and grandfather. Policies that Rajiv made not the smallest move to change.

It was not that Rajiv did not know that delivering economic change would win him the next election but he seemed unable to understand how to bring these changes about. When he failed politically to counter the damage done by the Bofors scandal the bureaucracy, ever-resistant to change, became stronger and imposed once more the centralized governance that their colonial administrative training had bred them to believe was the only way to govern India. Even when, under the influence of Mani Shankar Aiyar, who remained a close aide, Rajiv decided that the solution to problems in the country's governance lay in strengthening village councils or panchayats he created a system in which money would flow directly from the central government to the villages bypassing state governments. Powerful opposition chief ministers like R.K. Hegde in Karnataka immediately objected.

By 1988 I was writing a weekly political column for the *Indian Express* and I notice when I now read the pieces I wrote that year that nearly all of them make fun of what Rajiv and his government had become. There are references to the prime minister holidaying in the Andamans with Italian family and friends just months after the famine in Orissa, and to his attempts at reviving the spirit of the freedom movement by re-enacting events like the Dandi March as if they were meaningless exercises. His advisors convinced him that the best way to increase his popularity was to celebrate India's fortieth birthday as a nation and link it to Jawaharlal Nehru's centenary. So a committee was set up called the 40/100 Committee to devise events that sought to evoke nationalism and reverence for the dynasty that had given India three prime ministers. This committee persuaded Rajiv to lead a new Dandi March along the route the Mahatma had taken, without considering that Gandhiji had been protesting against an unjust salt tax and not just taking a long walk to the coast. The 40/100 Committee appeared not to have noticed either that the British Raj had ended long ago and that it was slightly bizarre for the prime minister to be re-enacting a famous protest march without having anything specific to protest against.

Then there was the Great Freedom Run in Delhi for which the prime minister and his ministers jogged from Vijay Chowk to India Gate to the soundtrack of *Chariots of Fire*, a film popular in India that year. I described the confusion in this attempt to improve the prime minister's image in these words in a column that appeared on 13 March 1988 in the *Indian Express*.

> I have a serious-minded friend who said she recently went to a village and puzzled villagers gathered around her to demand an explanation for the Freedom Run. 'I tried,' she said 'but when I told them about running to express our sense of determination to face external and internal threats to the country they only got more confused and said surely if these threats exist then we should work together solidly instead of running around.'

In the same piece I quoted Romi Chopra as saying proudly that, 'Like khadi, tracksuits are a great leveller.' He planned the Great Freedom Run along with Suresh Kalmadi who, decades later, when Sonia Gandhi became India's de facto prime minister, ended up in jail on charges of stealing money from the organizing committee of the 2011 Commonwealth Games.

When all attempts to revive the spirit of the freedom movement failed and when there were no signs of Rajiv becoming popular once again in India the bureaucrats in his inner circle succeeded in persuading him to concentrate on foreign affairs. They encouraged him to interfere in the internal affairs of India's neighbours like Sri Lanka and the Maldives and sent him off to travel to the capitals of powerful Western countries where local journalists still saw him and Sonia as a glamorous couple. Rajiv's foreign travels became so frequent that Delhi's *Sunday Mail* gave him a booby prize for being globetrotter of the year. It calculated that he made thirty-one visits to twenty-nine countries in eighty-seven days.

In private the officials who sent him globetrotting joked about the absurdity of some of his foreign policy decisions. When India blockaded tiny, landlocked Nepal for several weeks, causing terrible shortages of essential supplies, senior officials in the Foreign Ministry admitted, in off-the-record conversations with me, that this had been done for no real reason. The consequences of the blockade were hardly reported in the Indian press and I found out about the severe shortages of food and fuel Nepal was facing only because I happened to take Aatish on a holiday to Kathmandu. When I got back to Delhi I went to see a senior bureaucrat to find out why India was behaving like such a bully. He responded at first with the publicly stated reason, which was that Nepal was getting too cosy with China and had to be punished. Then with a short derisive laugh he said, 'That's the official reason. But the real reason is that Rajiv got upset because the King of Nepal refused to have breakfast with him in

New York on the grounds that he couldn't do a breakfast meeting because he was never up that early.'

With Pakistan relations were even more fraught because of a military exercise called Operation Brass Tacks that took place in 1987 and nearly caused a real war. The Indian Army described the exercise as routine but when whole divisions of the army were moved up to the front General Zia-ul-Haq became extremely nervous and responded by moving his own troops up to the border. It was a cricket tour of India by Pakistan's cricket team that brought hostilities to an end and Zia, ever smiling his horrible fake smile, came to India to try and improve his own image by taking advantage of cricket diplomacy.

Then suddenly Zia-ul-Haq was gone, killed in a mysterious plane crash on 17 August 1988. For me personally, it was an event I celebrated, as the vast majority of Pakistanis did, because of an aversion to military dictators that runs deep. Military dictators make democracy, even the dynastic kind, look good. With Zia's death everything in Pakistan changed. Benazir Bhutto came to power as the first democratically elected Pakistani leader in ten years opening up the possibility of an exciting new relationship with India, but again Rajiv was played by the bureaucrats as if he were a half-literate child. They allowed him to pose for pretty pictures with Benazir by his side, they put all sorts of nice-sounding statements in his mouth, but behind all this they remained as obdurately against peace with Pakistan as they had always been. It was the same old men in charge playing the same old games under the oblivious gaze of a prime minister who seemed happy with just the photo opportunities.

Zia's death gave me a chance to go back to Pakistan to do a story for NDTV and in doing so to become a bystander in a wonderful moment in history. NDTV came into being at about the time of the 1988 election in Pakistan and I was asked by Radhika Roy, who started NDTV with her husband Prannoy, if I would go to Pakistan to cover the election for the very first episode of a programme called *The World This Week* to be anchored by Prannoy. So I was in Karachi on the night Benazir won her slender victory and to this day I think of this election as the most poignant I have ever covered. After a decade of military rule so brutal that an elected prime minister could be executed, there was a tentative quality about the celebrations that night mixed with a joyous madness. I had dinner with my friend Imran Aslam, who went on to become one of Pakistan's most respected editors and head of Geo, one of Pakistan's first private television channels. At the time he worked for a newspaper in Karachi and played a vital role in explaining to me the nuances of the alliance that brought Benazir to power. We watched the victory processions from his balcony.

I stayed up almost all night unable to sleep because of the excitement. It was as if a lid had been taken off the country and unleashed political forces that nobody knew existed. The crowds who thronged the streets all night shouted slogans that mourned Zulfikar Ali Bhutto's absence and celebrated the victory of his daughter. The two that remain etched in my memory are, 'Bhutto *hum sharminda hain, tere qatil zinda hain.*' Bhutto we are ashamed that your killers are still alive. And, '*Jiye* Bhutto'. Bhutto lives. Two simple words but shouted with so much passion that they resounded in the air like background music. The revellers from Bhutto's Pakistan People's Party were matched by those who had voted for the MQM (Mohajir Qaumi Movement), which was part of the victorious alliance. Imran explained that the MQM was a new political party that was created to represent refugees who came to Pakistan in 1947. The word *mohajir* means refugee in Urdu. Trucks filled with women wearing bangles in MQM colours drove around the city till dawn broke. And in a country in which singing and dancing in public were banned under the military dictator's Islamic laws there was dancing and singing in the streets.

It was during this trip to Pakistan that I met Benazir for the first time in Sindh after spending a day following her around as she raced about the countryside in her Pajero trying to ensure that polling was free and fair. When I caught up with her she seemed tense and preoccupied and said she would answer all my questions after polling was over. Later that evening at the Bhutto family home in Larkana she gave a short audience to the army of foreign correspondents that had gathered and we were bewitched by her beauty and by that elusive quality called charisma that she exuded. She did not say much but what she said reflected her passion for democracy and the years she had suffered to bring it to her country. She seemed so much more intelligent and political than Rajiv that it was a contrast I found hard not to notice. She may have come to power because of her family name, as he had done, but unlike him she had fought a long and difficult political battle to get to the top. She carried on her fight for democracy even after her father was executed and spent many years in jail because of it. This gave her a gravitas that Rajiv did not have but in the end she could do little to make a new beginning with India because she was prevented from interfering in foreign policy by the generals in Pakistan with a vested interest in war rather than peace. A new initiative could only have come from India and did not because the know-all bureaucrats who surrounded Rajiv made sure that a real change of direction did not happen. India's foreign policy has been consistent since the time of Jawaharlal Nehru, they liked to say, as if this were something to be proud of.

While relations did not improve with Pakistan, they deteriorated seriously with Nepal and Sri Lanka. The only foreign policy triumph Rajiv could boast of was that he saved the government of the Maldives from being overthrown in a coup by Tamil mercenaries led by disgruntled Maldivian political leaders.

Once more I found myself in a toothpaste tube of a military plane that took seven hours to take us to Male. There were Indian soldiers everywhere and they were heroes in the eyes of the local people because they had prevented Male from being taken over by men who came at dawn to attack with rockets and heavy artillery. Despite the trauma of the attempted coup and the presence of soldiers everywhere this country of tiny islands did not lose its holiday atmosphere. We Indians accustomed to the dreary, socialist tourism facilities India offered in those days were startled by how far ahead of us this country in the Indian Ocean was on the tourism front.

We stayed in a resort called Kurumba that was a collection of white-washed bungalows covered in bougainvillea. The island was so small that every bungalow had a view of the emerald and turquoise sea. We ate an Italian meal that night in a restaurant built under a large, thatched roof and not only was the food delicious but a bottle of fine Chianti wine was available at a reasonable price. Such a meal would have been nearly impossible in India in 1988. Rajiv had followed his mother's policy of not encouraging foreign tourists to come to India either because the economic benefits did not occur to him or because his advisors viewed foreigners and foreign tourists with suspicion. It was not until after the economy was liberalized in the nineties that foreign tourists started coming to India in large numbers. By then countries like the Maldives and Sri Lanka, and most of Southeast Asia and China, had long understood the enormous benefits that tourism could bring to a country's economy.

While Rajiv was preoccupied with building his image abroad his former defence minister, V.P. Singh, spent his time travelling in the villages of north India spreading poisonous propaganda against his former boss. V.P. Singh set himself up as the anti-Rajiv, homespun hero who not only spoke Hindi perfectly but could break into rural dialects with fluency. Instead of the glamour and glitz that Rajiv and Sonia had come to symbolize, V.P. Singh went out of his way to show that he was just an ordinary man despite being a raja by birth. He travelled in a dilapidated Fiat and his driver was often a smalltime journalist whom I knew slightly and who invited me along on one of the tours.

We started in Lucknow where V.P. Singh was staying in a squalid guesthouse. I did not know then that the humble accommodation was part of the image he was cultivating. The journalists who surrounded him were not from big national newspapers but from small, mofussil papers and the fact that V.P. Singh had given up power and pelf to be with them in humble, if smelly, hostelries appealed to them. They followed him everywhere he went and spread his message far and wide. On the day I went with him we left Lucknow at dawn and travelled in a dusty convoy of rattletrap Ambassadors. We drove past Lucknow's ruined mosques and palaces and it saddened me to see another great Indian city destroyed. Most Indian cities had fallen to ruin after Independence because of the socialist disdain for aesthetics and town planning that our political leaders affected.

My father was posted in Lucknow in his army days and my childhood memories were of a city in which refinement had been carried almost too far and defined even the most mundane activities. As a child I remember being fascinated by how the city's scents changed with the seasons. In summer when we wore white muslin and pastel colours our clothes smelled of vetiver, tuberose, wild roses and jasmine. When the rains came the attar would become warmer and smell of wet earth and rain-washed evenings, and our winter clothes smelled of musk and ambergris. When people argued they did it in words usually found in poetry. Once I rejected a pavement seller's mangoes because they seemed a bit rotten and the old fruitseller said, 'Take them, your highness, they are pining in your memory.' Then in the eighties a rough, new breed of politicians came to power and sold chunks of the city to developers who built ugly new 'colonies' that paid no attention to the architecture of the old city.

It did not take long for the older, more beautiful part of the city with its mosques and minarets and quaint bazaars to get squeezed from all sides by the ugly, new city that rose like a vast shanty town around it.

Within minutes of driving out of Lucknow, that morning, we found ourselves in rural surroundings of the usual primitive kind. Women washed clothes at the edge of a drain, children defecated, dogs and chickens raced about and old men sat on string beds smoking hookahs and reading Hindi newspapers. Clouds of big, aggressive flies harassed us as we walked to the village's main square where an audience of villagers sat patiently under the shade of a magnificent old banyan tree. There was no stage, no microphones, none of the paraphernalia of a normal political rally. V.P. Singh climbed on to the little cement platform that surrounded the tree and made his speech. The audience consisted of about five hundred people. Women with veiled faces sat in the front, men in dusty kurtas and dhotis sat behind them and children, barefoot and half naked, scrambled about restlessly right under the platform the leader spoke from.

His message was simple and he wasted no time delivering it.

Rajiv was corrupt and had betrayed the people by not bringing about the changes he had promised. So the solution was to vote for V.P. Singh and his newly formed Jan Morcha because he would do all the things that Rajiv had failed to do. And he promised that within ninety days of his becoming prime minister he would catch the 'Bofors thieves'. The audience in that first village was unresponsive and silent. But as the day went on things improved and late that night when we stopped in a town whose name I no longer remember V.P. Singh's message was greeted with raucous slogans and an enthusiastic crowd. I returned to Delhi convinced that V.P. Singh could be prime minister one day.

As the end of his term drew closer Rajiv began to look more and more like a comical, half-witted prince with no idea of the country he was ruling or its problems. In the durbar around him there were now only sycophants. There were bureaucrats, like Mani Shankar Aiyar, who had long broken the boundaries that keep the civil service apart from politics. There were journalists, like M.J. Akbar, who had decided to give up journalism for a ticket to contest elections from Rajiv's Congress Party. There were sleazy businessmen whose only interest was in currying favour with the prime minister to further their business interests. And, there were those friends from the old days who had benefited hugely from being courtiers in Rajiv's durbar. Rajiv himself had little time for them because of the pressures of prime ministerial duties, but Sonia, still an apolitical if powerful housewife, had all the time in the world at her disposal. And they had all the time in the world for her because they knew that without her permission there was no access to the prime minister's house.

I saw these friends less and less partly because I was no longer in the same set and partly because there was so much political turbulence in the country that I seemed to spend all my time at political meetings. Rajiv had unleashed such terrible forces with his decisions to give Muslims their own personal law in matters of divorce and Hindus a new focal point for Hindu revivalism in Ayodhya that it was hard to keep up with the changes that were happening.

When it came to using Hindu revivalism as a political weapon nobody could beat the Bharatiya Janata Party and suddenly this political party was back in business. After having been reduced to two seats in Parliament by the wave that swept Rajiv to power in 1984 it had become a spent, forgotten political force until the Shah Bano case. When Rajiv allowed the unlocking of the Babri Masjid for Hindus to worship Ram the BJP could almost not believe its luck. The unlocking of the masjid's gates was a result of a court case in which a Hindu appellant had demanded the right to worship in what he said was a temple. A wiser prime minister would have found some way to defuse the tensions that inevitably arose. As Rajiv did nothing this was interpreted, by most political analysts, as an attempt to cultivate Hindu voters and when it comes to this the BJP is always hard to beat. Suddenly public meetings began to be held in Delhi in which tired old slogans like '*Gau-Mata ki Jai*' (Hail Mother Cow) were shouted along with new ones like '*Boliye Sri Ram Janmabhoomi ki Jai*' (Hail the temple where Sri Ram was born). At these meetings there were so many saffron-robed priests and weirdly dressed sadhus that it was often hard to tell if these were religious gatherings or political. But political they most certainly were since political leaders like Atal Behari Vajpayee and Lal Krishan Advani were always present. The new religiosity forced even someone like Vajpayee to announce that he was a proud member of the RSS and that he believed that the Babri Masjid should be 'bulldozed'.

This was at a meeting in Delhi's Ram Lila grounds in April 1989 and I remember being as stunned by Vajpayee's new mood as I had once been moved by the speech he had made on these very grounds at that first rally after the opposition leaders were released from jail in the winter of 1977. I had followed his career closely in the years that had passed and got to know him well personally, so I knew that he was uncomfortable with Hindu revivalism but he seemed to have no choice but to flow with the tide.

At this meeting, ostensibly held to commemorate the birth centenary of the founder of the RSS, Dr Keshav Baliram Hedgewar, a priest called Mahant Avaidyanath announced that the reason why ascetics like him had been forced to give up their prayers and meditations and return to 'real life' was because Hindu unity was in danger. 'There are those who say what problems can Hindus have when they constitute 80 per cent of the population, but let us not forget that this country was enslaved at a time when Hindus constituted 100 per cent of the population. How did we become slaves when we were at the height of our civilization? Only because we were disunited.'

In the speech he made that day Vajpayee did not target Muslims quite so directly but suggested, in a subtle reference to Muslims in Indonesia, that they had changed their religion but not their culture and continued to celebrate the Ram Lila every year. And, he added, the ancient capital of Thailand is called Ayodhya and their kings have been called Ram ever since the influence of India's mighty civilization spread to that country in ancient times. The implication was not lost on anybody and especially not on Muslims. Under Rajiv there had been terrible communal riots in Bhagalpur and Meerut but Muslims continued to see the Congress Party as basically on their side and the BJP as the enemy. The rise of Hindutva and the new aggressive language from supposedly moderate BJP leaders like Vajpayee fuelled hostilities which would two years later explode into the horrific violence that followed in the wake of L.K. Advani's 'rath yatra' to Ayodhya. It would also in a later election take the BJP's seats in the Lok Sabha from two to more than a hundred.

What helped reignite the BJP's engines more than anything else was Rajiv's decision to allow Muslims the use of Islamic law in matters of marriage and divorce. Even irreligious Hindus, uninspired by the campaign to turn the Babri Masjid into a temple, objected to Muslims being governed by a separate law. Ordinary people whom I talked to on my travels quoted the BJP slogan '*Ek vidhan, ek samvidhan*' (One law, one constitution) to me as if they had thought it up themselves. Many asked why Muslims wanted only a limited implementation of the shariat law. Why should Islamic punishments like chopping off the hands of thieves and stoning adulterers to death not apply as well? Less liberal Hindus remembered that India had been broken once before in the name of Islam and this could happen again if Rajiv was allowed to 'appease' Muslims. Appeasement was a word I heard so often those days that I got tired of hearing it but there was no escape from it because everywhere I went I saw signs of a resurgent Hindutva and the return of the RSS through its morning meetings called *shakhas* in cities and small towns across India.

Towards the end of Rajiv's term as prime minister when this wave of Hindu resurgence was beginning to spread into middle-class neighbourhoods in Delhi I got in touch with an acquaintance from my days in the *Statesman*'s reporters' room called B.L. Sharma 'Prem', who was not just a practising member of the RSS but a fanatical Hindu. He used to come to the reporters' room often to see if we could help him get information about his son who had been on a merchant ship that got lost at sea. He was a small, tired-looking man with sad eyes and lines on his face and his search for his lost son was so obsessive and so hopeless that I felt more than a little sympathy for him.

He came from a lower middle class Punjabi family that had come to Delhi as refugees in 1947 and like a lot of other people who had seen the violence of that time grown up with a passionate hatred of Islam. It was this that attracted him to the RSS and its ideology of aggressive nationalism laced with a deep hatred of Muslims and Islam. One of the earliest heads of the RSS, Guru Golwalkar, suggested in a book he wrote that the way to deal with Indian Muslims was the way Nazi Germany had dealt with the Jews. Prem never articulated views this extreme in front of me but when he did not find his lost son he filled the emptiness of his life with RSS work. He organized shakhas in middle class residential colonies in different parts of Delhi and because I was curious about what the RSS was up to I sometimes went along.

I knew something about the RSS from the Rajmata of Gwalior who had always been an ardent supporter but she had an exalted, nationalistic idea of its philosophy. She believed that all that the RSS was promoting was an assertive nationalism and this she considered a good thing for

India. She believed, like many Hindus did, that the only defence against the possibility of the country being broken up once more in the name of religion was to promote the aggressive nationalism of the RSS. Many rich Indians subscribed to this idea and were persuaded to donate vast amounts of money to the RSS and the BJP. What they did not see was the kind of RSS workers that I met through Prem.

From going with him to several morning shakhas I learned that there was a public face of the RSS and a private one. The public face was carefully harmless. Men young and old in shapeless, unflattering khaki knickers would gather at dawn in some park or open space and conduct activities that were self-consciously patriotic. The sessions began with the raising of the national flag which was saluted by everyone present. This would be followed by the collective singing of patriotic songs and an exercise in martial arts so feeble that it could not have saved anyone from an attack by a child. Then they would sing the national anthem, lower the flag ceremonially and go home for breakfast.

It was at these breakfasts that I discovered what was really going on. Sitting on the floor in small, middle class living rooms eating rich Punjabi breakfasts of parathas and oily potatotes I listened to Prem and his friends talk about how necessary it was for Muslims to be driven out of India. Where should they go, I remember asking more than once, and every time I heard the same answer. 'Pakistan. It was created for the Muslims. This is Hindustan and they cannot stay here.' Inevitably I would then ask if they seriously believed that a hundred and fifty million Muslims could be driven out of India and Prem would usually say, 'Not a hundred and fifty million. Two hundred and fifty million and the way they are breeding they will overtake the population of Hindus in a few years and then what will happen?'

Rajiv's policies as prime minister unleashed demons that should have died after the country was partitioned. An ugly, new form of Hindutva that became resurgent then would one day propel the BJP to a position that would make it the only national party in India capable of taking on the Congress. Did Rajiv not understand the consequences his policies would have? I believe that he did not.

19 THE LAST ELECTION

While Rajiv played into the hands of the worst kind of conservative Muslim by legislating to allow Muslims to be governed by Shariat personal laws, he did nothing about making the lives of ordinary Muslims more secure.

From the time I first started working as a journalist, I took a special interest in communal riots. Not just because I thought the horrible violence, caused mostly by petty disputes, made India seem like such a primitive country, but because I could never understand why the Indian state seemed so helpless in the face of violence. I took every chance to go to places where ethnic violence had occurred, and conducted a sort of amateur inquiry of my own. Nearly everywhere I went I found that the reason why more Muslims had been killed in a clash with Hindus, or Dalits in a clash with upper-caste Hindus, was because local officials tended to sympathize with the other side. The unstated reason for this was that most officials were upper-caste Hindus and were emboldened by the reality that when the violence ended all that happened was the setting up of an inquiry committee. It usually took so long to come out with a report that nobody ended up being punished for the dereliction of their duties. Rajiv could do nothing to change this because of his open justification of such violence in 1984, but that still does not explain why he took no action when in the summer of 1987 the Congress chief minister of Uttar Pradesh allowed his policemen to get away with massacring Muslims as if they were animals.

In Meerut in this bout of violence there were many days of murder and mayhem. And the city was under total curfew when police vans arrived one evening in an area called Hashimpura. They parked in a street in which there were mostly Muslim homes. Under the pretence of rounding up troublemakers, late on the evening of 22 May, the policemen filled a van with Muslim men, some as young as thirteen and some as old as seventy-five, and drove out of the city to the edge of a canal where they opened fire on the unarmed, helpless men while they were still in the van. Their bullet-ridden bodies were thrown into the canal. The story of what happened would never have been told had a few of the men not survived. One of them, Zulfikar Nasser, stayed alive by pretending to be dead after being thrown in the river.

Human rights activists helped him get to the All India Institute of Medical Sciences in Delhi for the treatment of bullet injuries that were to leave him with a permanent limp. Once he was brought to Delhi he was quickly discovered by reporters, who extracted every last detail of the massacre on the canal and brought it to public attention. Television was still state-controlled but the story of what happened in Hashimpura appeared in newspapers across India. From the government came only the usual cursory response that an inquiry commission would look into what had happened.

The policemen responsible for the carnage were dismissed from service but reinstated as soon as the fuss died down. The Congress Party Chief Minister Vir Bahadur Singh got away with the slightest public reprimand. Rajiv behaved exactly as Indian prime ministers always had when Hindu–Muslim riots happened. He ordered an inquiry knowing that by the time it came to any conclusions memories of the violence would have faded. Today more than twenty years later justice has still not been done and the Hashimpura massacre almost certainly became part of the reason why Muslims in Uttar Pradesh lost faith in the Congress. In nearly half of the state's eighty parliamentary constituencies, the Muslim vote is the deciding factor because of the Muslim community's tendency to vote collectively. The Congress Party's support has been so reduced in the state that despite an aggressive campaign led by Rahul Gandhi in the 2012 elections to the state legislature, the Congress managed to get only 28 seats in an assembly of 403.

Rajiv's attempts to appease both Muslims and Hindus ended up serving the purposes of only the worst elements in both communities. This muddled political strategy laid the grounds for his defeat in the 1989 elections by allowing two powerful enemies to loom larger and larger. One was V.P. Singh, who continued his campaign against Rajiv's alleged corruption, and the other was the BJP, which used Ayodhya as a foundation to build a new political structure of Hindu religiosity. With all manner of Hindu priests and ascetics on its team, it did not take long before word spread in small towns and villages that Rajiv and his foreign wife were anti-Hindu and so, automatically, anti-India.

By the beginning of his last year as prime minister, Rajiv had become unpopular with the very people who believed so much in his ability to bring hope in place of cynicism. He seemed oblivious of this and before the year ended did one more thing to tarnish his image. He banned Salman Rushdie's *The Satanic Verses* from being sold in India. It is often forgotten that the first people to notice that the book was 'anti-Islam' was the Government of India and not Ayatollah Khomeini. Was this a conscious choice on Rajiv's part? I believe not. I believe that because he had no real political beliefs himself, he became an easy victim of those who did.

For my part, I had fore-knowledge of the book's potential to create trouble by the strangest circumstances. Someone who had seen a proof copy of the book told me, laughingly at some Delhi party, that one of the characters in *The Satanic Verses* was a Sikh woman called Tavleen, a human bomb who blows up an aeroplane in the first few pages of the book. She is as minor a character as imaginable, but it seemed to me that a Sikh woman terrorist called Tavleen had the potential to cause serious problems for me since Rajiv had already hinted in the Lok Sabha that Raghu Rai and I had something to do with the hijacking of the Indian Airlines flight from Srinagar in July 1984. Until my father invented my name to save me from being given the usual gender-neutral Sikh names like Tavinder and Tejinder, Tavleen was not a name at all. There are now many Sikh girls who are called Tavleen (at one point there was even a tigress in Corbett Park named Tavleen!), but at the time when Rushdie wrote his book it was my name alone. It worried me that some bone-headed official in the Government of India might be inspired to reopen the file on my alleged terrorist activities.

I had met Salman Rushdie in Naveen Patnaik's drawing room, where, in the days before Naveen became a surprisingly successful politician, it was possible to meet such exalted personages as Jackie Kennedy, Mick Jagger and Bruce Chatwin as they wandered through India. Salman came with an introduction from Naveen's brother-in-law, Sonny Mehta, who was his publisher. On the evening that I first met Salman I had brought along my old friend, the cricketer Imran Khan, who when he went on to become a politician was to deny ever having broken bread with a man who caused 'immeasurable hurt' to Muslims. He told a lie, but since he was aspiring to become prime minister of Pakistan he may have had to.

In the summer of 1988, months before the storm over *The Satanic Verses* broke, I sought out Salman in London. I was there for the *Indian Express* to see if I could ferret out more information about the shell companies to which Bofors bribes had been paid. Arun Shourie was editor of the *Indian Express* at the time and was determined to expose every detail he could discover about where the money had gone. His resolve strengthened when in retaliation Rajiv ordered more than a hundred income tax raids on the newspaper's offices, showing that he did not believe much in a free press. When Arun asked me to go to London he gave me names of people about whom I was meant to make discreet inquiries. I was spectacularly unfortunate in this regard, and found that whatever leads I followed ended up with slammed doors or closed ones. What I did manage to do was meet Salman and appeal to him to change the woman terrorist's name in his book. He told me it was too late because the first copies of the book were already in print and compensated by giving me a proof copy of *The Satanic Verses* signed, 'For Tavleen, with apologies for the misuse of her name.' He said that this was all he could do. When I told him that his use of my name could get me into trouble in India, he said that he thought the one who was more likely to get into trouble was him 'with the mullahs'. An unfortunately accurate prophecy.

When the book was published, and before it became available in India, the first call I got was from G. Parthasarathy who was then the joint secretary in charge of external publicity in the Ministry of External Affairs. He had read *The Satanic Verses* and found it very funny that the Sikh woman terrorist had my name. 'I always knew you were a terrorist,' he said with a laugh, 'and now we have confirmation.'

Rajiv's government did not find the book amusing. As usually happens, the first people to draw the prime minister's attention to it were those who had neither read the book nor had any intention of reading it. In India books are nearly always banned at the request of people who do not read but whose literary sensibilities are easily offended. In the case of *The Satanic Verses*, the people who took immediate offence were the same fundamentalists who persuaded Rajiv to allow a separate personal law for Muslims. They came in delegations to demand that the book be banned and since they had the incomprehensible support of a section of Delhi's liberal intelligentsia Rajiv was easily persuaded. What made it easier for him to make the decision was that in Mumbai hysterical protests had already erupted because of what the Muslim community had 'heard' about the book. By then I had read the proof copy Salman gave me and found it heavy going but not particularly offensive. But then I am not Muslim and not a believer. And I do not believe books should be banned.

It made me sad that Rajiv, as a young and supposedly modern prime minister, had been so easily persuaded to take the side of fundamentalists and fanatics. And, as usual, when he had finished appeasing Muslims by banning Rushdie's book, he found it necessary to appease Hindus by way of compensation. He did this by beginning his election campaign in Ayodhya with the promise that if he won another term he would bring 'Ram Rajya' to India. With the BJP already demanding that the Babri Masjid be demolished to make way for a Ram temple, for 'secular' Rajiv to promise a return to Ram's mythical utopia was insanity, but by now I had learned to accept that Rajiv was so apolitical that he was capable of all sorts of mistakes.

It was becoming increasingly clear that he would lose the election. Even before Rajiv made this unwise start to his election campaign, even before I went out to cover the election, I predicted that he was going to lose. I had come to this conclusion from my travels with his main antagonist, V.P. Singh. When the foreign editor of the *Sunday Times* rang to ask me what would be the big story from the general election in India, I told her it would be the possibility that Rajiv could lose the election. She was an Australian woman with little understanding of India but huge confidence in herself. She asked me with a sneer in her voice who I thought would defeat Rajiv. I told her that I thought V.P. Singh would be India's next prime minister and she said scornfully, 'I don't think an unknown politician with big glasses and a funny hat can defeat a handsome and charismatic prime minister like Rajiv Gandhi.' I replied that it was possible that looks were more important in Australia than in India and reminded her that Gandhiji was not good-looking by any standards but she was not convinced and some other, more trustworthy journalist was sent from London to cover the election. I concentrated on covering it for my column in the *Indian Express*, which was not only more satisfying but also more interesting in terms of the places to which it took me.

When Rajat Sharma suggested that I go with him and the actor Shatrughan Sinha on a journey by road that would start in Patna and take us across Bihar into eastern Uttar Pradesh and on to Lucknow, I happily agreed. Sinha was not a politician then but was campaigning for the BJP with the intention of joining its ranks one day. As the most famous Bihari in Bollywood he was a big star in Bihar and drew huge crowds everywhere we went. I remember endless meetings on dusty playing fields and in squalid village squares, and sometimes just wherever crowds gathered because they had heard their beloved 'Bihari Babu' was passing through.

Sinha spoke with the studied eloquence of an actor and made the same speech everywhere, the main message contained in a single verse: '*Kaun kehta hai aakash mein suraakh nahin ho sakta, ek patthar to tabiyat sey ucchalo yaaron.*' Loosely translated it means, 'Who says it is not possible to make a hole in the sky? Just try to throw a stone upwards with all your heart.' He would begin almost every speech with this verse so that everyone understood he was urging them to have faith in the opposition's ability to defeat a prime minister as seemingly invincible as Rajiv. The crowds responded fervently in the decayed, disorderly towns and villages we drove through. But it was not till we got to the former princely kingdom of Dumraon, at the edge of eastern Uttar Pradesh, that we saw how effective the opposition campaign against Rajiv was proving to be.

One of Rajiv's ministers, a famous sycophant called K.K. Tiwari was contesting from here and on our first evening as we were driving to the maharaja of Dumraon's broken-down palace our car was stopped by a mob of Tiwari's supporters. A man leaned in through the open front window and slapped Rajat so hard in the face that his glasses broke. We drove on without waiting to find out why but assumed that Tiwari's supporters were so nervous that they were trying to frighten away Shatrughan Sinha. The slap was meant for him.

Sinha was staying as a guest of the maharaja in his charming, dilapidated little palace while Rajat and I were relegated to spending the night in what may once have been a fine hunting lodge. It was in ruins, with holes in the roof and its main drawing room bereft of all furniture. It was in this vast, rancid-smelling hall full of political workers sleeping on rough bedding on the floor that we spent the night. It was an especially uncomfortable night for me. I was the only woman in the dormitory and going to the foul lavatory meant that I needed Rajat to stand guard outside because the door had no locks on it.

The next morning I discovered to my huge relief that Nandini Mehta, editor of the *Express*'s weekend edition in which my column appeared, was staying in considerably more luxury as a guest of the maharaja. I scuttled off to the palace as soon as I was up and found Nandini awake and reading the morning newspapers in a room filled with sunlight and the scent of a hot breakfast. She was more than happy to allow me the use of her clean and comfortable bathroom for my morning ablutions. Afterwards, we sat and chatted over boiled eggs, buttered toast and hot tea and she confirmed that the election did not look good for Rajiv. She said she had travelled all over Bihar and had noticed an overwhelming sense of disappointment. A majority of the people felt that their hopes had been betrayed, and on top of that there was the Bofors scandal and the very effective opposition propaganda that Rajiv was really a foreigner because of his distance from Indian realities. We exchanged notes about our travels and agreed that one of the signs that things were not going well for Rajiv was that people were making jokes about him. She said that one of the jokes that was popular and had been turned into a slogan at public meetings taunted Rajiv by saying that Jawaharlal Nehru was sending his grandson a warning from the heavens that he would face defeat. In Bhojpuri it went like this: '*Swarg se nana ki aayi pukaar, ab ke naati tu jaibe haar.*'

I said goodbye to Nandini after breakfast and after attending an opposition rally in Dumraon we drove across the border into Uttar Pradesh and on towards Rajiv's constituency, Amethi. Everywhere in the filthy bazaars of small towns were posters of Rajiv smiling happily but there were no signs of improved living standards. Except in the streets in which officials lived, where there was order in the rows of neat gardens and bungalows, the towns had grown organically out of villages without any attention to urban planning. I have never understood why the Gandhi family's pocket boroughs, constituencies that are almost their private estates, look so very uncared for. Many other political leaders have made sure that their own constituencies look so good that people vote for them in the hope that they will replicate what they have done in their constituencies on an increasingly larger scale.

What I saw in Uttar Pradesh and Bihar on this long drive reminded me of one of the saddest examples of poverty caused by political neglect that I have ever seen. It was in a village in Bihar's Palamau district a year earlier. I had been invited by the social activist Swami Agnivesh to see the work he was doing to release workers in Bihar from bonded labour. This is a peculiarly Indian form of slavery in which a small debt enslaves generations of a family because somehow the debt continues to remain unpaid. In one village I met bonded labourers who had never left the farm they worked on to even go to the nearby town of Daltonganj less than 10 kilometres away, never seen money and never heard the name of the country in which they lived. They had heard of elections and voted regularly. When I asked them who they voted for they said simply, 'We vote for whoever they tell us to.' 'They' were the landlord and his henchmen. It sickened me to see the degradation in which these people eked out an existence on the handful of grain that the landlord gave them at the end of the day. Had Rajiv's grandiose, computerized anti-poverty schemes worked better the repugnant, shameful practice of keeping human beings in 'bondage' should at least have stopped. But when I came back to Delhi and discussed this with his officials, they said I could not possibly have met bonded labourers in Bihar because bonded labour had been legally abolished during the Emergency.

Somewhere along the way on my travels with Shatrughan Sinha in Uttar Pradesh we ran into V.P. Singh's campaign convoy and attended a meeting he held on the edge of town. I remember thinking that the crowd was huge by rural standards and that people seemed to be actually listening to what he told them. Whenever he mentioned Bofors, they responded with glee and jeers. He made it the cornerstone of his campaign and came back to it over and over again in different ways so that it seemed there was nothing more important for India than to catch 'the thieves who had stolen the people's money'.

On 2 December 1989, V.P. Singh was sworn in as India's seventh prime minister at the head of a government that was doomed from birth because of its fractured nature. The prime minister did not have enough seats for even a simple majority in Parliament and needed the support of several disparate parties. From the moment he was chosen to lead this rickety coalition, he earned the enmity of the man who had thought he would be prime minister until Indira Gandhi's assassination made it seem like a silly dream. Chandrashekhar.

Chandrashekhar, who walked from the southern tip of India to New Delhi to show that he was serious about understanding the problems of the ordinary people of India. Chandrashekhar, who went to jail during the Emergency rather than compromise with Mrs Gandhi. Chandrashekhar, who was so passionate about his socialist ideas that he did not change them even slightly in his many decades in politics. With this impressive political record behind him, Chandrashekhar showed his first signs of pettiness when he refused to accept V.P. Singh as prime minister and started to make trouble for the new government from day one by storming out of the meeting in which V.P. Singh was chosen as leader.

Even without Chandrashekhar's sulks the new government had enough troubles. The day after V.P. Singh became prime minister, his Kashmiri home minister Mufti Mohammad Sayeed's daughter was kidnapped by the Jammu Kashmir Liberation Front (JKLF) and returned only after the government released a large number of important secessionist leaders. When these militants returned to Srinagar, they were publicly welcomed by armed comrades who fired automatic weapons in the air in celebration. Kashmir's armed insurgency had begun and V.P. Singh soon showed that he had no idea what to do. His handling of India's most serious political problem was so inept that Rajiv, whose policies had created this new phase of the Kashmir problem, started dictating what should be done as if he were still prime minister. He demanded that an all-party delegation be sent to the Valley and behaved as if there had been no Kashmir problem at all until V.P. Singh became prime minister. The wobbly, unsure new prime minister let him.

It was not just in dealing with Kashmir that V.P. Singh showed he was not a real leader, but in almost every aspect of governance. It is true that his own colleagues were plotting against him from the day he took office, but had he shown a hint of being a real leader he could have rendered futile their attempts to unseat him. Rajiv saw what was happening and quickly realized that the government was unlikely to survive a full term so he lost no opportunity to attack the government in public. It did not survive a year. But before it fell V.P. Singh, in a cynical and desperate attempt to garner popular support, announced plans to reserve thousands of government jobs for lower-caste Hindus. The castes he included in this plan were not traditionally untouchable castes or castes that had ever been oppressed. These castes represented powerful peasant clans who needed no affirmative action on their behalf. So when Singh announced that he was implementing the suggestions for affirmative action recommended in a long-forgotten report called the Mandal Commission it was seen by upper-caste Hindus as a deliberate attempt to divide the Hindu vote. It was to prevent this that the BJP's powerful cadre-based progenitor, the RSS, decided it was time to take action. So Lal Krishna Advani, till then a man in the shadows and not a mass leader, was pulled out of the BJP's backroom and ordered to set off on a 'yatra' from the Somnath Temple in Gujarat to Ayodhya.

The route chosen for his journey was full of Hindu symbolism. The legendary wealth of the Somnath Temple had caused it to be looted and destroyed at least six times by Islamic invaders. It was in ruins in 1947 when India became independent and one of the first things done by the government of Jawaharlal Nehru was to restore its former glory by reconstructing a magnificent new temple at the ancient site. Advani's rath yatra began in Somnath ostensibly to remind Hindus that if a new temple could be built in Somnath it could just as easily be built in Ayodhya. The real purpose of the yatra was to consolidate Hindus, always fragmented by the caste system, into an integrated vote bank.

Would there have been a yatra at all if the actions of Rajiv and V.P. Singh had not paved the way for it? Perhaps not. To give Advani's journey a touch of Hindu mythological melodrama, a Toyota truck was embellished to look like Ram's own chariot may have done. And, when Advani stopped to greet the crowds that lined his route, he stood under an embroidered umbrella like gods do in old Bollywood movies and more recent TV serials. It was a shameful exercise in exciting hatred against Muslims but it was horribly effective.

I followed for a while in the rath yatra's wake and came upon town after town in which ordinary Muslims had been massacred and their homes destroyed by militant Hindu groups who seemed to never leave the killing grounds without painting Hindu religious symbols on blackened walls. These militant Hindus were always, without exception, linked in some way to the RSS and so to the BJP.

Advani did not get to Ayodhya. He was arrested in Bihar but managed to enter Delhi still riding his 'chariot'. Overnight, he became the BJP's new mass leader and his battle cry was 'end pseudo-secularism'.

Urban liberals like me may have been disappointed by the new genre of politics Advani created, but to the ordinary Hindu he was a hero and it was because of his chariot ride that the BJP was able to rise spectacularly from its humiliating diminishment in 1984. Aggressive Hindu nationalism took the party from strength to strength and by 1998 it was in a position to make Atal Behari Vajpayee India's first BJP prime minister. Advani was graceful enough to concede to Vajpayee, but perhaps he did this because he understood that to be prime minister you needed more than Hindu support. With his decision to reserve government jobs for lower-caste Hindus, V.P. Singh successfully identified the fault-lines of caste and by the time his unstable, hopeless government fell in November 1990, India was engulfed in political violence. In campuses across the country upper-caste students protested, some even setting fire to themselves, against his job reservations.

It was a bad time to hold another general election so soon after the last one and in such a fraught atmosphere. And Rajiv, sounding magnanimous and statesmanlike for the first time since his defeat, offered to use his 197 MPs in the Lok Sabha to support (from the outside) a government led by Chandrashekhar. So Chandrashekhar finally became prime minister, but only after making a humiliating compromise. With no more than 64 of his own MPs, he became head of a government that relied totally on Rajiv's grace and favour.

Chandrashekhar did not last long as prime minister. He was sworn in on 10 November 1990 and by March of 1991 was forced to resign because it became impossible for him to rule at Rajiv's behest. He remained caretaker prime minister till 21 June 1991 but was a real prime minister for only the first three months. Even in those months he could take almost no decision without Rajiv's permission. Rajiv's immaturity as a politician became more evident during the months of Chandrashekhar's rule than at any other time. He behaved like a spoilt prince whose kingdom had been wrongfully taken away from him and took to ordering the prime minister around as if he were an underling.

Chandrashekhar had inherited a government that was nearly bankrupt.

The financial situation was so bad by early 1991 that there were rumours that the Government of India was on the point of dipping into its gold reserves to pay its debts. Chandrashekhar's inflexible socialist worldview prevented him from coming up with new ideas or imaginative solutions to the crisis. But even if he had he would have been allowed to do little by Rajiv Gandhi who in Parliament and in public made it clear, often and loudly, that Chandrashekhar was prime minister only as long as he wanted him to be. When Chandrashekhar tried to think for himself or do something without Rajiv's permission, Rajiv always made it clear who was in charge.

His interference reached absurd levels when the first Gulf War began. Saddam Hussein's invasion of Kuwait happened while Chandrashekhar was prime minister and Chandrashekhar decided that it was in India's interest to allow American warplanes to refuel in India. Rajiv saw this as a departure from the anti-American foreign policy he had inherited from his mother and threw a public tantrum about Chandrashekhar's disobedience. He then flew off to Moscow to try and get Mikhail Gorbachev to prevent the Americans from launching a ground war against Saddam. It was a foolish thing to do since not even the Russians were on Saddam's side by then. His sycophantic advisors deluded him into believing that even if he was no longer prime minister, he was so important a world leader that he could stop the United States from launching a ground war.

In the end it was not some grand act of disobedience that caused Chandrashekhar's government to fall, but the silliest reason imaginable. After Rajiv lost the election, he and his family moved from the prime minister's house on Race Course Road to a smaller house, 10 Janpath. This house would one day become famous as the most powerful address in India, but that was more than a decade away. In the spring of 1991 it was just another large house at the edge of a roundabout on one of Delhi's busiest roads. As soon as the Gandhis moved in the gates of the house that opened on to Janpath were sealed and high walls built for reasons of security. The only entrance to the house that remained open was through a heavily guarded cul-de-sac.

One morning Rajiv decided that the prime minister was violating his privacy by posting two constables from Haryana in his house to spy on him. If the prime minister of India wanted to spy on someone he would not need to rely on ordinary constables. In Delhi, in the paranoid atmosphere that Mrs Gandhi's horror of the CIA had created, there was a huge and very discreet infrastructure that could have been used. But Rajiv was adamant and went public with his charges.

These new accusations were so odd that they appear to have made Chandrashekhar realize that his position as prime minister was not much more exalted than one of Rajiv's flunkeys. Gathering together what remained of his tattered dignity he surprised everyone by going quietly to a Doordarshan studio and announcing on national television that he was submitting his resignation as prime minister and ordering the dissolution of the Lok Sabha. Chandrashekhar's decision to resign appeared to take Rajiv more by surprise than anyone else. Political pundits agreed that all Rajiv had been trying to do was assert his dominance over the prime minister, not cause the government to fall. But perhaps what was happening was beyond the power of mere human beings, perhaps there were energies in the cosmos that had come into play that were bigger than we knew.

When Chandrashekhar announced his resignation, the first hot summer winds were beginning to sweep through Delhi, bringing people like me intimations of the nightmarish journeys that lay ahead on the campaign trail. My plans were to start my travels in Rajiv's constituency in Uttar Pradesh. but I did not expect to interview Rajiv in Amethi. I had not seen either Rajiv or Sonia socially or at a personal level in a long time and responses to my requests for an interview with Rajiv could have frozen a Delhi summer. Then unexpectedly something happened.

My friend, Louise Fernandes, a colleague from my days in the *Telegraph*, had married Salman Khurshid, a Congress Party politician. Louise covered south India for the newspaper and after coming to Delhi to marry Salman did some legal reporting for the *Telegraph* until the pressures of bringing up four children (including a set of twins) and being married to a politician made her abandon journalism altogether. In 1991, Salman and Louise lived in a house that was directly opposite 10 Janpath. I had kept in touch with Louise as she sank into domesticity and often, when I dropped in for a meal or coffee, she would urge me to end my 'hostilities' with Rajiv. I always told her truthfully that the hostilities were not of my making and it was not in my hands to end them. She suggested that an accidental meeting be arranged at a social event so that I could talk to him and find out why he was angry.

Louise arranged such an 'accidental' meeting just after Chandrashekhar resigned. It was the month of Ramzan, and Salman and Louise were having an Iftaar party. Rajiv had promised to come and Louise suggested that I come as well. I knew there would not be too many people at their Iftar party and agreed that there could not be a better chance for me to try and resolve my differences with Rajiv. I made it a point to arrive early so as not to miss him. A little too early, I found, because I reached as the maulvi led the prayers before the breaking of that day's fast. The men had gathered to pray in Louise's kitchen garden, the sun gilding the tops of mango trees and flights of parrots wheeling about noisily. I watched with the wonder of an unbeliever at the faith that inspired so many millions to starve themselves for so many days every year. The thought of fasting for a whole month made me hungry.

By the time dates were brought around with glasses of juice for the believers to break their fast, I had already filled a plate with delicious, spicy kebabs and was about to start devouring them when Rajiv arrived. The prayers were still in progress so I was among a handful of people who noticed his arrival. He came surrounded by armed commandos but I found myself face to face with him as soon as he walked in. He smiled cheerfully when he saw me and I grabbed the chance to speak with him alone. This is how I remember the conversation we had.

'When I have criticized you,' I said, 'it has been in your role as prime minister or leader of the opposition. There isn't anything personal about this and I can't understand why you should behave as if it were a civil war.'

His smile widened and he said that he never saw it as a civil war and there was no problem at all as far as he was concerned. Pushing my luck as always I told him that I was going to Amethi in a few days and would love to interview him if he was going to be there. He said he was and that I should call R.K. Dhawan and fix a time for the interview. Mrs Gandhi's old stenographer had not only been totally exonerated of the charge that he was involved in her assassination but had been rehabilitated, extraordinary though this sounds, as a member of Rajiv's personal staff. I said I would call Dhawan the very next day. That is all I had time to say before Rajiv was swept away by a crowd of adoring guests. I noticed from the glazed expressions on their faces that he had lost none of his famous charisma, at least for the people in this Delhi garden.

The next day when I called Dhawan to fix an appointment in Amethi he said that Rajiv had spoken to him about an interview and it would be arranged. I think I asked him why if it was so easy to get an interview with him now it had been so difficult all these months, and he said something like 'there are problems on the domestic front'. This became abundantly evident from the icy reception Sonia gave me when I turned up with my television crew at Lucknow airport in readiness for the drive to Amethi. When I saw her that morning, she was standing among a crowd of women political workers and ignored me pointedly when I tried to speak to her. So I stopped trying and spent the day following them around the villages they visited. Rajiv drove himself and Sonia sat, her head covered, beside him in the front of an SUV. Every time they stopped to meet people, or for a roadside meeting, I would leap out of the rickety Ambassador I was in and urge my cameraman to take every shot he could from every angle. Whenever I caught Sonia's eye, she looked the other way. She was so obviously displeased to see me lurking at every turn that I was beginning to worry that my interview with Rajiv would be cancelled. This meant that I would have wasted not just my time but the time of the crew who had come along to record the interview for the video magazine that I worked for at this time. In the end I did get my interview. But it was brief and Rajiv seemed uncomfortable because in the small dak bungalow in which we talked, Sonia would almost certainly have been able to hear every word from the next room.

It was the last time I saw Rajiv.

Two weeks later, on 21 May 1991, the last day of the election campaign, Rajiv Gandhi went to Sriperumbudur, a town in Tamil Nadu that almost nobody had heard of.

Afterwards, Congress Party campaign managers told me there was no reason for him to have gone there. It was late in the evening and from all accounts Rajiv was exhausted and running an hour late, so it was not till around 10 p.m. that his convoy of white Ambassadors arrived at the rally that was being held to support his candidate, Maragatham Chandrasekhar.

It has continued to puzzle those who investigated the assassination how Mrs Chandrasekhar survived, as did every other senior Congress leader at the rally. Usually when an important political leader arrives at a public meeting the people who surround him include the candidate and other local leaders. But among the fourteen people who died with Rajiv that day there were no Congress leaders. In the huge crater that Dhanu, the human bomb, made they found mostly the bodies of his security personnel. This has inevitably led to conspiracy theories that have never been proven. A Tamil journalist, who shall remain anonymous, tried to conduct his own investigations into Rajiv's assassination and was warned to stop. He never told me who warned him but did say that he had been puzzled by the material he had gathered because it revealed that Dhanu was on surprisingly friendly terms with Mrs Chandrasekhar's daughter, Latha Priyakumar. They had been on picnics together and met often enough for Dhanu to have been allowed into Rajiv's innermost security perimeter.

Rajiv Gandhi's assassination came at the end of the first phase of the election campaign and helped his party win more seats in the second phase than they were expected to. But not enough for the Congress Party to return to power with a full majority. Sonia Gandhi was given her first chance to appoint the prime minister of India. She had no official position in the Congress Party then but her authority was taken for granted. She chose P.V. Narasimha Rao, whose loyalty to the Gandhi family had never wavered.

EPILOGUE

After Rajiv's death Congress Party leaders announced that the only person they considered worthy of taking over India's oldest political party was the dead leader's widow.

Sonia was born in Italy, did not become an Indian citizen for nearly twenty years after coming to live in India, spoke almost no Hindi, understood little about Indian politics or India and yet was considered the tallest leader in the Congress Party by men who had ruled large Indian states. When they offered the leadership of India's oldest political party to Sonia Gandhi they set a dangerous new precedent but, for reasons I have never understood, nobody objected. The media behaved as if it were perfectly normal for an Italian housewife to become the prime minister of India and the few small voices, like my own, that were raised in protest were shouted down by everyone, including opposition politicians. My own objections were based not just on Sonia's foreignness, and these were strong, but on her having always been not just apolitical but against all things political. Why would someone who had never expressed anything but disdain for Indian politicians and politics decide to become an Indian politician?

Sonia, more aware of her limitations than the men who offered her the job of leading the Congress Party, chose for a year to keep away from public life. She lived in semi-retirement behind the high walls of 10 Janpath. But her retirement was so very semi that her picture appeared on the front pages of Indian newspapers almost every day. She was never out of the public eye, because news photographers always seemed to be present when foreign dignitaries came to visit her. They visited her more often than the prime minister she had chosen as her proxy, P.V. Narasimha Rao. Rao was prevented from getting too big for his very small boots not just by her but by everyone in the Congress Party. Even small-time leaders defied him openly all the time and got away with it by going afterwards to pay obeisance to Sonia. For someone ostensibly uninterested in politics, she seemed to be meeting politicians all day during her period of mourning. I pointed this out in my column in the *Indian Express* more than once and more than once got berated by her friends.

From tidbits of information I gleaned from these friends, it was easy to work out that her only reason for staying away from public life for a year was that she needed that much time to prepare. When she refused to become Congress president on the night Rajiv died, it was probably because she knew that if she took the job, she would be quickly exposed. In her year of semi-retirement she learned to speak Hindi well enough to read out a speech written in the Roman script, and studied carefully the politics of her mother-in-law. There were rumours that she watched videos of the late prime minister Indira Gandhi so she could learn to imitate her mannerisms.

At some point, she appeared to have noticed that left in the hands of its senior leaders, the Congress Party would, before long, disintegrate completely. Rajiv had continued his mother's practice of filling the party with courtiers and sycophants whose political future depended on the dynasty's vaunted charisma, so its roots had weakened as had its organizational structure. It was no longer the party's leftist ideology that was its glue but the Gandhi family. Years later, the ultimate subscriber to the idea of democratic feudalism, Mani Shankar Aiyar, admitted in a television interview with Karan Thapar that the party was not just proud of its dynasty but knew that it was the 'adhesive' that held things together.

Narasimha Rao ran a corrupt but efficient government that lasted its full term despite not having a full majority in Parliament. It was under him that India made the changes that moved the country away from stagnant socialism towards a more open economy. It was under him that the licence-quota-permit raj, which had held India back for decades, began to be slowly dismantled and it is this that resulted eventually in India transiting from being an economic basket case to becoming an 'emerging economic superpower'. But by the time of the 1996 election Narasimha Rao had made the Congress Party unpopular enough for it to be in no position to win.

The Babri Masjid was torn down by Hindu fanatics on 6 December 1992 and this lost the Congress Party its crucial Muslim vote bank. Another reason was that small caste-based parties like the Bahujan Samaj Party became powerful enough to steal away the Dalit vote. And from the casteist churning created by V.P. Singh's Mandal politics were born leaders like Mulayam Singh and Laloo Yadav who began to build their own vote banks out of castes that fell in an intermediate category. The upper castes were lured away by the Bharatiya Janata Party for whom the demolition of the Babri Masjid was a boon, whatever its leaders may say.

The Congress Party lost the 1996 general election but nobody else won. So a shabby, leftist, 'secular' government was put together with Congress Party support. This support was withdrawn in two years by Sonia Gandhi. The reason she gave was that the investigation into her husband's assassination was not being taken seriously. She wanted the fragile coalition government, that existed only because of support from the Congress, to take action against the Dravida Munnetra Kazhagam (DMK) which happened to be part of the coalition government. The DMK, led by M. Karunanidhi, had never concealed its support for the LTTE but Sonia's demand for action against it was baseless and this got exposed when the DMK later became her staunchest ally. When she made her speech in Amethi, asking people to understand her '*vedna*' (pain) at action not being taken against her husband's killers, she was really only indicating that she was ready to become a real politician.

By the time of the 1998 general election, Sonia was ready to claim her political inheritance. She agreed to campaign for her party and addressed her first public rally in Sriperumbudur on 11 January 1998. I was there.

Giant cardboard cut-outs of Sonia in a sari with her hands joined together in a namaste were erected all over Sriperumbudur. The sycophancy she inspired was stunning and for me, as an Indian, shaming because it was inspired not by her political achievements (she had none at this time) but by her white skin. The songs of praise the people sang compared her to god, and a little less generously to Mother Teresa. When she finally appeared on stage in a green Tamil sari, with her daughter beside her in an orange sari, the crowd went wild. It was as degrading a display of servility as I have ever seen. More songs about 'white-skinned goddesses' were sung. 'You are god, you have white skin,' they sang, 'we worship you.'

Sonia Gandhi did not succeed in winning that election for the Congress, but in 2004 she did. Although she refused to take the prime minister's job, everyone in India knew she was the real prime minister. After 2009, when her government won a second term in office, she has worked tirelessly to ensure that nothing stops her son, Rahul, from claiming his inheritance whenever he wants.

So the dynasty continues, and its example is emulated by almost every political party in India with dangerous consequences for Indian democracy. In 1997, when Laloo Prasad Yadav as chief minister of Bihar was jailed on corruption charges, he appointed his semi-literate wife, Rabri Devi, as his proxy. Rabri Devi had never stepped beyond the boundaries of her home, nor did she claim to be anything more than a housewife and mother of Laloo's nine children, when she was quite suddenly appointed chief minister of one of India's largest and poorest states.

At the time Rabri Devi became chief minister of Bihar, I used to do a weekly television programme called *Ek Din Ek Jeevan* for Star Plus. The programme was popular and I had interviewed for it prime ministers like Atal Behari Vajpayee and Inder Gujral as well as movie stars like Amitabh Bachchan and Shahrukh Khan, so my request to spend a day with Rabri Devi was eagerly received by the officials handling her public relations, and I was invited to Patna to interview Bihar's new chief minister.

When I arrived, I rang the chief minister's home and asked if I could come over with my crew for a casual chat with her to plan the interview that was set for the following morning. The official I talked to said there would be no problem at all and to the surprise of all of us, we found Rabri Devi waiting for us and ready to be interviewed. My producer whispered that we should seize the opportunity so that we had more material to play around with when we were editing.

I interviewed Rabri Devi in her little sitting room filled with bric-a-brac that consisted mostly of trophies and mementoes that had been collected by her husband in the course of his chief ministerial duties. Rabri Devi told me how she had burst into tears when Laloo informed her that she was going to be chief minister instead of him. She said she had been in the kitchen when she got the news and had been terrified because all she had ever done was look after her home and children. When I asked if it had been difficult for her to adjust to her new role as the leader of Bihar, she admitted that it had not been easy and that she would not have been able to manage without her husband's help.

Laloo was out on bail. When I met him that day he was holding court in an outhouse behind the main residence. He was dressed in a white dhoti and vest, and a small army of officials and politicians had come to call on him. He chatted to me in a friendly way about this and that and allowed himself to be photographed. The programme needed visuals of Rabri Devi going about her daily activities and she happily agreed that evening to show us the pond in which she was breeding fish and the cattle shed in which she kept her cows. So imagine my shock the next morning when she refused to see me at all.

We arrived early to get shots of her while she did her morning puja, but were told by a servant that she was busy and that we should wait outside. We waited for more than four hours before she agreed to meet us in her office and, to my surprise, she was not just cold but rude. When I asked her why she seemed so upset with me she said that she had heard that I had described her in my Hindi column in *India Today* as illiterate. I told her, truthfully, that what I had written was that she was the Sonia Gandhi of Bihar. This pleased her and the interview began on a pleasant note, but at some point I made the mistake of asking if she did not think that people who entered politics should be literate and she had a fit. She saw this as a reference to her own limitations with the written word. Could people who were not literate not see and hear, she asked me angrily and on camera. Could they not understand things? Was my cameraman literate? When I said that literacy helped a great deal when it came to governance, she said 'officials run governments' and brought the interview to an end.

Rabri Devi was such an obvious example of the dangers of dynastic democracy that she came in for more public approbation than others but she still managed to rule Bihar for more than one term. I admit to being delighted when, in the 2010 assembly elections, Rabri Devi and other members of her family were resoundingly defeated.

I have often puzzled over why India's fiercely independent television channels and newspapers have not been more incensed by something that has caused such severe damage to the political fabric. Is it because journalists have become part of the game? Journalists who do not speak out against parliamentary constituencies being treated like private estates, and hereditary succession becoming the norm rather than the exception, usually get treated very well by governments. In an insidious form of bribery they are offered not just access to leaders and foreign junkets when such leaders travel abroad, but nominated seats in the Rajya Sabha, subsidized housing and all sorts of other perks that are usually available only to politicians and high-ranking government officials.

The price for such media complicity has been paid by India. Political dynasties now flourish across the country and because of this, legislatures are increasingly becoming private clubs in which the unworthy heirs of political leaders, with little knowledge of governance and even less political acumen, have privileged access. Like feudal potentates they surround themselves with sycophants and courtiers. The sort of Indians who entered public life during the freedom movement out of a desire to serve India no longer exists. With a handful of rare exceptions, most Indian politicians enter politics today not for reasons of ideology or public service but because they believe that their own interests and the interests of their family are best served this way. All of this has happened because of the example set by the dynasty in Delhi. In almost every Indian state chief ministers use their power to send their wives or sisters to the Lok Sabha from constituencies that are not pocket boroughs but private estates. There are almost no political parties left that do not practise dynastic politics, and increasingly there is evidence of a collusion to keep this diminished form of democracy alive.

Would this have happened if Indira Gandhi had not led by example? I believe not, which is why the story of Rajiv Gandhi is so important. It was with him that it all began.